MW01146312

THE

BLOODY FUNNY HISTORY OF ROME

VOLUME ONE
THE ROMAN REPUBLIC

THE CONQUEST OF ITALY
AENEAS TO PYRRHUS

Brett A. Clark
www.bloodyfunny.com

PHILOLOGOS MEDIA

Printed in USA
ISBN 0-9779526-0-6 (Volume 1)

The Cover painting of David's *Rape of the Sabine Women* shows Hersilia trying to separate her husband Romulus from her father Tatius, while Cupid fires love-arrows from above. Rubens' foreground painting is of a mangy wolf suckling Romulus and Remus, lying next to a comic theater-mask mosaic from the emperor Hadrian's Villa. "Venus brandishing her sandal," one stuffy critic has written, "is one of the most disliked statues in classical scholarship, due to the bad taste of her ridiculous nipples!" (See p.163, which illustrates her points more clearly.) Venus is spanking two bald heads - a comic actor and an austere senator - with more to come. The back cover sports a statue of a boy wrestling a goose.

Overleaf the popular Etruscan double-flute player pipes in the entry (Vulci, 480 BC).

Page iii shows drunken old *Silenus* (Swilling-wine) riding a wineskin while piping an invocation to the Muse (Vase painting, 350 BC).

Page v dedication is an Etruscan bronze Pan blowing his panpipes (500 BC).

Page 4 illustration of Roman mythology on silver plate (Mildenhall, 400 AD) depicts the god Oceanus center, with dolphins poking out of his hair, surrounded by four sea-nymphs cavorting with a seahorse, sea-duck, sea-deer, and seaman. The encircling Bacchanalia festival depicts (from top, clock-wise) upside-down Bacchus straddling his panther being served wine by old Silenus, Pan playing panpipes chasing two girls, a double-flute player serenading three dancers, a drunk supported by two slaves barfs on a mortified lion, and a nudist attacks a Bacchante.

Invocation to the Muse

Laugh O a Muse and sing
of life and love with zing
this Funny tome
on Bloody Rome
and every ruddy thing!

DEDICATORY INSCRIPTIONS

"Don't touch or steal me, I'm not yours!"
(Common Latin inscription on movable articles)

"An ancient historian superintended the building of this book
built of plunder from other tomes, at his own expense
as an offering to a Muse. May lovers hate you and stand aloof
unless you praise me and give your blessing!"
(Adapted suppliant dedication)

"Slaves use rear entry"
(Front entry warning)

"I've run away. Catch me. If you take me back to
[insert your name here] **you'll be rewarded!"**
(Slave collar-tag)

"*EIN THUI ARA ENAN*"
"DON'T YOU DARE, DO ANYTHING HERE!"
(Etruscan hex curse from the *Tomb of the Hex Curse* 600 BC)

"To Lisa - ego amo te!"
(*Domus Matrona*)

Casual Dating

Romans measured time as *Ab Urbe Condita* (From the Foundation of the City) or AUC for short.

The sixth-century monk Little Denis calculated (wrongly) that Jesus was born in 753 AUC, so invented a new dating system by changing 754 AUC to AD 1 which was the first *Anno Domini* (Year of our Lord). The year before AD 1 should be AD 0, but instead became 1 BC (Before Christ). Missing out the year zero means that someone born in 10 BC who died in AD 10 would officially be aged 20, but really be only 19 (which was great for recruiting underage monks). It also means that AD 2000 is really AD 1999, but the good news is that you're a year younger than you think you are.

The monks later realized that Jesus was actually born under the reign of King Herod the Great who died in 750 AUC (4 BC). This means that Christ was born at least four years Before Christ (which is another miracle).

Some politically correct scholars change BC and AD to BCE (Before Common Era) and CE (Common Era) but keep the first system's common error. AB CD would be easier to remember (*Anno* Before, Christ *Domini*), or even BC (Backwards Counting) CF (Counting Forwards). AUC is a lot easier, since the ever-practical Romans never did anything backwards and always went forwards.

CONTENTS

1 INTRODUCTION

Slave's address

Tell the reader, *Salve*,[1]

Welcome to Bloody Funny History, the study of antic-witty, where we laugh at your ancestors. Ancient readers were illiterate and required an educated slave to read aloud to them, so for an authentic historical experience you should have a friend do the same for you - while serving hot honeyed-wine[2] and massaging your feet.[3]

The purpose of history is to give us a laugh (for if we really learnt anything from it we'd stop repeating our mistakes), and since nobody can ever remember the good jokes, we write them down.

"You remember what you laugh at," grumbled the Latin poet Horace, "much easier than what's good or holy!" "Men might praise the tragic epics," snorted Martial, "but they read the funny stuff!" "After tedious study," advised Lucian's bogus *True History*, "scholars should relax with a book like this!" "Literature, like life, should mix serious with funny," added Pliny, "so we're neither too pompous, nor too silly!" Nothing funny has been written about Rome since the Romans wrote, so we're going to make history...

Abridged too far

This book presents Rome's rise from barbarism to decadence without culture in-between. Chapter 2 squashes early Rome between the great Etruscans and Greater Greece. Roman history begins in Chapter 3 with the fabulous Greek fable of Aeneas fleeing Troy to start the Roman race. Virgil's famous poem the *Aeneid* illustrates how this origin myth was used to justify world conquest: "We Romans are pious, honest, hardworking farmers who fight only because you provoke us!" The Romans didn't want all the land in the world but, like typical farmers, only whatever abutted their boundary.

Rome is founded in Chapter 4 as a free haven for bandits, criminals and runaway slaves, where animal rights mean that even wolves can adopt babies. Chapter 5's legendary Seven Kings of Rome build the city-state out of Greek myth mixed with an Etruscan wolfman cult. Chapters 6-8 broach the birth of the Republic, the fights with the neighbors, and the

---

[1] *Salve* is a Roman greeting, and applied to wounds inflicted by arriving legions.
[2] Make sure your slave pours only *Falernian* (best wine). "This book's best read drinking," advises Martial's *Epigram* 11.17, "before the sober thinking!"
[3] *Footnote*: remind your slave to massage between your toes!

Gallic attack that almost snuffed out Rome's existence stillborn. Chapter 9 records Rome's subsequent recovery and expansion across Italy. The alarmed south Italian Greek cities hire a foreign Greek army to fight Rome in Chapter 10. Their defeat stuns the civilized Greek world, which demands to know: "Who are these upstart Roman barbarians?" Chapter 11 covers Roman vices, bad habits, and how to knot tie a toga - I sheet thee knot! Chapter 12 has Chapter 11 bankrupt Roman religion with foreign loans.

False truths

This book has been researched from primary sources, with no tome left unturned. The more amazing events have their authors and works cited, so you can follow up for further info.[4] The modern English translations of the Latin and Greek texts are of varying quality. The Penguin editions are annoying because they're abridged, and the Loeb editions because they're not. Loeb translates the obscene Latin passages into Italian, so the Italian edition probably has them translated into English. "Nobody mess with my poems," warned the cranky poet Martial, who would die to see them translated into limericks.

Despite faithfully following the ancient accounts, I can't swear that everything recounted here is true, but they say it is: "You'll be amazed to read this," the Roman historian Tacitus explains in his *Histories*, "but to amuse with fiction isn't the purpose of this work!" Truth is funnier than fiction, so when the historical records contradict, the strangest version must be right. "The historian's highest job is to commemorate good deeds," added Tacitus, "and to ensure that evildoers fear posterity's condemnation - in books like this!" History also has more dates than Cleopatra, so only the most important times BC (Backwards Counting) or AD (Altered Dates) have been noted, like whether a war was fought before breakfast.

Many ancient authors are mere fragments, figments, frauds, or known only because later writers mention them, usually to say, "They're no bloody good!" Titbits come from Aulus Gellius' *Attic Nights* written to liven up long winter evenings in his attic, Valerius Maximus' forgettable *Unforgettable Doings and Sayings*, and Dio Cassius' *Roman History*, which some scholars argue was really written by Cassius Dio.

The poets Horace, Juvenal and Martial also deserve mention: "You never know when the gods might strike you down," wrote the Greeks, "so call no man happy until he's dead!" "I was happy yesterday already and not even the gods can take that away from me," retorted Horace, "so

---

[4] Searching the Internet for ancient authors is like a modern archaeology hunt, since old links disappear while others are newly discovered, but most texts are online. The songs are available at www.bloodyfunny.com.

let them do their worst, nyah!" And once you've read this book, you can say the same. "Live today, die tomorrow," advised Martial, "in that order!" "Vaccera praises dead poets," he added ruefully, "but I'm not dying just to please him!" Remind your reading-slave that poetry is to prose, what singing is to talk - so all poems should be sung.

All ancient *manuscripts* (handwritings) have been copied repeatedly down through the ages, so any mistakes you spot in this work should be blamed on the lazy scribe who copied the previous scroll. Most mistakes were accidental, but occasionally a copyist would decide to 'improve' a book by making their own additions (*interpolations*). This was especially true of Plays where some actors complained that their lines were too short so added their own dramatic speeches - which were then handed down as being part of the original. Scholars often argue over which parts of ancient texts are genuine, but you can be pretty sure most of this book is, apart from this paragraph I added.

Anonymous scribes very often jotted notes (*scholia*) on old manuscripts commenting on (or disputing) various passages, so you too can be a Scholiast by scribbling your own comments in the margin for the next reader to ponder.

"I avoid weird words," said Julius Caesar in his book *Good Grammar*, "like I do a rock!" Unfortunately Latin's full of weird words, but where these occur there's a *gloss* (definition) given in brackets, for example: *barbarus verbosus* (weird words), *saxus* (rock), *barbarus saxus* (weird rock), or *rolling stones* (weird rock band).

Other historical sources include museums and archaeological digs, many of which display amazing feats of engineering. For instance, the entire Temple of Jupiter at Pergamum has been shifted into the Berlin Museum, the Parthenon roof at Athens has been shifted into the British Museum, while half the Coliseum at Rome has been shifted into local homes by stone-robbers.

DON'T CONFUSE YOUR SCHOLIA (RUNAWAY FOOTNOTES) WITH SCOLIA (GREEK DRINKING SONGS)!

The Pope's Secret Collection is kept locked in the *camera segretta* (secret room) of the Naples Archaeological Museum and was only available for viewing by serious male scholars or monks until recently. Such was the demand by monks to eyeball this antique pornography hoard last century that wads of permission tickets were printed and a revolving door almost fitted. Saddam's Secret Collection has been removed from the Baghdad Museum, but is open for viewing on the black market.

"Consistency makes for a poor book," wrote Martial, "while a great book consists of three parts: Good, bad and indifferent!" In order to be inconsistent, we've got three types of jokes: Funny (*guffaw*), bad (*groan*) and those you don't get (*duh?*). "Many corrections can't improve your jokes," Martial tells me, "but one rubbing out can!"

It's said that the only accurate quotation is a misquotation, the one duty we owe to history is to rewrite it, and the very best humor always offends somebody - so there should be something here for everyone! *Vale*,[5] an ancient Historian.

Succeeding historians' precision	History is indeed
should be held in high derision	nothing but the screed
for their knowledge increases	of mankind's mistakes
(as their sources ceases)	unlucky breaks
in pompous disquisition!	and criminal misdeeds!
	- After Gibbon[6]

---

[5] *Vale* is a Roman farewell, since departing legions usually left you under a shroud.

[6] From Eddie Gibbon's *The Decline and Fall of the Roman Empire* - a whole book of footnotes. "Another damned, thick, square book," complained William Henry, the Duke of Gloucester, upon receiving the 2nd volume from the author in 1781, "Always scribble, scribble, scribble, eh, Mr. Gibbon?"

2 SEX PLEASE, WE'RE ETRUSCAN

Herd of Cow Land?

Italy is shaped like a big boot kicking Sicily (which it did quite often), and means Cow-land, so-called because the Greeks thought that the barbarian women were cows, or were cowed by them, but since most ancient *etymology* (true-reason) is guesswork, it might also be full of bull.

Right: Putting the boot in. Italy may mean Calf-land because the Greeks admired her nice shapely leg. Rome is located on the kneecap, mis-named *Caput Mundi* (Head of the World), beside the Tiber River, which gives Italy water on the knee.

Around 5000 BC New-stone Age farmers discovered that "the pen is mightier than the sward," so herded their cows off the *sward* (grassland) into pens. New nomads arrived in Italy in 1000 BC and settled down to become the *Villa-novans* (House-new) or *Villa-no-vans* (House-no-wagons).

Right: Villanovan bronze statuette (730 BC). A warrior fondles his wife's breast as she steadies a water jug on her head while grabbing his groin, which shows they balanced work with play.

The archaeological traces of round Iron Age huts have been found copied as miniature baked-clay funeral urns, which proves that primitive

Romans lived in mud huts before and after they died.

Right: An early Roman tries on a miniature baked-clay Iron Age mud-hut replica funeral urn for fit. After cremation, one size fits all.

The cremation urns were buried in pits (*pozzo*), but burying bodies in trenches (*fossa*) became popular until the Romans caught enemies desecrating their corpses, which got them burnt up enough to be cremated again. Those too lazy to dig just stuck their dead inside hollow tree-trunks.

Trenched in a *fossa* fits
while a *pozzo* is the pits
but I'll urn cremation
so exhumation
won't mess my body bits!

Early Rome was squashed between the mighty Etruscan League above, and the mightier Greek Empire below. Lower Italy was once so overrun by Greek colonists that it was known as Greater Greece (because it boasted more Greeks and temples than Greece itself), so the Romans can be called Lesser Greeks since they copied their statues, paintings, plays, gods, laws, myths and history.

Unfortunately, they followed the Etruscans in fashion, who gave them the toga, curly-toed red shoes and funny haircuts.

Sybaris and bad Sins

The Greeks first colonized *Pithekoussai* (Monkey Island) off *Naples* (New-city), before founding many southern Italian cities, like Sybaris and bad Sins (720 BC). Wealthy Sybaris was so devoted to pleasure that they banned all noisy tradesmen and roosters so everyone could sleep in. "I still didn't sleep very well," a Sybarite complained, "because the rose petals I sleep on were crumpled!" "Well, I saw a farmer digging,"

DEARIE ME! JUST LOOKING AT YOU READ THIS BOOK MAKES ME TIRED!

complained his friend, "and the sight gave me a rupture!" "Stop it," he retorted, "just hearing your story has made me ache!"

Rich Sybaritic women hired experts to teach them the finer points of lovemaking, and only accepted party invitations a year in advance so that they'd have time to get ready. Unmarried girls were allowed to take lovers and taught that the best way to catch one was by showing their breasts.

Right: Carved stone relief (570 BC). A girl catches a naked

man, but instead of showing her breasts, she lifts her dress. This technique seems just as effective. Another Etruscan statue of a woman lifting her dress has missing legs, prompting some scholars to argue that perhaps she wasn't showing her pubes, but that she had bird-legs (as shown on p.154).

The Sybarites so loved banqueting that they were known as "Slaves to their own bellies" and when dining they each held a portable urinal between their knees to save leaving the table. For after-dinner entertainment, they taught their horses to dance, which unfortunately proved to be a big disadvantage in battle. An enemy army advanced on the city playing flutes. This caused the Sybarite horses to begin cavorting, which tossed the cavalry into disarray. The other Greeks diverted a river over Sybaris to clean it up. Today *sybarite* is still a derogatory term for uninhibited fun-lovers.

SYBARIS CAN-CAN

ENCORE!

Sex please, we're Etruscan

Not much is known of the mysterious Etruscans since their writing is rather scanty, like *arse verse* (beware fire), and the longest piece found is a linen text reused as an Egyptian mummy's loincloth. Besides books, the Etruscans used linen for awnings, sails and see-through dresses. "They originated from famine stricken Lydia (modern Turkey)," claims the Greek historian Herodotus, "where they ate on the even days and gambled on the odd days to take their minds off the hunger," which no doubt worked if you won the loser's food ration.

Right: Gilded ivory statuette (660 BC). An Etruscan woman squirts milk into a cup to breastfeed herself.

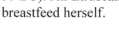

Right: Engraved Etruscan mirrors depict games between naked couples. The inscription records their conversation, She: "I'm going to beat you!" He: "I do believe you are!"

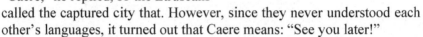

The Etruscans starved off the inedible, landed in Italy, and set siege to a local town. A soldier began chatting with the enemy, asking, "What's your city called?" "Caere," he replied, so the Etruscans called the captured city that. However, since they never understood each other's languages, it turned out that Caere means: "See you later!"

"Etruria is a free and easy place," the Greek historian Theopompus explained, "because most of their customs are copied from Greece, like the hairdressers that abound to pluck their private parts and every other body hair, apart from the head. They love music so much that the women knead bread, wrestle and whip slaves to the sound of flutes. Oh, and the slave-girls wait on you naked!"

Right: A drunken dancing scene from the *Tomb of the Lionesses* (520 BC).

The faded Etruscan funeral frescoes feature frolicking flute-players, and women in heavy makeup, see-through dresses, dyed blonde hair, and false beauty moles, which means that they used any excuse to party.

Theopompus advised that if you visit an Etruscan gentleman, the door-slave will candidly announce, "The master's making out with the maids, but please, do come in," since they prefer sex with people watching. "They usually sleep with courtesans and boys," Theopompus confided, who must have liked to watch, "but occasionally even with their own wives - each other's, that is - and when they're totally exhausted, waiting young men leap into bed to take their place. The women are heavy drinkers who like to dance nude, and because their husbands insist on sharing them, the kids are raised not knowing who their real Dad is, just like some kind of ancient Hollywood!"

Right: The *Tomb of the Bulls* (550 BC). A depiction of a hetero-sexual couple happily performing beside a cute sleeping cow, contrasts with a frantic homosexual couple being chased by a huge enraged red bull, which proves that when making love outdoors you really must choose your paddock carefully.

Left: The *Tomb of the Bulls*. It looks like the Etruscans invented the idea of using a slave when there wasn't a bed available.

Right: A humorous sculpture of a satyr waving a snake to scare a nymph, while he reaches round to cop a sneaky feel of her breast. Obviously, nymphs weren't as easy as Etruscan wives were.

Sex is the Etruscan word for *Girl*, who earned a dowry by openly engaging in prostitution so she could afford to buy a decent husband. She was naughty, and the goddess she worshiped was *Nortia* (Got-Lucky). However, some modern historians try to snub the idea that the Etruscans were fun-loving sex-maniacs, by insisting that they were as miserable as everyone else. Staunch prudes, the Romans themselves considered dancing as almost a criminal offense. "Anyone who dances," declared Cicero, the loudmouthed 1st century orator who had an opinion on everything, "is either very drunk or raving mad!"

A modern road repair (AD 1823) accidentally uncovered a tomb containing an Etruscan corpse that

still danced. "The body became agitated with a sort of trembling, heaving motion which lasted a few minutes," reported the workmen, "and then quickly disappeared, dissolved by contact with the air!"

Left: *Acquarossa* (Red-water) mass-produced terracotta plaques decorating many houses, with scenes of orgiastic music drinking and early breakdancing. (The guy spinning on his head better be careful!)

Left: Etruscan wine jug (630 BC). These crudely incised figures baffle scholars.

The Etruscans had such a great life that they didn't want death to stop the fun, so they built bulging round tombs decorated with lively frescoes. One Tarquinian tomb depicts a crouching man defecating beside his name, so it's believed he's the artist, who perhaps added this touch because he hadn't been paid. Stone markers outside tombs indicated how many were inside, with phallus-pillars for males, and boxes for females. Inside the tombs, sculptured sarcophagi depicted the deceased still living it up after they were dead, with couples embracing, using wineskins for cushions, and letting animals drink from their holy libation dishes. Others depict a parade of the deceased heading to the Underworld, accompanied by lictors, flute players, and carts lugging all the junk they want to take with them. One tomb has painted plaster models of food, a cat catching a rat, and the occupant's slippers by the bed, ready for when they wake up. The good living caught up with the men, because they later display increasingly fatter naked bellies, and even breasts. The deceased are depicted smiling at the viewer, although one sculpture shows a youth fallen asleep waiting, or perhaps sleeping off a drunken hangover.

The Etruscans formed a League of 12 Cities so they could refuse to send help to each other when Rome picked them off one by one. They built a string of watchtowers along the coast to keep a lookout, not for foes but fins, since fishing was a favorite pastime. Port temples dedicated to the love goddess, Uni, provided rows of beds for ritual prostitution so that lonely sailors could "achieve communion with the divine."

During the Roman invasion, the Etruscans could do little but boast, "Hey! We think we're the victorious Greeks who once defeated the Trojans (Romans) in the Trojan War!" The sarcophagi no longer depict fun, but death scenes from Greek mythology, such as Minerva beating a giant to death with his own severed arm.

Right: Etruscan temple sculpture illustrating the Greek myth of the *Seven against Thebes*. The goddess Minerva carries a potion of eternal life for heroic *Tydeus* (Thumper), but changes her mind when she sees him eating his dying enemy's brains.

Below: Etruscan temple sculpture reconstruction depicting the Greek myth where Bacchus discovers Ariadne asleep (lost heads added).

A local Etruscan favorite was Plow-Hero, which depicts a naked farmer killing some soldiers with his plow, which was probably a common fantasy of disgruntled farmers bullied by arrogant Roman soldiers.

At Chiusa grave goods were sculpted from the local limestone *pietra fetida* (stinky stone) which retains a strong sulphuric odor, hence the name. The gullible Romans bought the Etruscan's *bucchero* (black-clay) pots, brightly buffed to resemble burnished bronze. The Romans may've wised up, because the Etruscans later began coating their clay pots with a tin wash to pass them off as embossed silver. The breast was significant in Etruscan art, and a red-figure cup shows Pasiphae nursing the baby bull-headed Minotaur on her lap, giving cows milk

Right: An Etruscan *Bucchero* cup. Eight nude dancers let it all hang out.

The famous Francois Vase (570 BC) was discovered in Etruria by Francois, who reconstructed it from 1000 fragments. This giant wine bowl features the marriage of Thetis and Peleus that started the Trojan War, along with other Greek myths (see p. 173), such as Achilles killing

Prince Troilus because he was sick of always letting him go free.

Fortunately, in AD 1900 a disgruntled museum guard smashed the vase, which allowed some more recently discovered pieces to be added.

Polished bronze mirrors buried with dead women were rendered useless by the inscription: *suthina* (belongs to the corpse). The engravings on the rear vary from rather crudely scratched images to masterly detailed works of art. The four mirrors below (300-200 BC) illustrate how the myth of the twins Castor and Pollux became more complex with the addition of their mother Leda (who hatched them from an egg after sex with a swan) and sister Helen (the most beautiful woman in the world).

Left: Etruscan athlete celebrating his victory, sports arm bangles and the famous fancy boots that Julius Caesar later liked to wear.

Right: Set for action, a typical Etruscan warrior wears an impressive hat, but no underwear.

Right: A two-legged headless chicken pot. The (missing) stopper was the chook's head.

Left: The *Tomb of the Floggings.*
A woman clasping an old man's hips has her bum hit by a boy. This seems a bit foolish and the old man appears to be calling a halt to the fun before love hurts.

Etruscan farmers played flutes to lead their pigs, and to hunt wild animals, which were captivated by the sound. "We did adopt one Etruscan battle innovation," the Romans grudgingly admitted, "The trumpet!"

Following the conquest of Etruria, an exceptionally handsome Etruscan lad, Spurinna, was so molested by noble matrons that he resorted to defacing himself. "Ugliness," he sighed, "is the only protection from lust!" The Romans besieged *Viterbo* (Old-town) due to the beauty of *Galiana* (Haughty), but agreed to leave after she offered to appear nude on the ramparts. The Gauls captured an Etruscan frontier town, and not knowing what to do with it, used it for burying their dead in the abandoned houses, barns, and wells. The doddering old Emperor Claudius wrote a 20-book-long *Etruscan History*, which fortunately is lost, so this is a short chapter. However, Old Pliny was able to report, "At Fufluna, the Etruscans have carved a statue of their wine god, Fufluns, from a single vine!" Claudius also penned an authoritative work on dice gambling called *Playing for Money, or Playing with Nuts*. A common English word derived from Etruscan is *person*, from the Latin

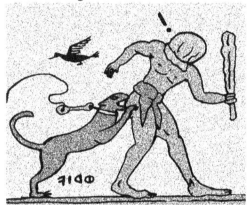

personna (mask) adopted from the masked dancer *Phersu* depicted in the *Tomb of the Augurs.* This tomb shows the Etruscan custom of forcing gladiators to fight at funeral parties (Left). Sometimes these match-ups weren't very even. The hooded man with a club fights a dog, but to be fair, it should be blindfold too.

An Etruscan master may say
it's not my wife I lay
nor my maid
being laid
but we're lying anyway!
- *Free translation of an undeciphered Etruscan inscription.*

Above: A mysterious Etruscan inscription that baffles modern scholars. Remember, Etruscan is read right to left.

The 18th century rediscovery of the mysterious Etruria burial tombs created an Etruscan craze in modern Europe. "We're descended from the Etruscans," boasted the city of Florence, in an effort to be important, "who were the 12 Tribes of Israel led by Noah after the Biblical Flood to become the chosen people of Italy - That's why we once had 12 cities!"

The ignorant locals dug up the tombs looking for pretty painted pots to sell (which were Greek imports) and smashed all the genuine plain black-clay Etruscan vases, declaring the *poca roba* (small stuff) to be "cheaper than seaweed!" "Destroy all new discoveries," ordered Napoleon's brother, "so that they won't devalue my own Etruscan collection!" Fashionable upper-class supper-parties were held in the tombs, where the smoke from picnic-fires, and guests scratching their autographs, destroyed the paintings. Many sepulchers were reused as farmers' pigsties, or knocked down for building rubble. Mixing up sarcophagus lids was common, so many museums now display women reclining on battle scenes, and men lounging over birth days.

Lady Gray was a vicar's wife, ordered to winter in Italy due to her poor health. "The previous vicar was chased off by his knife-wielding wife," she wrote, "and he carried a pail of water to throw at her if she caught him!" Her best-selling book *Tour of Etruria* described the awful hardships she endured, such as having to substitute egg yolk for milk in her tea. "I looked in a tomb and saw the awful face of an Etruscan chief looking back at me," she wrote, "and I could almost fancy he frowned on me as an unwelcome intruder in his last resting-place!" Lady Gray tried to translate Etruscan by using any Latin, Greek or Hebrew words that looked the same, so that she interpreted *cives Ana* as "Citizen Ana - a priestess." Her artist romanticized the copies of the Etruscan frescoes, toning down the nudity for Victorian sensibilities. A banquet scene of a lecherous drunken woman throwing her arms around her drinking companion is naively described by Lady Gray as "an afflicted mother consoled by her remaining son."

Above: Lady Gray's version of an Etruscan tomb painting.
Below: The same painting by the Scottish artist Byres, who is accused of 'improving' the original to suit 18th century artistic mannerisms.

The archaeologist Dennis quickly published *Cemeteries of Etruria*. "I hear Mrs. Gray is writing a fourth edition of her book," he wrote, "and I would fain put a full stop to her erroneous progeny!" Dennis endured big bedbugs, shepherds' rabid dogs, and "traveling on a feather bed strapped to a coach roof with a pretty young lady who sang all night long!" "I'm an old hackneyed horse still in harness," Dennis later wrote, sad at his lack of literary success, "while other racy writers win the Derby!"

Above: An artistic copy by Byres of a tomb that is now lost.
The slaves offer golden chaplets.

Left: Bed-time story.

Diverse tombs

Etruscan influence briefly extended past Rome down into southern Italy, as evidenced by the unique painted Greek tomb found at *Paestum* (Neptune-city). The *Tomb of the Diver* depicts banqueting scenes, drinking games, and a drunken reveler piped home by a boy. But since Paestum was founded by the fun-loving Sybarites (600 BC) they probably didn't need much excuse to party. The tomb ceiling sports a diver (positioned over the body of the deceased) which has been interpreted by scholars as the leap from life to death, or known to unknown (or dry to wet!).

Above: A *symposium* (Greek drinking party) in the *Tomb of the Diver* (480 BC) depicts *cottabos*, a drinking game that involves tossing your

wine dregs into a cup, while a happy drunk tries to seduce a zither-playing boy. *Cottabos* losers lost their shirts, and some proud tossers rated their skill as superior to that of javelin throwers. A variation is to toss it onto a bald man's head.

Paestum also produced the *phlyakes* (gossip) farce, a very obscene comedy featuring actors wearing five types of masks (youths, girls, ugly old men, hags, or slaves) with costumes sporting large, padded-behinds, and long penises (the original big swinging dick) as depicted on the vase painting shown left. "Lewd *Fescennine* poetry doesn't derive from the Etruscan town of Fescenna," claimed jealous Roman poets, "but from our Latin *fascinum* (phallus)!" *Atellan* farces performed at Atella developed into mimes because they were performed in the local Oscan language, which nobody could understand. An extant pantomime plot unfolds as follows: "The wife loves her slave, who loves another slave, so she kills them both, then embraces her lover's body. She gets drunk to forget, loves a new slave, and poisons her husband. As she pretends to mourn, her husband's corpse comes back to life…" The rest of the script is missing.

The Samnites (savage Italian hill people) overran southern Italy around 400 BC, and their many tombs depict warriors, weapons, duels, chariots, and hardworking women spinning wool (instead of yarns). There is absolutely no fun or dancing, and the women are all shown bawling at funerals - a practice that continues today.

Above right: Samnite women scratch their cheeks, tear their hair, and beat their breasts to celebrate a funeral. **Right:** Bloody Samnite warriors fighting nude, in barbarian style.

The Romans in turn took over Paestum (273 BC) but were too superstitious to destroy the Greek foundation shrine, so instead just dug a big hole and buried it. The gigantic Greek temples at Paestum are the best preserved in Italy because the place became a swamp during the Middle Ages and the stone-robbers were afraid of catching malaria. The richness of the farming soil engendered the proverb: "You get rich in a year - but you die in 6 months!" Many of the thousands of Etruscan tombs have been demolished and ploughed over to make more farmland, whereas other sites turn up so many artifacts by plough or rain that irritated farmers have termed them the 'field of jewels.'

THEY SAID I WAS DAFT TO BUILD A TEMPLE IN A SWAMP! BUT IT STAYED UP!

Left: The so-called Temple of Neptune at Paestum.

Luna (Moon) was the northern most Etruscan frontier town, renowned for gigantic cheeses stamped with the moon symbol. The city was sacked by the Vikings in the Middle Ages when their leader pretended to convert to Christianity and shammed dead to get a Christian burial. He then sprang back to life in the church, killed the priest with his sword, and opened the city gates to his army. "We had the last laugh," the Lunatics boast, "because the ignorant Vikings thought that they had sacked Rome!" An alternate version claims that the Roman emperor's wife fell in love with the Lunatic king, pretended to die, and then resurrected herself in his bedroom. However, the emperor found out and sacked the place.

Art of the steal

The Etruscans and Romans loved depicting Greek myths in their artwork (paintings, mosaics, sculptures, etc) with their

favorite subjects being the 12 labors of Hercules, the voyage of Odysseus, and the battles of Achilles. Determining the exact myth can be tricky, but generally Hercules carries a club, Achilles carries a grudge, anything with snakes for legs is a giant, and anything with wings is a harpy, a genius, a cupid, or undeterminable.

Left: The fashionable Etruscans liked to keep abreast of current affairs (Votive bronze, 400 BC).

Right: The Etruscans began depicting themselves as taller than Romans (Volterra bronze, 300 BC).

19

3 ROME ANTICS (1200-753 BC)

The uncensored story of Rome begins with what they tried to make up, and ends with what they tried to hush up. The simple Romans were quite happy fighting all comers until they met the sophisticated Greeks who bragged, "Haw! You missed out on the first battle of history - the Trojan War!" Mortified, the abashed Romans hastily rewrote history to include themselves. Obviously they couldn't be the Greeks, even though they'd won, so snorted, "We were there too - since we're descended from the Trojans!" This came in handy when they later trashed Greece, declaring, "That's for Troy!"

Around 800 BC the blind Greek poet *Homer* (*Ho Meros* means The Thigh, so-named for his hairy crotch) wrote an *epic* (wordy) poem about the Trojan War called the *Iliad*, our first great work of western literature. The war-mad Romans loved the bloody battle scenes. Ilus founded Troy, so Homer called it Ilium, but perhaps we should rename the *Iliad* as the *Triad*, since it was a war between Greeks and Trojans - and apparently a secret society of Romans! Greek epics, like this book, always begin with an invocation to the gods: "Sing me, O a Muse..." This is because the Greeks believed that the Muses spoke through the poet, which was handy whenever poets messed up, since they could blame it on the gods.

Illogical *Iliad*

"I want to rape the water-nymph Thetis," laments Jupiter (the king of the gods), according to Greek myth, "but an oracle said her son will be greater than his father." "Nobody should be greater than me," he decides, "so Thetis must marry the lowly mortal Peleus!" Much miffed, Thetis tries changing shape to scare Peleus off, but he clings onto her until she changes into something more comfortable. Thetis begets Achilles, who she dips in a magic river that makes him invulnerable, except for the heel he's held by. "You've a choice of dying young in fame, or living old in ignominy," a seer tells Achilles (to which Napoleon famously replied, "Fame is fleeting, but ignominy is forever!").

Strife isn't invited to Thetis and Peleus' wedding, so sends a gold apple marked: "To Sexy." "That's me," each goddess insists, and Jupiter sighs, "I'm staying out of this one!" "You can judge the world's first beauty pageant," he orders the dopey Trojan shepherd Paris, who admits, "I'm better qualified to judge the prettiest goat than goddess!" The goddesses display their heavenly bodies, and wonder, "How will we keep Paris down on the farm, after he's seen them?" "Pick me," begs war goddess Minerva, "and I'll make you smart!" "Pick me," growls Queen Juno, "and I'll make you strong!" "Pick me," winks love goddess Venus, "and I'll get you laid!" Paris picks Venus. "No wonder our Roman judges

PARIS JUNO VENUS MINERVA

accept bribes," complained the cranky latter-day poet Apuleius, "when the first judicial decision in history was sold for a roll in the hay!" Venus gives Paris the beautiful longneck Helen, who'd hatched from an egg after Jupiter had raped her mother disguised as a swan.

Right: Leda laid-a egg! A Roman lamp engraving depicts Leda who seems to be wringing the cheeky swan's neck, while Cupid helps by pushing from behind (AD 50). "Don't start with the egg!" was a Greek maxim that meant don't start the Trojan War (or any story) by going too far back.

Unfortunately, Helen is already married to Greek Menelaus, so Paris kidnaps her. "My real name is Alexandros," laughs Paris, "but I tell the women I bed that my name's Paris so their husbands can't find me!" Menelaus complains to his big brother King Agamemnon, who orders the well-aggrieved Greek army to go get her back, thus starting the Trojan War.

Not satisfied with a mythological explanation, the historian Herodotus wrote *History*, our first history book, to show that the war between East and West was really started by wife-stealing: First, the Phoenicians kidnapped Io from Greece, so the Greeks kidnapped Europa from Phoenicia. Then, the Greeks kidnapped Medea from Colchis, so Paris kidnapped Helen. "The Greeks were wrong to declare war," says Herodotus, "because no girl gets kidnapped unless she wants to!" "Io wasn't kidnapped either," the Phoenicians complained, "She got pregnant to our ship's captain so sailed away in shame while her kid napped!"

The Greeks prepare for war by attempting to dodge the draft. The wily *Odysseus* (Hurts) pretends to be crazy, while *Achilles'* (Aches) mother dresses him as a lady and hides him in a king's harem. Odysseus sows his farm with salt, but is proved sane when the suspicious Greeks place his infant son in front of his plow. Achilles is exposed by being tricked

21

into picking up a sword placed amongst some ladies' toiletries, as wily Odysseus tells him, "Ya mother dresses ya funny!" While hiding in the harem Achilles got a girl pregnant, who named her baby Pyrrhus, after Pyrrhia - the girl who had fathered him! That name was too sissy for the Greeks who later renamed *Pyrrhus* (Redhead) as *Neoptolemus* (Odd-fighter).

Right: A fresco from old Pompeii depicts Achilles' embarrassment at being exposed by Odysseus hiding in the harem.

Cross-dressing became a popular subject of Roman art, but was performed by only the very greatest of heroes, such as Achilles, Jupiter, and Hercules.

"Helen's face launched a thousand ships," the poets boast, "since she makes everyone keel over!" "Agamemnon once bragged that he was a better hunter than me," complains the goddess Diana, "so I won't let the wind blow unless he sacrifices his daughter!" Taking his daughter to the altar in pretence of a marriage to Achilles, Agamemnon sacrifices her (Pompeii fresco, below), and his wife's wailing blew the boats off.

"We'll avenge Helen," wise Old *Nestor* (Nester) tells the enthusiastic army, "by each bedding a Trojan wife!" Old Nestor proves himself the Greeks' most experienced warrior by out-drinking all-comers with his giant cup, and endlessly recounting his youthful heroic exploits: "I beat the hairy beast-men (*centaurs*)! We were much tougher in the good old

days!" Ovid tells how Nestor was once chased by a wild pig and so used his spear as a vaulting pole to leap into the nearest tree.

Homer's *Iliad* begins with the Greeks camped before Troy (*Ilium*), and dividing their war booty. "Haw! You haven't got a prize," laughs Achilles at King Agamemnon, who replies, "I'm confiscating your prize!" Achilles' prize is a pretty slave-girl, Briseis, so after handing her over he retires to sulk in his tent, play his lute, and ask Jupiter for divine aid. "Don't help the Greeks," Jupiter orders the gods, "so that they'll have to beg Achilles to come back!" Juno tricks Jupiter into bedding her, and then while he's asleep the gods help the Greeks. "Agh!" cries Jupiter when he wakes up, "I told you not to do that!"

Achilles' boyfriend is called *Patroclus* (Father-famous), which is a trick name since *Patra-cleos* backward forms *Cleo-patra* (Famous-father). "The Trojans are thrashing us," laments young Patroclus, "so I'll wear Achilles' armor and scare them off!" Troy's greatest warrior Hector kills Patroclus. "I wouldn't fight when Agamemnon offered to give me my girlfriend back," growls Achilles, donning his helmet, "but killing my boyfriend is too much!"

Divinities usually foretell of any hero's impending death, but in Achilles' case, it is announced by *Xanthus* (Brunette), his horse:
"A horse is a horse, of course, of course,
Patroclus and Achilles got a divorce,
You never heard of a talking horse?
Well listen to this: I'm the famous Mister X!"

Achilles attacks prince Aeneas, who resorts to throwing stones, but is saved by some gods who've decided to leave at least one Trojan alive. A river god splashes Achilles in retaliation for polluting his waters with so much enemy blood. "Please don't kill me," begs young prince Troilus, and Achilles demands, "Why? I've killed better men than you!"

"Don't attack Achilles," cries prince Hector's mother from the battlements, waving her naked breasts at him, "Come and suckle on these!" Hector considers his choice and prefers to fight, but is killed by the goddess Minerva who is still mad at losing the beauty contest. Achilles ties Hector's corpse to the back of his chariot for a drag race around three laps of Troy, so old King Priam rolls in cow dung and begs for the body back.[7]

---

[7] In honor of Britain's Prime Minister Neville Chamberlain signing a peace treaty with Adolf Hitler (1938) the English poet laureate Masefield wrote: "Nev in the night, divinely led - Unto the Nazi fuehrer said - As Priam to Achilles for his son - I'll end a war not yet begun - And beg back bodies not yet dead!" (That poem was considered the first atrocity of World War II!)

Achilles consents, in order to get smelly old Priam out of his tent, by trading Hectors corpse for its weight in gold. At this point Homer's *Iliad* ends, so other poets have continued the tale...

EVER SINCE HE HID IN THAT HAREM ACHILLES LIKES TO SLIP INTO SOMETHING MORE COMFORTABLE AFTER WAR!

GRRR!

WORLD'S FIRST DRAG RACE | HECTOR

The Greeks fight the *Amazon* (Breastless) warrior women, whose name derives either because they sliced off one breast to shoot their bows straight, or their refusal to breastfeed (to prevent drooping, which seems more likely, since Amazons are always depicted with two tits). After killing a warrior whose helmet falls off to reveal the beautiful Amazon Queen, Achilles gazes into her eyes and falls in love as she dies. "Haw! Achilles is a *necrophiliac* (corpse-lover)," laughs a fellow Greek, *Thersites* (Cheeky), prompting the embarrassed Achilles to kill him too.

Finally Achilles falls in love with the Trojan princess *Polyxena* (Many-strangers), reveals his weakness (Achilles' heel) to her, and she betrays him. Paris shoots a poison arrow at Achilles' ankle, and crows, "I got the heel!" "If I had to die because of a woman," croaks Achilles, "I'd rather it had been an Amazon!" Paris dies from an arrow shot in his crotch by *Philoctetes* (Everything-lover), who is turned gay in revenge by the angry love goddess Venus.

Right: Funnily enough, the best-selling vase of Achilles didn't depict him in combat on the battlefield, but being beaten by Ajax in a game of dice. They were too engrossed to notice the Trojan attack.

AJAX! YOU CHEAT!

Previously, Hector had fought the giant Greek warrior Big *Ajax* (Eagle) to a standstill, so they decided to swap gifts as a sign of respect. "I got the best deal," gloated Big Ajax, who took Hector's sword in exchange for his belt. "Wait until he's fighting," snorted Hector, "and his pants fall down!"

24

The Roman poet Ovid's *Metamorphoses* (Changes) Book 13 records the contest over Achilles' armor: "Give the armor to me," Big Ajax tells the Greeks, "and not to Odysseus, because he's all talk! The coward tried to evade the Trojan War by pretending to be mad - if only we'd believed him! He ran from the Trojans, and was only saved from certain death by hiding behind my own giant shield! Why does Odysseus want new armor when his own is still in brand new condition - while mine has a thousand holes! The weight will only slow him down as he runs away, and if the shield slips, it will squash him! His puny neck can't support the weight of Achilles' huge helmet, and the sun's reflection on it will give away his hiding place! Achilles' gold armor will give the Trojans no cause to fear Odysseus - but to rob him! And even if he loses this contest, he'll still be famous for having matched himself with me!" (Odysseus had earlier won the Funeral Games Footrace by tripping Ajax on the finish line to make him fall face first into a dung pile.)

"Who better to give Achilles' armor to," answers cunning Odysseus, "than the man who tricked him into coming to the Trojan War? Since I was the one who made him come here, everything he did or had belongs to me! Big Ajax said I didn't want to come to war, which is actually insulting Achilles, because he didn't want to come either - and at least I didn't hide in a dress! Also, Big Ajax doesn't appreciate the intricate carvings on Achilles' shield, so it should be given to an art connoisseur like me!" "Look, I'm covered in scars from fighting for the Greeks," declares Odysseus, stripping off his clothes, "while Big Ajax doesn't have a mark on his body!"

(Ajax is unmarked due to his fighting skill. "Those who slay crowds are 'harvesters' since they mow down nothing remarkable," Ajax boasted, "but those who kill heroes are 'wood-cutters'!")

Outraged that the dead Achilles' armor is awarded to the blabbermouth Odysseus, Big Ajax gets drunk, and slaughters all of the Greek leaders in revenge. Waking with a bad hangover, Ajax is ashamed to discover that he really only slaughtered a herd of sheep, and so kills himself with Hector's sword (his first and only wound). Achilles actually had two sets of armor, so they could've got a set each. Odysseus lost the prized armor when his boat sunk. Philostratus (AD 230) records that shepherds later blamed Ajax's ghost for making their flocks die, and one quoted Homer, singing, "Ajax fled Troy!" causing an awful voice to howl from Ajax's grave, "I did not!"

"We'll win by horsing around," decides wily Odysseus, who builds a gift Wooden Horse that the unsuspecting Trojans wheel into Troy. "Beware Greeks bearing gifts!" their prophet warns, but should've said, "Beware gifts bearing Greeks!" Helen is suspicious, and so calls out to the Greek warriors hiding inside the Horse by mimicking their wives' voices, but Odysseus throttles those dumb enough to answer. Odysseus opens the gates of Troy from the inside, and the Greeks sack the city.

Achilles' son Pyrrhus celebrates by killing Hector's father King Priam, and marrying Hector's wife Andromache. Menelaus catches Helen in bed with the Trojans (Pompeii fresco, right) so is about to kill her, but on the topless towers of Ilium she shows him her breasts. "Even though I won," he sighs, "I get the booby prize!" They live happily ever after.

"Helen was never at Troy," wrote Herodotus, "but living in Egypt! Otherwise the Trojans would've given her back to stop their city being sacked! Homer knew this, but didn't want to ruin his poem!"

Tragic *Trojan Women*

The Roman poet Seneca's tragedy *The Trojan Women* (AD 60) describes how the Greeks draw lots to divide their captives. "Amongst all these beautiful women, nobody wants to draw my lot," laments ugly old Queen Hecuba, "so at least one Trojan name still holds terror for the Greeks!" "You Trojan women are lucky," complains Helen, "because there's a chance you might be picked by a handsome Greek, while I'm stuck with smelly old King Menelaus for sure!" Odysseus draws Hecuba, who complains, "He already won Achilles' armor, and now he wins Hector's mother as an accessory!" "But my revenge," she cackles, "is that I stopped Odysseus from getting a pretty girl!"

Andromache hides her son *Astyanax* (Town-prince) in Hector's tomb. "Where's Hector's son?" demands Odysseus, and Andromache truthfully tells him, "He lies entombed with the dead!" "Oh blast, now we can't kill him in revenge," replies wily Odysseus, "so instead we'll knock Hector's tomb down!" Realizing Astyanax will be squashed, Andromache gives him up, and he's hurled off a high tower. "Splat! He's unrecognizable!" reports a messenger, and Andromache boasts, "His father's likeness still! Hector died looking a mess too!"

"My brave dad's ghost demands the sacrifice of Polyxena," Pyrrhus informs King Agamemnon, "and if you try to keep her for yourself, like you kept his last concubine, then I'll sacrifice *you*! King Priam would like some royal company!" "Achilles wasn't so brave when our ships burned," snorts Agamemnon, "while he lazed singing in his tent!" "Achilles' singing was more terrifying to the Trojans," Pyrrhus retorts, "than all your soldiers' slinging!" "You sacrificed a girl to get here," the soothsayer informs Agamemnon, "so you must sacrifice another to get back! Just pretend that Polyxena is going to marry Pyrrhus, the same way you pretended your daughter was going to marry Achilles." "It's not so bad marrying Pyrrhus," Helen tells Polyxena, "you get to change your rags for nice clothes and jewelry!" Pyrrhus pretends to marry Polyxena, until the priest announces, "You may kill the bride!" Polyxena dies, marries Achilles' ghost, and leaves Pyrrhus jilted at the altar in the most bizarre wedding ever. Agamemnon's daughter already died in a marriage ceremony with Achilles, so his ghost is committing bigamy.

Aggrieved *Agamemnon*

Seneca's tragedy *Agamemnon* has Little Ajax rape *Cassandra* (Mantrap) on Minerva's sacred shrine (Pompeii fresco, right). To avert Minerva's wrath the Greeks vote to kill Ajax, but can't because he clings to the same shrine. Minerva sinks their ships in revenge, and borrows Jove's thunderbolt to throw at Little Ajax, but misses. "Haw! Gods, Water, and Fire can't kill me!" sings Little Ajax, gleefully dancing on a rock, until he slips, cracks his head, and so dies from Earth. The few Greeks who do make it home find that they've all been cuckolded, except for Nestor (who's too old to care anyway).

"It's amazing what the gods charge for sea travel," joked the satirist Lucian, "Agamemnon got a fair voyage to Troy for a King's daughter, while Nestor got a safe return trip for only nine bulls!" "So! You've married a Trojan slave!" sneers Agamemnon's wife, when she spies his new concubine, Princess Cassandra. "Apollo gifted me with prophecy in exchange for sex, but when I reneged on the deal, he cursed me never to be believed," laments Cassandra, and Agamemnon snorts, "Who'd believe that?!" "Your wife and her lover will kill you in the bath," predicts Cassandra, and Agamemnon laughs, "Yeah, right!" They do.

Odious *Odyssey*

In the epic *Odyssey*, also written by Homer (or another poet with the same name), the cunning Greek hero Odysseus tells a long story to explain to his wife *Penelope* (Ducky - another bird related to egg-born Helen) why it took him ten years to get home from Troy.

First, he landed in the commune of the lotus eaters, who lay about blissfully drugged. Then he blinded the *Cyclops* (Round-eye) by getting the monster drunk and ramming a stake through his single eye. "I'm Nobody," Odysseus told the Cyclops, who calls for his brothers, screaming, "Help! Nobody blinded me!" "Nobody blinded him?" his brothers snort, going back to their caves, "He must be drunk!" The wind god *Aelous* (Blow-hard) gives Odysseus a bag containing all the winds except the one needed to blow him home. Just as they reach their home isle of *Ithaca* (Happy), Odysseus' idiot crew open the bag, expecting to find gold, and they're all blown away again. The witch *Circe* (Circler) turns all of Odysseus' crew into pigs, but by chewing a weed, Odysseus' breath overpowers Circe who becomes his lover. "I'll never change him," she complains, "He's already a sexist pig!" After a year in bed,

Odysseus visits *Hades* (Unseen) where he meets his dead friends. "I was murdered in the bath by my wife," laments King Agamemnon's ghost, "for my daughter-slaughter!" "I'd rather be a live slave," whines Achilles' ghost, "than a dead king!" "I'm still not talking to you!" growls Big Ajax the Sheep-Killer's ghost.

The sound of the seductive Sirens' songs caused sailors to leap into the sea, so Odysseus listens while tied to the ship's mast, as his deaf crew row blissfully by, suffering from a bad case of ear wax. Finally Odysseus is shipwrecked, spends seven years making love to the nymph *Calypso* (Cover-girl), and returns home exhausted. Outraged to find 108 suitors entertaining Penelope, Odysseus kills them all. "How do I know you're really you?" demands Penelope, and Odysseus retorts, "Because your bush is in my bed!" (Odysseus had built their bedroom around a tree he couldn't be bothered shifting.)

His own son finally killed Odysseus. "Idiot! You should've recognized your Dad," his mother Circe scolded, "Since he looks just like you!" Penelope and Circe didn't miss Odysseus however, since they married each other's sons, and so got younger toy-boy versions.

Hitting a Homer

Modern historians spend a lot of time trying to retrace Odysseus' exact route. "If you want to find Homer's geography," wrote the geographer Eratosthenes, "first find the tailor who sewed the winds up in a bag!" "Instead of worrying about where Odysseus sailed," added Seneca, "we should rather make sure that we don't get lost too!"

In 240 BC, the Greek slave Livius Andronicus translated the *Odyssey* into the Latin *Odusia* that eventually became a boring schoolboys' textbook, and the latter-day poet Horace records, "My teacher Whacker Orbilius beat it into me!" (The later poet Juvenal in turn complained of having to study Horace by lamplight until the book was burned black with soot). Greek concepts shocking to Roman ears were toned down, for example, Patroclus "gave advice as good as the gods'," became "was a godly good advisor," and "Odysseus soiled himself," became "Ulysses spoiled himself." Greek sex was right out.

Gullible Roman tourists to Greece paid to see temple treasures such as Old Nestor's giant drinking cup, Paris' mirror and curling tongs, one of Leda's eggs, Achilles' harem-dress, Helen's bosom-band, Aeneas' invisible cloak, and the clay out of which the gods fashioned men.

The Greekless Middle Ages couldn't read Homer, but thrilled to the translated Latin eye-witness accounts of warriors who were actually at the Trojan War. Dictys of Crete (a Greek general) wrote his *Diary of the Trojan War* and Dares of Troy (a Trojan priest) wrote *The Insider Story of the Fall of Troy*. Unfortunately, these are now known to be clever fakes written around AD 300. The *Second Sophistic* (Double Speak) of the Roman Empire (AD 60-230) saw 'correcting' Homer become almost a literary sport. "I got the idea while herding my sheep," wrote the shepherd Quintus of Smyrna whose *In-Between Homer* explained what happened during the gap between the *Iliad* and the *Odyssey*. "Originally named *Outis* (Big-ears) due to his looks," wrote Ptolemy the Quail, "*Odysseus* (Hurts) was renamed by his mother because she was tired of carrying him!" "I was killed in the Trojan War and I've been reincarnated," explains a talking cock, in Lucian's *The Cock*, "and I can tell you that Homer wouldn't know what really happened at Troy, because he was a Bactrian camel at the time! Big Ajax wasn't so big as they say, or Helen as beautiful, and Achilles was always in his tent singing. Helen had a very long neck, so I knew she was a swan's daughter, but she was long in the tooth too, as old as fat Queen Hecuba!"

Hearing *Big Heroes* (AD 230)

Philostratus (Layer-lover) wrote his dialogue *Big Heroes* between a grape-grabbing priest and a gullible sailor to expose more of Homer's mistakes, omissions, and the 'true' heroes of the Trojan War.

"The ghost of the first Greek killed at Troy, *Protesilaos* (First-killed)," boasts the priest to the sailor, "told me what really happened during the Trojan War!" "Where's the ghost now then?" asks the suspicious sailor. "Usually at Troy, his tomb, or having his wife in Hades," the priest brags. "The ghost also assists lovers to pick up boys," he adds, "but he won't help adulterers, because they give love a bad name! He once made a dog bite a couple making love beside his shrine on the buttocks, so that the cuckolded husband found them out!" "Well, what's this ghost look like?" asks the intrigued sailor. "Just like his statues, except he's even better looking naked," the priest confides "And he stays in shape by shadow boxing, because he says archery is for cowards and wrestling for the lazy. He even lets me hug and kiss him!" "What did he say about the Trojan War?" asks the amazed sailor. "He said…Homer is Troy's true founder, because the sacked city is only remembered because of his poem! The ghost won't say which city Homer came from, since so many cities claim him as a citizen, and he doesn't want them all to be disappointed. But, he told me these secrets:

"Great Jupiter, enfolded by sheep, horse and mule," wrote the cheeky poet Pamphos, "-dung!" Homer cleaned up this insult by writing, "Great Jupiter, enfolded by clouds, rain and sky."

The Greek hero *Palamedes* (Calculator) was so clever that he invented letters, numbers, dates, money, and checkers. "I would've invented medicine too," boasted Palamedes, "but since somebody else invented it, I don't think it's worth learning!" "Look! The cranes invented letters, not you," said Odysseus, pointing at their v-shaped pattern of flying, and Palamedes retorted, "Those cranes are flying to fight the Pygmies of Africa, but you've never seen a v-shaped battle charge, you coward!"

"Why don't you own slaves?" Achilles once asked Palamedes, who held up his hands, and replied, "What are these?"

"Yes, you should take more," the Greeks told Palamedes, when they split up the war spoils, and he answered, "No, you should take less!"

Jealous Odysseus finally outsmarted Palamedes by hiding gold in his tent to frame him as a traitor, and had him stoned to death. Achilles was so angry about this that he got drunk and composed a song called "Palamedes rocks."

"I'll tell you what really happened during the Trojan War," Odysseus' ghost later told Homer, "but in return you must praise me as the smartest Greek in your poem the *Iliad*, and don't mention Palamedes at all!" "Everybody will believe an honest poet like you," Odysseus explained, "and I'm punished less in Hades so long as mortal men think I'm not guilty!" Homer agreed, which is why Palamedes ain't in the *Iliad*.

Once, a farmer owned a dog so cunning that he named him Odysseus and constantly beat him. Palamedes' ghost was so pleased that he rewarded the farmer by showing how to use boxing gloves to knock hailstones away from his grape vines! As for the story about Odysseus listening to the Sirens' songs, Protesilaos says it is better to fill your own ears with bees-wax so you can't listen to such nonsense, since Odysseus was much too old and ugly to make love to goddesses.

Homer deliberately made no mention that Hiera was a warrior-woman who was even more beautiful than Helen, since that would've ruined his poem's theme. Hiera was so sexy that when she died the Greek elders had to order their army to stop sleeping with her!

"Make me a good singer so I can sing songs about myself," Achilles asked the gods, who replied, "Stick to fighting! We're sending Homer to sing about you!" Dead Achilles married Helen's ghost, and now sings nonstop about love, the Trojan War, and Homer. "Sing divine Homer, about how great I am," Achilles wails, "so Troy doesn't fall, I don't die, and Patroclus is still mine!" "Truly," the priest assures the sailor, "that's the true Troy truth! The End."

The epic a musing Aeneas (1200 BC)

The Romans adopted the Etruscan's chief god *Tina* (Tinkle-bell) under the manlier name of *Jupiter* (Day-Dad) or *Jove* (Dave) to his friends. Jupiter (spelt *Juppiter* by the Romans, but we'll *p* him off) was the weatherman who hurled down divine retribution in the form of lightning bolts, although the skeptics wondered how come he blasted his own temple so often.

"I'm always getting berated by my wife Juno," lamented Jove, "because I bed women who are beneath me!" In Roman mythology, Jupiter had 115 different consorts, which hardly compares with the Emperor Claudius' wife who had that many in a single night when she challenged the Prostitutes Guild to a consorting contest.

"I blame the goddess of love, Venus," Jove growled, "so I'll wreak poetic revenge by making her fall in love with Anchises, a lowly mortal beneath her!" If you're starting to think that early Roman history is fantasy, you're not myth taken.

Anchises got lucky with Venus
who said he's a lovely peon us
two shall embrace
to start a race
that'll end as the Roman genus!

Right: A theoretical reconstruction of the armless Venus de Milo (found on the Island of Melos). Some scholars argue that Venus wasn't so modest and the arms should be positioned behind her head.

The Roman race began when Anchises ran up Mount *Ida* (Bush) and down the delta of Venus. Venus gave birth to *Aeneas* (pronounced *Any-ass*) the first Roman, which is why Romans think they're all such great lovers. Latin pronounces *v* as *w* so the Romans called her *Wean-us*, and as Mother of Rome, that's what she did.

"Don't kiss and tell!" Venus warned, but rather smug at scoring with a goddess, when asked, "Where were ya last night?" Anchises bragged, "Ida Mount!" then added, "Goddy style!" Angered at his cheek, Jupiter smote Anchises with a thunderbolt, which left him limp. This seems a bit unfair, since Jove set the date up, but in Greek mythology the gods always sleep with you and never respect you in the morning.

The Greeks won the Trojan War, sacked the city of Troy, slaughtered everyone, and the pathetic Trojan loser Aeneas was sold into slavery, and never heard from again. That was the Greek version. In the new improved Roman version, the exceedingly brave and handsome Trojan hero Aeneas not only fought his way out of the burning city, but did it while piggybacking his limp old Dad at the same time.

Aeneas piggybacked old lame
Anchises through the Trojan flame
the Greeks let 'em through
'cos they thought the two
were just playing a funeral game!

Aeneas sailed off with a boatload of fellow Trojans who'd also piggybacked their fathers out, landed in Italy, and greeted the local Latins by pillaging the country side.

"Oops," he noticed, "they've sent Latinus to flatten us!" Aeneas made peace by marrying King Latinus' daughter Lavinia, who gave birth to a town called *Lavinium* (Animal-bath) and a son called Little Juli (*Iuli of Ilium*) who founded the Roman race as mixed Italian-Trojans.

"This means war," growled King Turnus of the Rutulians, "since Lavinia turned me down when Aeneas turned up!"

An angry king called Turnus
says he's gonna learn us
we took his wife
now he wants strife
in t' urns to turn us!

Turnus killed his prospective father-in-law, Latinus, which severely ruined his chances with Lavinia. "It ain't fair," he moaned, "when Aeneas was late in!" "That's right," agreed Aeneas, "I'm Latin, and one of you, so forget I lost the Trojan War already!"

They've taken the welcome-mat in
but I got a marketing pattern
to rebrand our guys
we'll advertise:
old Trojan's now new Latin!

"Back me up," Turnus promised his Etruscan allies, "and you can drink all the wine in Latium!" The Latins went one better by instead promising all their wine to Jupiter, and so won the war, although Aeneas was killed. Turnus hoped this would give him a better chance with Lavinia. It didn't.

Annoyed *Aeneid* (19 BC)

Zooming forward in time past Rome's conquest of the world, past the bloody civil wars between competing warlords, which saw more Romans killed by each other than any enemy, and down to the fall of the Roman Republic, we meet Augustus, who became the first Emperor by being the last Roman standing. Sick of the braggart Greeks' world cultural domination, Augustus' first act was to re-rewrite history, by ordering the poet Virgil to pen a Latin epic poem in praise of Rome.

Virgil began by copying Homer's *Odyssey*, and ended by copying Homer's *Iliad*. "So," the Romans boasted, "it's twice as good!" "No," the Greeks retorted, "it's just Odd and Ill!" "Why don't you try ripping off Homer?" snorted Virgil to his critics, "You'll find it's harder than stealing Jove's thunder!"

"Who would listen to another poet?" asked Theocritus, "Homer is sufficient for all!"

"If I had a second life to live," snorted Cicero, "I still wouldn't find time to waste reading Greek lyric poets!"

However, the Greeks had already tried to rewrite Homer prior to Virgil's attempt. Sotades the Obscene rewrote the *Iliad* in jocular verse ("The Wooden Horse poops Greeks"). Timolaus doubled the length of the *Iliad* by adding the subtitle *Troicus* and repeating every line in different words. Since the *Iliad* was divided into books according to the 24 letters of the Greek alphabet, the poet Nestor rewrote the poem without using the letter 'A' in Book 1, the letter 'B' in Book 2, the letter 'C' in Book 3, and so on. Tryphiodorus rewrote the *Odyssey* without using the letter 'S' so it became the *Odyey* of Odyeu. The Romans changed Odysseus' name to *Ulysses*, but forgot to rename the *Odyssey* as the *Ulyssey*.

Because Homer's poems were originally spoken aloud they contain repetitive epithets to remember who the characters are, like: *well-greaved* Greeks, *sly* Odysseus, *perfect* Penelope, *hector* Hector, *heavenly-haired* Helen, *fast-footed* Achilles (even when he's sitting), *fair-armed* Andromache, *cow-eyed* Juno, *dog-eyed* Agamemnon, and *anxious* Aeneas. Virgil renamed him *pious* (dutiful) Aeneas, and by not repeating himself made his written poem half as long as Homer. "Our hero's mother was a goddess," boasted the Romans, "but Achilles' mother was just a watery fish girl (sea-nymph)!"

Like Homer, Virgil wrote in dactylic hexameter. A *dactyl* (three-bone-toe) stresses the first of three syllables, e.g. Enemy (EN-em-ee), Panicking (PAN-ick-ing) and Run away (RUN-a-way), which are all terror dactyls. A dactylic *hexameter* (six-footer) runs on six metrical feet of dactylic toes, e.g. Virgil is | rhymed in | dactylic | sounding | so oddly | idyllic! (Dactylic hexameters aren't used in English poetry because they're too damn hard to make!)

Originally, Virgil's poem was titled *Mighty Deeds of Rome*, but that didn't sound Greek enough, so he renamed it the *Aeneid*, after the main hero Aeneas, although the *Augeid* or *Guseid* would be better titles since the poem was political propaganda to justify the emperor Augustus ruling the world. Virgil wrote the story first and then hastily converted it into poetry so as to create a finished poem. "My poem is a towering edifice," boasted Virgil, "and the awful bits are just temporary props to hold the rest up! Don't worry, I'll go back and fix them later!" Unfortunately, Virgil found many of his half lines too hard to complete, even after ten years of trying, so left them like that.

Upon Virgil's sudden and mysterious death, his will ordered that his unfinished poem be destroyed, but Augustus proudly published it, boasting, "The bit about me is okay!" It was rumored that Augustus poisoned Virgil because he'd been about to make improvements, by deleting the bit about him. "Troy almost got incinerated twice," a wit joked, regarding the poem's rescue.

The Other Secret Roman *Iliad Homerus Latinus Ilias Latina*

Augustus may've hedged his bets, since an anonymous poet also penned an epitome of Homer's *Iliad* in Latin for those that couldn't read Greek. The humorous *Homerus Latinus* contains all the great fight scenes, plus praise for Augustus' Julian house that Homer had forgot to mention. Suspected authors include Homer, Pindar, Virgil, Ovid, Nero - or Italicus, whose name is spelt out with acrostics in the poem's last lines: "**I** Tell **A** Lengthy *Iliad* Cut Ultra Short."

34

Here's an even shorter epitome of the *Ilias Latina* epitome, complete with acrostic:

Achilles cries for a lady
Until he sighs for a laddie
Great Gus' rewriting
Iliad's fighting
Ends with Hector's Daddy!

An anorexic *Aeneid*

The 12 Books of the *Aeneid*, considered the greatest Latin poem ever wrote, are summarized in the following few pages with the poetry and boasting about Rome mostly left out, but the funny bits left in.

Book 1. Virgil's cautious editor confessed he'd had to alter the poem's opening line, which originally read: "I once blew a shepherd's pipe, so I've penned a poem to cheer up my neighboring farmers because the greedy senators rob them - For rams and demands I sing!" This was revised as: "For arms and de man I sing!" Cheeky wall graffiti from Pompeii (AD 79) reads: "For launderers and the owl I sing, not arms and the man!" (The owl was the patron bird of the laundry washers, who bleached clothes by jumping on them in a vat of urine.)

Epics always start with an invocation to the gods. "Sing me, O a Muse," sang Homer, who really did sing the *Iliad* accompanied by a lyre, but since the *Aeneid* was only read, Virgil copied with: "Tell me, O a Muse." Hundreds of handsome warriors were violently killed in the *Iliad*, but gay Virgil's poem instead does that to the pretty women.

"Aeneas is the son of Venus," Virgil begins, just like the story so far, but then he changes the plot: Aeneas' Trojan wife Creusa becomes the mother of Little Juli (*not* Latin Lavinia) so when Troy burns, poor Aeneas not only has to piggyback his old dad Anchises, but his wife and son too. Virgil seems to have a grudge against Latin women (by excluding Lavinia), but on the other hand he also has poor Creusa burn to death in the flames. "Sail to Italy," Creusa's ghost tells Aeneas, who obviously never listens to a word she says, since in the next Book he has forgotten where to go already.

"Jove raped Electra, and the Trojans are descended from her son Dardanus," growls Juno, "so I hate them! Paris made me lose the beauty contest, and Jove keeps the cute Trojan prince Ganymede as a Troy-boy!" Juno blows Aeneas off course to African Carthage (which wasn't actually built until 800 BC).

Right: Campanian fresco dog caricature.

The Romans must know they're a bit ugly, because Venus has to use magic to make Aeneas appear handsome in order that the widowed Queen *Dido* (Tramp) will fall in love with him.

Of arms and the man I serenade
whom jealous Juno did degrade
but never fair
Venus did his hair
so that he'll get laid!

Dido's first date is translated by Charles Cotton (AD 1670) in this burlesque passage:

Dido led Aeneas in kind fashion
toward her Grace's habitation
and made a curtsy at the door
and prayed him to go in before
but he most courteously cried no
I hope I'm better bred than so
but let him say what he fay could
Dido swore Faith and Troth he should
Well (quoth Aeneas) I see still
Women and Fools must have their will
and thereupon without more talking
enters before her proudly stalking
scarce were they got within the doors
and Dido called her Maids all Whores
and a great coyl and scolding kept
because the house was not clean swept!

Book 2. "The Greeks couldn't beat me in a fair fight," Aeneas brags, trying to impress Dido at the dinner table, "so the cowards hid inside a wooden gift horse, and then fought me while I was asleep!"

I beat the wily Grecian mob
but they pulled an inside job
and in they snook
so always look
a Greek horse in the gob!

Right: A Cycladic storage jar depicting the Trojan horse (670 BC). Presumably, the Greeks at the windows could pull down blinds to hide behind when the Trojans appeared.

"Troy was all ablaze and I was in sheer terror," Aeneas explains, "Because dead Hector's ghost appeared who advised me to run away!" "The house burnt down of my neighbor *Ucalegon* (Doesn't-care) – but I did!" he continues, "I tried sneaking out disguised in Greek armor, which fooled the Trojans but not the Greeks, so I was attacked by both sides! I hurriedly climbed up on the roof and fought them by throwing stuff on their heads! Then I saw Pyrrhus kill old King Priam, and that gave me the cunning idea to sneak out by hiding under my dear old dad, Anchises! But he refused to leave, until we saw Little Juli's hair burning and I told him - You're fired!"

Book 3. "I've sailed everywhere Odysseus did," Aeneas belches, recounting his travels, "looking for a place to found."

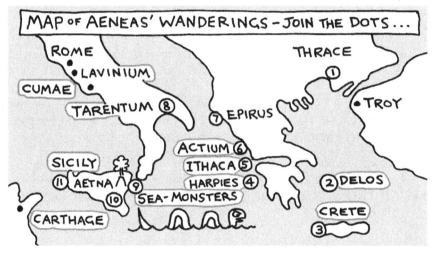

Key to Map:

1. Thrace. Aeneas visits the Thracian First National Bank where the Trojan gold was deposited for safekeeping and makes a withdrawal.

2. Delos. "Indiscrete Aeneas," decrees the Oracle of Apollo, in obscure riddles, "return to your Mother's alley."

3. Crete. "In dis Crete," announces Aeneas, "we'll build our city." "No, not dis Crete," the gods tell him, sending a plague, "It-alley of your mother not!" "I-tally the dead," the confused Aeneas complains, "so it-illy?"

AENEAS MAKES A WITHDRAWAL !

Eventually he works out that the gods mean Italy.

4. Harpy Isle. "You'll be so hungry," caws an upset *harpy* (snatcher) whose feathers Aeneas ruffled, "that you'll eat your table!" This curse is later humorously fulfilled when Aeneas spreads his bits of food onto some dry bread like a table, and then eats that too, thus inventing the first pizza (This is Virgil's only joke).

THE HARPY'S REVENGE

5. Ithaca. The crew hurls insults at the isle of Ithaca, since that's where the *Odyssey*'s Odysseus came from, and the *Aeneid* is better.

6. Actium. The crew has a party, because Virgil knows this is where the emperor Augustus defeated Mark Antony and Cleopatra. Aeneas nails a Greek shield up in a temple, inscribed: "I tweaked the Greeks!" (Since nobody there knew that he hadn't.)

7. Epirus. Aeneas is amazed to find that after Achilles' son Pyrrhus got bored bedding Hector's captured wife Andromache, he married her off to Hector's brother, Helenus, joking, "Now my supply of Trojan slaves won't run out!" Pyrrhus was killed (while abducting Helen's daughter Hermione), and so Helenus has taken over his kingdom - or at least the half with slaves in it.

The *Greek Anthology* Riddle 14.9 reads:
"My father-in-law killed my husband! My husband killed my father-in-law! My brother-in-law killed my father-in-law! My father-in-law killed my father!
Who am I?"[8]

"Aeneas, settle where you see a sow with 30 piglets," prophesies Helenus, "called *Alba Longa* (Blonde Long)!" The crew accepts this as a good omen, since it means bacon all around.

LONG BLONDE

8. Tarentum. The crew prays to Juno to be nice to them. She isn't.

9. Sea-monsters. The whirlpool *Charybdis* (Sucker-down) and sea-monster *Scylla* (Mangler) shipwrecked Odysseus and drowned his crew, so to prove that he's a better sailor than those Greeks, Aeneas makes it past them.

---

[8] *Answer:* Andromache. 1. Achilles (father of her second husband, Pyrrhus) killed Hector. 2. Pyrrhus killed King Priam. 3. Paris killed Achilles. 4. Achilles killed her father Eetion.

"Hideous Scylla has a womb full of blue barking dolphin-tailed wolves, whose mouths shoot out to eat up sailors," Aeneas explains, then thoughtfully adds, "but she does have quite nice tits!"

Right: Scylla combs her hair, while her dog heads munch sailors, having fish and ships for lunch. Emperor Tiberius kept a similar statue at Sperlonga.

10. Aetna. On Sicily, the Trojans are affrighted by a creature with a scraggy beard, wild staring eyes and clothes held together by thorns, which screams, "Help, I'm a Greek castaway that Odysseus left behind!"

Aeneas taunts the giant Cyclops that Odysseus blinded. "Hah, Odysseus might say he's No-Body," he yells, "but I'm Any-Ass!" Bravely uncowed by all manner of monsters, Aeneas sheepishly admits to Queen Dido that the rumble of the Mt Aetna volcano on Sicily did leave him a little nervous.

I've braved gods and harpies weird
and tweaked Cyclops' fearsome beard
I jeered ghost grumble
but only Aetna's rumble
has really made me scared!

"Mount Aetna flings fearful fountains of fire into the sky," wrote the accurate Greek poet Pindar, which Virgil copied here as: "Mount Aetna vomits groaning balls of fire to lick the stars." "Only a tongue can lick things, Virgil," complained his literary critics, "not balls, and certainly not stars, they're too far away!"

11. Sicily. Aeneas' dear old Dad Anchises dies, and Juno blows the ships off course over to Carthage (which is back in Book 1 where we started).

Found in translation

Translating Latin into English is an amusing art, as one of Virgil's early translators here cheerfully acknowledges:

Such's our Pride, Folly, or Fate
Virgil's *Aeneid* to Imitate
by heating his Fame
with Ashes not Flame
Those who can't Write: Translate!
- After Sir John Denham (1669)

The first English translator of the *Aeneid* was Chaucer, who "pray that my English be understonde, God I beseech!" He needn't have worried, since he was followed by Gavin Douglas' *Eneados* in Scottish verse, who wrote:

Mast reverend Virgill, of Latyne poetis prince
Gemme of ingine and fluide of eloquence
I mene thi crafty werkis curious
sa quik, lusty, and mast sentencious
Na, na, ma vulgar blabring mak ya wince!
- After Gavin Douglas (1513)

Douglas was praised for his description of Venus as a huntress: "Hir skirt kiltit til hir bair kne!"

"Gentlemen amateurs dabbling in Virgil are mere Holiday Authors," complained the poet Dryden, who then proceeded to incorporate their work into his own translation. "Okay, I copied Lauderdale's unpublished manuscript," the rather wet Dryden admitted, and in revenge Lauderdale's later published book bore the Virgilian inscription: "*Sequiturque sequentem*" (He follows the follower).

"It's only fair, that the Latin which made us cry as boys," explained John Phillips, in his parody of Virgil, "should make us laugh as men!"

This seems a good place (as any) to give examples of various authors' attempts to translate Latin into English, paraphrased here in Virgil's romantic Book 4, more coarsely known as the *Libido of Dido*.

Book 4. Even though Venus made Aeneas look handsome, his boasting isn't enough to impress Dido. Venus orders Cupid to remove his wings, pretend to be Aeneas' son, and drive Dido crazy with love.

Dido so young, so lusty, so glade
that if God, who the earth made
left off heaven's governance
and had half a chance
with her woo he'd be waylaid!
- After Geoffrey Chaucer (1400)

Chiefly Dido coming ill
strives in vain desire to fill
She views Aeneas by turns
insatiable looks gazing burns
She's troubling for a spill!
- After Wordsworth (1832)

"Aeneas is alive, and your husband is dead," Dido's sister helpfully reminds her, "and ghosts ain't that good under the sheets!" As a last resort, Venus zaps Aeneas invisible.

VENUS' PLAN TO SEDUCE DIDO...

1) MAKE AENEAS HANDSOME 2) PUT CUPID TO WORK 3) ADVICE FROM ANNA 4) AND INVISIBLE CLOAK

Mosaic 1: A series of mosaics depicting the romance of Aeneas and Dido grace the floors of a luxury Roman villa's bathhouse at Low Ham in Britain (AD 300). In this first scene, Venus appears in all her glory, ably assisted by Cupid (left) and Stupid (right) who has apparently got himself tangled in her robe.

Mosaic 2: Venus introduces Aeneas and Little Juli to Dido.

Venus enflames Dido with love, who decides to slip into something a little more comfortable.

Venus then swaps Cupid for Little Juli, who looks like he is up way past his bedtime.

41

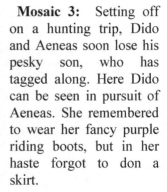

Mosaic 3: Setting off on a hunting trip, Dido and Aeneas soon lose his pesky son, who has tagged along. Here Dido can be seen in pursuit of Aeneas. She remembered to wear her fancy purple riding boots, but in her haste forgot to don a skirt.

Mosaic 4: Aeneas looks back nervously and notices that Dido is in hot pursuit.

Like Dido, Aeneas too is also distracted by love, so has similarly donned his fancy purple riding boots, but has absentmindedly forgotten to wear his clothes. Dido catches him.

Mosaic 5: Juno sends down a thunderstorm, so the couple runs to shelter in a cave, both frantic not to get their nice cloaks wet. Aeneas did Dido. Notice how Aeneas rides his horse naked, but makes love dressed in full combat gear.

"Shush," Dido warns Aeneas, but a rumor of their affair soon spreads.

"Homer says: Strife starts small, and then grows to the heavens. Virgil copies him here as: Rumor starts small, and then grows to the clouds," complained the critic Macrobius, "But when rumor grows, it's no longer rumor - it's gossip, and then common knowledge!" "Also," he adds, "Homer reaches the heavens - but Virgil's only a sky scraper!"

One Cave in her dark bosom doth afford
shelter to Dido and the Trojan lord
the hapless Queen to various fame
doth her Crime in Hymen's name
Perchance because she's getting bored!
- After Sidney Godolphin (1643)

Not one poor dram of consolation
O vile woman in desperation
what shall I do in this condition
to keep me from the World's derision
at African-Trojan miscegenation!
- After Charles Cotton (1670)

Dido frets, and blames Anna's encouragement for her predicament.

Ah, sister, sister! Hadst not thou
played Mistress Quickie's office so
and soothed me up till I grew jolly
I never had committed folly
and bade the saucy Knave: 'No!'
- After Charles Cotton (1670)

"Dad, I've heard that Aeneas did my girlfriend Dido," complains King Iarbas, who is Jupiter's son by the rape of an African nymph. "Aeneas shouldn't be having fun with strange women," growls Jove, "That's my job!" He sends Mercury, the messenger of the gods, to remind Aeneas, "You're not here to lay about, so go roam!" Aeneas is warned to look after his son.

Mercury rattled him: 'Thou lousie
mangie, careless, drunken, drowsie
coxcomb! How oft must I be sent
hither from Jove to complement
your worship to a reverent care
of the young Bastard here, your heir?'
- Charles Cotton (1670)

Dido gets wind that Aeneas is about to leave, and begs him to stay.

The Queen beheld as day appeared
the Navy sailing the Haven cleared
thrice her Naked Breast she knocks
and tears upon her Golden Locks
O by Jove she's acting Weird!
- After Sir John Denham (1669)

Aeneas: O Queen of Carthage wert though ugly-black
with blubber'd cheeks, I'd still love thee back!
Dido: No farewelling, carry me to your fair dwelling
kidnap me, my Paris - I'm your second Helen!
- After Christopher Marlowe (1593)

"But we're not even married," Aeneas complains, unaware that Dido considers sex in a cave during a thunderstorm with the gods watching to be a Punic wedding ceremony.

Although I did the thing you wot
Jove be my Judge, I meant it not
indeed I took it for a kindness
to be familiar with your Highness
and thought you just put out a lot!
- After Charles Cotton (1670)

"Ungrateful wretch," Dido complains, "I found you as a starving shipwrecked beggar, and gave you Bed and Broad!" Dido tries making an effigy of Aeneas, but it just isn't the same. "Make me big-bellied with a baby," she coos, "then I'd have something to remember you by, and those nasty African kings won't want me!" Her pleading fails to retain Aeneas, so Dido resorts to cursing him.

Go! Seek thy farm, I hope 'twill be
I'the very bottom of the Sea
altho' in Proverb old is found:
Who's born to hang, will never be drowned
I place my very curse on thee!
- After Charles Cotton (1670)

As soon as I can turn to a ghost
which will be in a week at most
then in the midnight sleep I'll wake thee
and ride thee worse than any hackney
I'll terrify thee day and night
nay if thou do'ft but go to shite
there will I stand with burning taper
to fizzle thy tail instead of paper!
- Charles Cotton (1670)

May none give house-room to the mongrel
but let him perish on some dunghill
and when his treacherous Soul's departed
let his foul carcass be deserted
to Hogs and Dogs, and Kites and Crows!
- Charles Cotton (1670)

Aeneas thanks Dido and sails off for Sicily. "Don't expect me to wait up for you!" she warns, which the Romans claim explains Carthage's great hatred for them.

"I'm building a huge fire to burn your bed," Dido tells the dismayed Aeneas. "Ha! Fooled you," Dido gloats, as she instead falls onto his sword and into the flames, "Just like you fooled me!"

Mosaic 6: Aeneas makes good his escape.

The Low Ham mosaic is taken as evidence of an educated Roman appreciation of great literature.

Dido's real name is Elissa (*Dido* is a nick-name for the Punic moon goddess, given due to her lunacy).

I gave Aeneas my home
but now he's off to roam
I got the shove
so don't love
any-ass in a Roman poem!

Farewell to fair Elissa
but I ain't gonna miss her
when I looked back
she gave me a smack
right on the kisser!

"I didn't weep when I read the true story of how Christ was nailed on the cross," Saint Augustine revealed in his *Confessions*, "but as a boy I bawled when I read Virgil's fiction about how Dido died!"

Commentary on the *Aeneid*

"Virgil didn't copy Dido's love scene from Homer," Macrobius pointed out, "He copied it from the Greek *Voyage of the Argonauts'* Medea and Jason love affair. Everybody knows that chaste Dido would never sleep with ugly Aeneas, but artists like to turn a blind eye, just so they can depict lurid lusty love scenes!"

Macrobius may have a point, since the witch Medea helped Jason steal the Golden Fleece, and they slept together in a cave. But there the similarity ends. Unlike Dido and Aeneas, Medea sailed away with Jason in his ship the *Argo* (Speedy). (Medea chopped up her little brother and tossed the pieces into the sea to slow down her father who was in hot pursuit. When Jason later took another wife, Medea killed both his bride and her own children out of spite! Medea's witchcraft was also credited with miraculously making the old young again, which some suspect was due to the early use of hair dye and wrinkle cream.)

Other commentators argue that Dido really represents sexy Helen (with Paris), or Calypso (with Odysseus) or Cleopatra (with Marc Antony) who all drove their lovers crazy. Otherwise, she's big hairy Ajax (who, like Dido, killed himself with someone else's sword).

Servius (AD 400) wrote a very long *Virgil Commentary, which* exhaustively analyzed every last detail of the *Aeneid*, and an example of his Book 4 reads like this:

"Some foolish people say Book 3 and 4 don't join, because one is about Sailing and the other is about Love – but I say instead that they're very cleverly joined, because Book 3 ends with Aeneas saying he's tired, while Book 4 starts with Dido saying she can't sleep. "Dido's heart is pierced with love" means she's been shot by Cupid's arrow. "Dawn bathed the earth with the Sun's lamp" means that Aeneas must've been talking all night, and "Bathed" means cleaning the earth, because darkness is dirty. "Ah!" means Dido loves Aeneas. When Anna says "Will you fight against pleasing love" she means "Dido repels unpleasing lovers, but will she distain a pleasing lover too?" and "Fight against" is Greek, because we Romans say "Fight with." "Unbridled Numidians" means they have no bridles. "Support of the gods" means the gods carried Aeneas to bed Dido. "Two-toothers sacrificed to Ceres, Liber, and Apollo" means sacrificial sheep with buck teeth, and since Dido wants to marry Aeneas she appeases the anti-marriage deities, like the goddess Ceres (who's angry because her daughter is Pluto's wife), the drunken wine-god Liber (who had to kidnap a wife), and Apollo (who doesn't have a wife)."

Macrobius was so impressed with Servius' *Virgil Commentary* that he made Servius into one of the characters in his own book about Virgil (*Saturnalia*) so Servius could quote himself.

Book 5. In Sicily, Funeral Games are held for Aeneas' dear old dead Dad Anchises. "I threw my helmsman overboard for not sailing closer to the rocks," complains a losing Boat Race captain, while another helmsman chuckles, "I sailed into the rocks - but at least the captain didn't throw me overboard!" "Give me first prize, because no one will fight me," boasts the young boxing champion, until the old champion comes out of retirement and knocks his teeth out. The leading Foot Race runner slips face first into some dung, so churlishly trips the next runner, which allows the third runner to win. Due to their loud complaints, Aeneas has to award three First Prizes.

"We're burning the boats," growl the Trojan women, "because we're sick of sailing in circles!" Dismayed to find himself stranded in Sicily, Aeneas is relieved when divine Jupiter douses the flames with a piddle from on high. "I'm setting sail for Italy with only the very toughest men," Aeneas snorts at those who elect to stay behind, which the Romans claim explains why the Sicilians are so soft, and why it's called *Sissy-ly*.

The Trojan women's peeve
do brands of fire heave
but the boats were spared
when Jove declared
I decided to relieve!

Right: A relieved Hercules statue from *Herculaneum* (Hercules-town).

Book 6. Aeneas' first landfall in Italy is at Cumae (the oldest Greek colony) where he makes a sacrifice to thank the gods. An enemy Greek unexpectedly approaches, so Aeneas quickly turns his back and pulls his toga over his head so that he's not recognized. The ruse works, and so the later Roman priests adopted that ritual for all of their sacrifices.

Aeneas meets the mad old Sibyl who lives in a cave that is the entrance to Hell. Today gullible tourists are shown the "genuine" Sibyl's cave (which is a long rock cut military tunnel). Known as the *Phlegraean* (Fiery) fields, this volcanic area stinks of sulfur with a rotten eggs smell and contains Lake *Avernus* (Birdless - because the gases kill all birds flying over). The region suffers from the geological phenomenon of *bradyseism* which causes ever changing undulating landforms, with the most recent arrival being *Nuovo* (New) Hill which demolished a local town when it appeared almost overnight (AD 1538).

Homeric legend credits *Baia* and *Misenum* as being named after two of Odysseus' Greek sailors (Baios and Missin'-him). This was too much for the patriotic Virgil, who instead claimed that the coast was named after Aeneas' drowned trumpeter, and his old nurse, whose epitaph read: "I suckled Aeneas whom we admire - who saved me from Troy's fire - to cremate me on this pyre!"

Bradyseism has since sunk Baia into the sea, and underwater archaeology has revealed submerged fishponds and a *Claudian nymphaeum* (a temple featuring statues of the emperor Claudius' family, and Bacchus the wine god) whose unpatriotic centerpiece is a sculpture of Odysseus and Baios getting the Cyclops drunk (with internal pipe work to squirt real wine).

Right: A theoretical reconstruction of the Claudian nymphaeum wine-fountain. Baios squirts the wine cask into the Cyclops' big gob, while Odysseus catches the drips.

The emperor Tiberius also had a nymphaeum displaying Cyclops and Odysseus in his grotto at Sperlonga, further up the coast. A central pond featured Odysseus sailing away from the sea-monster Scylla who was busy devouring his crew. This mythical spectacle symbolized the hero's *apotheosis* (transformation into a god) which Tiberius almost experienced himself when part of the cave roof collapsed on his head. The fishpond outside was used for *ichthyomancy* (predicting the future by the way fish swim).

The mad old Sibyl guides Aeneas into the Underworld, and Virgil writes, "May the gods not blast me for revealing the Secrets of the Afterlife!"

"Beware," Sibyl warns, "here dwells Famine, Disease, Agony, Anxiety, Grief, Old Age, Sleep, and Guilty Joys!"

"I'm not afraid," Aeneas boasts, "of those last two!"

At the Stygian Marsh, Aeneas meets the unburied who are doomed to wander the earth (even though three handfuls of dirt chucked over a corpse was considered a decent burial). "What are you doing here?" demands Aeneas, when he spies his helmsman's ghost. "I fell asleep, fell overboard, and drowned!" the ghost sheepishly replies, adding, "Can you bury me at Velia?" (An impossible task, since at that time it hadn't yet been built - Virgil must be confused by too much spirits).

The Sibyl brandishes a gold branch to threaten Charon unless he ferries them across the river *Styx* (Hate). "Hey fatty, you're sinking my boat," complains Charon when Aeneas hops in, since it's designed only for ghosts who weigh nothing.

On the far bank, Aeneas notices that the 'Beware of the Dog' sign has been changed to 'Beware of the Three-headed Snake-backed Serpent-tailed Puppy!' Sibyl drugs Hades' triple-headed guard dog Cerberus with a poison doggy-treat.

At the Mourning Fields, Aeneas is annoyed to find the dead Queen Dido two-timing him with her first husband's ghost. Aeneas meets the warriors of the Untimely Dead, and doesn't recognize his friend *Deiphobus* (Cut-scared), who has had his nose and ears chopped off. "What happened to you?" Aeneas exclaims, and the ghost mutters, "I didn't hear the Greeks sacking Troy, so Menelaus surprised me in the sack with Helen!"

In Homer's Underworld, Odysseus met Tiresias (a man who'd turned into a woman, then back again), and so not to be outdone, Virgil has Aeneas meet Caenis (a woman who'd turned into a man, then back again), also called Caeneus (since the Romans didn't think a man should have a woman's name). "Men enjoy sex more than women," Juno had once complained, to which Tiresias replied (who'd been both), "No! Women enjoy sex nine times more than men!" Outraged at his cheek, Juno struck him blind.

Aeneas hurries past Pluto's Palace and fiery Tartarus where the wicked are punished, which Sibyl warns him to avoid. Eventually, at the happy *Elysium* (Thunderstruck) Fields, Aeneas meets the great Romans who either killed lots of enemies, or were good poets. The Roman idea of heaven was listening to your enemies being tortured in Tartarus next door, while recounting old war stories.

The emperor Augustus decided to decree himself as a god, so that when he died he could live on Mount Olympus with all the mischievous Olympian gods, rather than at the Elysium Fields with the boring good Romans.

"Augustus is the greatest!" proclaims Anchises' ghost, since Augustus paid Virgil to write that, and adds, "It's Rome's duty to rule the world! We'll give you great monosyllables like *lex*, *mos*, *jus*, and *pax* (law, order, justice and peace) after we've beaten you!"

The Greeks may have fancy schooling	It's Rome's artistic destiny
philosophy, science, rhetorical fooling	to conquer all barbarity
music and art	if they fight
they think they're so smart	give 'em shite
but remember, it's Rome that is ruling!	if they yield, let 'em be!

Anchises explains the workings of the universe, and foretells the future of all Roman history, which culminates in Augustus' glorious reign. This poetical technique is very effective as it makes Virgil appear omnipotent by predicting future events that his contemporary Roman readers would know have indeed come true.

However, as W. H. Auden pointed out in his poem "No, Virgil, no" (paraphrased here, along with his Blonde joke), this literary effect dates rather quickly, since the modern reader wonders why Virgil's predictions all stop at 30 BC, and why Augustus wasn't told that his Empire would fall or that the last Roman emperor's name was *Augustulus* (Little Augie).

The *Aeneid*'s future prediction	Virgil's a refugee rhetorician
now seems a silly fiction	whose prognostic composition
when Anchises don't see	convinced a blonde prince
past 30 BC	that Providence
to Rome's final dereliction!	gave Blondes the top position!

Why doesn't Anchises recall
that Rome will one day fall
and to Augustus proclaim
the last ruler's name:
Augustus the Small!
- After W. H. Auden (1960)

However, during the Middle Ages the *Aeneid* was held in such superstitious awe that a method of foretelling the future called Virgilian Lots became popular, where you simply opened the tome and picked a line at random (I tried it on this book, and I tell you it works!). Therefore a reply to Auden's "No, Virgil, no" might be an *Audeid* that reads:

Yes, Virgil, yes!
we put it to the test
and your foresight's
exactly right
while Auden has to guess!

While in Hades, Aeneas also spies Augustus' son-in-law who has just died, and during a live poetry recital, the canny Virgil told Augustus: "Marcellus is doing just swell, down there in Hell!" Marcellus' mother was listening, fainted outright, and when she recovered paid Virgil ten sesterces for each verse.

Finally, Aeneas views the ghosts waiting to be reborn, who must drink from the River *Lethe* (Forgetfulness), including Augustus, who's in for a pretty long wait (1000 years - the time it takes to purge their sins). "Sleep has a horny door for true dreams," explains Anchises, "and an ivory door for false dreams!" "Hades is easy to enter, but hard to exit," cackles the old Sibyl. "Well, I'm not really horny," replies Aeneas, so sneaks out with the false dreams.

Book 7. Aeneas sails up the coast to Latium, and while passing Cape Circe listens to the howls of the men that the witch Circe has turned into animals.

"I knew you were coming because my daughter's hair caught on fire and I saw a bee-hive," King Latinus tells Aeneas, "which our oracle said portended the arrival of a flaming busybody!"

Latinus was convinced when a mysterious voice from a bush said, "Don't marry your daughter to ugly old King Turnus! Marry me to that handsome Trojan stranger instead!" "Don't marry Lavinia to Aeneas," screams Latinus' wife Amata, "you know those Trojans are always starting wars by stealing foreign women!"

"What's Amata?" Latinus asks the Latin matrons, who chant, "Juno has driven her and us all mad, so we're going into the hills to perform parts in a depraved Bacchanalic orgy!" (Virgil has a definite grudge against Latin women.)

War breaks out, but in Virgil's version, the Latins become baddies fighting for Turnus because Little Juli shot their pet deer, while the Etruscans are now goodies fighting for Aeneas, since Augustus' best friend Maecenas was Etruscan, and also paying Virgil's bills.

When the Trojan army rides
confused Aeneas chides
Etruscans hug
but Latins mug
'cos we've all changed sides!

Turnus' troops are well-armed (with acorn-firing slingshots) but aren't well-legged (having only one boot each) so he asks the exiled Greek warrior Diomedes for help.

In Homer's *Iliad* the fierce Diomedes bashed Aeneas, pummeled the messenger god Mercury, speared the war god Mars in his guts (who screamed louder than 9000 men), and stabbed Venus in her hand (as she dragged her son Aeneas off the battlefield to save his life).

Virgil patriotically writes that Diomedes is now too scared to fight Aeneas! Maybe Diomedes is afraid to face Little Juli, who could justly complain, "You gave my Granny the finger - you prick!" "I've killed too many Trojans," Diomedes sighs, "I'll not kill another!"

Book 8. "Go ask the Greek king, Evander," the Tiber river god tells Aeneas, "to turn on Turnus."

Forget Turnus' slander
that the Rutulians are grander
seek the Greek
'cos if you're meek
don't get mad - get Evander!

Evander (Good-guy) rules the Greek town of Pallanteum, set on the Palatine hill, so even with Augustus' rewrite, the Greeks still built Rome first. "Look, we can prove Evander really existed," the Greeks claimed, when questioned by skeptics, "because Hercules says he met him there while traveling!"

"One day this will all be Rome," boasts Evander, pointing about, "and where those cows are grazing will be the forum!" However, Evander doesn't predict that in the Middle Ages the forum will be renamed the *Campo Vaccino* (Cattle Field) and cows will graze there once again.

"Not only has Virgil offended literary taste by using Greek words and weird expressions," complained Macrobius, "but morality too, since he has Venus beg her husband Vulcan to make a gift of armor for her illegitimate brat!"

Venus gives Aeneas a magic shield depicting great moments from Roman history (retold in the next chapters): the babes sucking the wolf's teats, the rape of the Sabine women, Mettius Fufetius pulled into four pieces, Rome beaten by Porsena and the Gauls, and of course in the middle - Augustus' great triumphs. At ten sesterces a verse, who can blame Virgil for ranting on?

Book 9. While Aeneas is gone, Turnus attacks the Trojans, but before he can burn the ships, they turn into mermaids and swim away. In a rollicking rewrite of one of Homer's *Iliad* battle scenes, Turnus escapes by jumping in the lake.

I jumped in Tiber's flood
to wash off all the blood
how can you say
I run away
when I'm stuck in the mud?

Virgil's most romantic scene has the lovers Nisus and Euryalus creeping about at night to murder the unsuspecting enemy lying drunk asleep. Euryalus steals a shiny gold helmet that reflects the dawning sun and so betrays his position to the waking enemy. The lovers are killed together.

Book 10. Venus and Juno engage in a fierce slanging match over the fate of the Trojans and Latins. "I won't destroy the Trojans who've badmouthed you," Jove sighs, to placate Juno, "but as a fitting punishment I'll make their descendants all have to mouth bad Latin!"

After slaying Evander's son Pallas, whom Aeneas had promised to protect, Turnus proudly dons Pallas' engraved sword belt that depicts the 50 Danaids murdering their husbands on their wedding night. Turnus then proceeds to chase the fleeing Aeneas, who turns out to be a ghost that Juno created in order to save Turnus' life by drawing him away from the battle. "Darn it," Turnus curses, when he discovers the ruse, "Now everyone will think I ran away again!"

Book 11. Literal revenge is taken on Rome's old enemies the Volsci by making their best warrior be a woman, Camilla. As a small baby, Camilla was saved by her fugitive father who hurled her across a river to safety, tied to a javelin. Fighting with a sword and one bare breast, Camilla shows off her cleavage, but Virgil kills all the women in his poem off horribly, so she gets a nipple piercing.

In the *Aeneid* thriller
the Volsci maid Camilla
squashes enemy pates
between her breast plates
she's a real lady killer!

Book 12. Jupiter decides to help in his usual manner by raping Turnus' sister, Juturna. She hides in the Tiber river and the bamboozled Jove can't find her until an informer squeals. To dry her tears, Jove puts her in charge of rivers. She uses her new powers to help Turnus, until Jove warns, "You don't Turnus on anymore!" Juturna now lives in a forum well.

"I'll fight that Asia-Minor-runaway Aeneas," Turnus boasts, "in single combat for Lavinia!" Lavinia blushes bright red, and scholars have taken this to mean that she loves Turnus, or loves Aeneas (or maybe is just plain embarrassed?). The battle rages. "I think Turnus has lost," sobs Amata, who hangs herself. "The Trojans are sissies who wear tunics with sleeves," laugh the enemy, "and ribbons to keep their bonnets on!" "I can sing vipers to sleep and cure snakebite," advises Turnus' doctor, "but I've no antidote for the sting of a Trojan sword!" In the climactic finale Aeneas is about to spare Turnus, but observes he's wearing dead Pallas' belt, so spears him, growling, "Pallas belted you, not me!" The last line reads: "Turnus chills out, as his life spills out!"

Virgil doesn't say how Aeneas dies, but it must be in bed, since he writes: "After Aeneas died, Lavinia gave birth to his son called Silvius who founded the Roman race as mixed Italian-Trojans." However, Augustus' Julian clan claimed descent from Little Juli, and Virgil fails to specify how. We don't know who Little Juli's wife is (but the only other woman left alive at the end of Virgil's poem is the mad old Sibyl!).

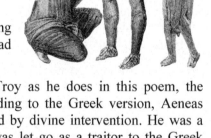

The end

Right: A Pompeii fresco depicting Aeneas either having an arrow head removed or his legs plucked.

If Aeneas had fought as well at Troy as he does in this poem, the Trojans never would've lost. According to the Greek version, Aeneas was only saved from Achilles' sword by divine intervention. He was a coward for hiding on Mt Ida, and was let go as a traitor to the Greek cause.

If Homer wrote the *Aeneid*
of exploits that Aeneas did
in the Trojan war
it'd be no more
than the title: *An 'e hid*!

Vegius was so upset by the ending that he penned Book 13 of the *Aeneid*, where Aeneas marries Lavinia to live happily ever after.

In Ovid's version, Dido's sexy sister Anna arrives, weeping, "The horrible Numidians attacked Carthage after Aeneas left, and I had to flee! I've no clothes and no where to go!" She moves in with the newlyweds, much to Lavinia's jealous chagrin.

Aeneas became worshiped as the minor god *Indiges*, so some Romans had an extra course at their sacrifice feast for Indigestion.

Aeneid criticism

The poem was considered boring enough to be compulsory reading for all schoolboys for a long time. "My pupil's parents demand impossible standards," complained Juvenal in *Satire* 7, "and surprise them on their way to the public baths with questions such as: Which breast was Anchises nursed on? What steps did Anchemolus' stepmother take? How many jars of Sicilian wine did the Trojans drink?" (All of which have no answer.)

Not all schoolboys paid attention however, since Trimalchio recalls, "I remember the story about how fat Cyclops poked out Odysseus' eye with his thumb, and during my school trip to Cumae I saw the shriveled up old Sibyl hanging in a jar saying that she wanted to die!" (Sibyl eventually died from touching a stamp seal made of clay from her homeland, whose earth she was forbidden to return to.)

Priscian (AD 500) gave dismayed Latin students tricky *Exercises* on the first line of each book of the *Aeneid*, such as: "Proposition prepositions' suppositions impositioned indisposition's depositioned composition." (How many prepositions are there in that line?)

Literary critics published many commentaries on the *Aeneid*, entitled *Faults*, *Thefts*, the more kindly *Resemblances*, *Aeneidomastix* (Aeneid-whipper), and the more severe *Virgiliomastix* (Virgil-whipper). "I wrote my commentary because none of the other commentators made any sense," wrote TC (Tiberius Claudius) Donatus in his book *Interpreting Virgil* and interpreted every single part of the poem as praise for Augustus.

"Virgil didn't copy everything from Homer," insists Macrobius in his *Saturnalia*, "some things he copied from other Roman writers, which they had copied from Homer!" For instance, Homer says: "Shield against shield, helmet against helmet, man against man." Furius copies Homer: "Foot on foot, sword on sword, man on man." And Virgil copies Furius: "Foot stands on foot, man jams man." Also, Homer says: "I don't have 10 tongues and 10 mouths." Hostius copies Homer: "I don't have 100 tongues or mouths and can't sing." And Virgil copies Hostius: "I don't have 100 tongues, 100 mouths, or iron tonsils." "If from Virgil you quote it," brags Macrobius, "I'll name the poet who wrote it!"

"Virgil's ghost appeared to insult me," explained Fulgentius (AD 500) in his book *Exposing Virgil's Secrets*, "and then explained the secret meaning of the *Aeneid* to me, which is really an allegory about you! The shipwreck is your birth, Dido's funeral pyre is your self-consuming hot teenage passion, going to Hell is school, and Aeneas' final battle is where you fight off rage and wickedness!"

Virgil's ghost became a tour guide through Hades for the Italian poet Dante in his epic poem *Inferno* (AD 1300), which is a Christian Hell, so contains many more elaborate tortures for sinners than the *Aeneid* did.

Virgil's many imitators included Fracastoro's epic *Syphilis, or the French Pox* (AD 1500) in which the cheeky shepherd Syphilis was cursed by Apollo with an awful venereal disease.

Camoes' epic *Lusiad* (AD 1550) sails Vasco da Gama's *Lusitanians* (Portuguese) to India to fight the Mohammedans. The love goddess Venus champions Vasco (like Aeneas), while the drunken wine god Bacchus backs the Mohammedans (even though they're teetotalers). "Christianity is our religion," complained his critics, to which Camoes replied, "Yes, but my poem can't have the holy angels flying around doing the depraved things that the Roman pagan gods do!"

In Milton's epic *Paradise Lost* (AD 1667) Satan tricks Adam and Eve into eating the Apple of Knowledge to realize they're naked, so that God kicks them out of the Garden of Eden. "Better to reign in Hell, than serve in Heaven," says Satan, reflecting Julius Caesar's comment: "I'd rather be chief of a stinking barbarian village - than the second-ranking man in Rome!" "Milton's a true poet," wrote William Blake, "but on the Devil's side and didn't know it!" "It's a good poem," said Sam Johnson "but nobody ever wished it was longer!" Dryden decided Milton was as good as Homer and Virgil combined, hence his epigram:

Two famous old poets ain't wiltin'
cos Homer has lines that are liltin'
and Virgil has groove
Nature couldn't improve
so added them both to make Milton!

HOMER & VIRGIL

HEY! I CAN SEE AGAIN!

The fascist Italian World War II dictator Mussolini ordered his troops to read Virgil, in the hopes that this would inspire the Romans to take over the world again. It worked too, for a while.

"He who writes last, writes best," declared the philosopher Seneca, "Since you just have to rearrange whatever you copy to make it look new. That's not stealing, because nobody owns words!" Under Roman law whoever owned the parchment owned the words written on it, so a poet had no copyright.

The Greeks may have expected Roman plagiarism, since they were having trouble thinking up new ideas themselves. Way back in 400 BC the Greek poet Choerilus had gloomily complained that everything had already been written about. "I have my shiny new chariot all yoked-up," he whined, "with nowhere to drive it to!" He did manage to write one thing:

Blessed the poet remote
who could pen an original quote
while I'm dressed so
with nowhere to go
and that's all I wrote!

"Sing me, O a muse..."
is a line that I don't use
for everyone uses
Homer's muses
but... I refuse!
- Pollianus, *Palatine Anthology* 11.130

MY CHARIOTS READY WITH NOWHERE TO GO! BECAUSE THE ROMANS HAVEN'T BUILT ANY ROADS YET!

Some ignorant Romans who weren't aware of the Official Story recount other versions, such as: "The Trojans sailed to Italy where a seasick woman named *Rhome* (Super-girl) secretly burnt the ships, leaving them stuck there. The men were very angry, so the women invented kissing to make up."

Brutish Brut of Britain

Geoffrey of Monmouth (AD 1150) read the Roman tale of Aeneas, and decided that Britain needed a famous Trojan ancestor too.

"Little Juli's son secretly got a girl pregnant," wrote Geoffrey in his *British King History*, "and the soothsayers predicted that the baby would kill his mother and father." This turned true when the mother died in childbirth and little Brut grew up to be such a bad bowman that he accidentally shot his father while aiming at a deer.

Brut was exiled from Italy, so moved to Epirus where Helenus and the rest of the Trojans were still enslaved by the Greeks. "To the Greek King," wrote Brut in a letter (which was longer than what I have recorded), "we are sick of being your slaves, and have gone to live in the forest on bugs and berries." The outraged king sent his army into the forest, which discovered that their Trojan slaves had been breeding like rabbits, and now outnumbered them. "We will kill you," Brut told the captured king, "unless you give us permission to run away!" The bemused king agreed, and the Trojans sailed off to Britain, stopping only to sack France on the way, where Brut founded the town of Tours (named after Turnus to remind the French that Aeneas had killed him). Brut named Britain after himself, and renamed Crooked Greek (the Trojan language) as brutish British. The Trojans were renamed as the barbarian British tribe *Trinovante* (Troy-new), and their capital city New

Troy, until King Lud renamed it *London* (Lud-town). Lud's brother Ninny complained that it was an awful name…

[Geoffrey's history continues on, to recount how a British king kindly sailed his 30 Trojan daughters to Rome when he heard that Romulus had no wives for the Romans, so that they wouldn't have to rape the foreign Sabine women. This generous offer wasn't taken up, so Geoffrey claims that another 'British' king, Brennus, avenged the insult from Rome by going and sacking the place!]

Is Troy for real?

In AD 1695 the *Renaissance* (Rebirth) reached Britain and collectors began buying (and stealing) all things ancient. Modern fakes appeared, and some antique statues were in museum displays for years before it was noticed that they were wearing Victorian underwear. Scholars built reputations by criticizing the ancients, and each other.

"Homer was just a poor bard who earned drinking money at Greek festivals," claimed England's greatest classical scholar, Bentley, "by singing his violent *Iliad* to cheer the men, and his romantic *Odyssey* to seduce the women!" "A pretty poem, Mr. Pope," Bentley announced, regarding Alexander Pope's translation of the *Iliad*, "but you mustn't call it Homer!" "Claret," added the tippler Bentley, "strains to be port!" "Where Bentley late tempestuous wont to sport," retorted Pope, in his epic *Dunciad* (Dunce), "in troubled waters, but now sleeps in Port!" "Thomas Hobbes' translation of Homer," Pope churlishly added, "if writ on purpose to ridicule that poet - has done very well!" This erudite correspondence ushered in modern classical criticism, with scholars searching for more fakes, and better insults.

Bentley translated the *Greek Anthology* poem 11.235 ("The Greeks reek, except Geek, but Geek's Greek!") into English as: "The Germans in Greek are sadly to seek, except only Hermann, but Hermann's a German!" However in 1873 the German H. Schliemann seeking Greeks surprised the world by discovering Troy, since until that point Homer's Trojan War was considered to be a mere fable.

Two Turks who owned *Hisarlik* (Tower) Hill allowed Schliemann to dig, provided they could use the stones he uncovered to build a bridge. The Turks soon had enough stone and ordered the digging to stop, much to Schliemann's frustration, who had uncovered phallus-shaped objects that seemed to point in the right direction. Schliemann promised to split any treasure, so the Turkish Government provided a guard and allowed digging to resume. Pretending it was his birthday, Schliemann got the guard drunk, and then secretly split an unearthed horde of gold jewelry amongst his friends, before splitting for Athens. Studiously following Pausanias' ancient *Guidebook to Greece* he excavated Agamemnon's Greek hometown of Mycenae. "I've gazed on the face of Agamemnon," Schliemann boasted, when he discovered the beaten gold funeral mask of an even earlier king. He also announced the discovery of a circular bronze shield, which turned out to be a frying pan. "The spade is the sword of archaeology!" declared Schliemann, "Dig it?" "Troy was sacked twice," complained his critics, "first by the Greeks, then by Schliemann! And he did the greater damage!"

The new science of archaeology saw Napoleon Bonaparte invade Italy to rob Roman art for France, while English Lord Elgin stole the Parthenon temple sculptures from Athens to display in his amateur museum. "They're better than anything Bony stole!" he proudly boasted. "Elgin's grand saloon's a general mart," wrote the poet Lord Byron, "for mutilated blocks of art." "I brought back the statues to instruct the English in sculpture," explained Elgin, to which Byron retorted, "Hmph! The English are as capable of sculpting, as the Egyptians are of skating!"

Wasting money on Phidian freaks
chasing fame by hoarding antiques
sniff blockhead Elgin
and you'll smell gin
so the mute stone speaks!
- After Byron
English Bards and Scottish Reviewers.

To prove that the English were defacing Greek antiquities, Byron carved his name across the forehead of a huge statue at Paneum. Elgin lost his marbles, which are now in the British Museum.

Today the tourists to Troy can view a dirt mound cut through with trenches, layers of stone marked as levels 1-12, and a clunky wooden horse surrounded by anxious Turkish street-vendors selling everything from the original Golden Apple to Achilles' Armor.

Beware Greeks bearing gifts!
Through the stalls I sifts
while a pick my pocket lifts
I get a break
then find it's fake -
Beware Turks selling gifts!

4 WOULD A ROME BY ANY OTHER NAME SPELL AS NEAT?

(753-715 BC) Longa tales

After drowning, Aeneas was all washed-up, so the Latins and Etruscans fixed the Alba River as the boundary between them, and Little Juli's son, Romulus, founded Rome in 753 BC. Then the Greeks ruined the story by insisting, "The fall of Troy occurred in 1200 BC, nyah!" Not to be outsmarted, the Romans inserted a string of 12 kings to cover the missing 400 years.

Lavinia ruled Lavinium, since Little Juli wasn't old enough, but when she finally kicked him out of home at age 30, he built a long city on the *Alban* (White) hills that he named after his pet pig, *Alba Longa* (Long Blonde). The archaeological evidence shows Lavinium, Alba Longa and Rome were actually all founded about the same time, but the Greeks have spoilt the tale once already, so let's forget that.

Little Juli was going to call his son Romulus, but changed his mind and named him *Silvius* (Woods-born, or Woody for short) since the chariot didn't get to the midwife in time. Silvius' son Aeneas Silvius' son Latinus Silvius' son was still called Silvius, showing that they really needed a faster chariot. Another four sons later came Tiberinus Silvius, who drowned crossing the Alba River, so they renamed it the Tiber in his honor.

Tiberinus was a big wine imbiber
in his honor, wrote the inscriber:
Don't cross Alba drunk
or you'll be sunk
that's why we now call it the Tiber!

"I reckon I'm better than Jupiter!" decided Remulus Silvius, and to prove it, built a hideously noisy contraption that let off loud thunderclaps. Whenever he heard real thunder in the sky, his soldiers were ordered to make hoots and banging noises to drown it out. Sick of the racket, Jove sent down a lightning bolt to shush him up. His son, Aventinus, named the hill he was buried on:

When Remulus was hit by lightning
Aventinus said it's frightening
in rain, don't climb
the hill Aventine
or we'll get a-vent-in-us brightening!

Rhea Silvia, Rome's Mama Mia (Around 780 BC)

"Amulius and Numitor, you have a choice," offered King Proca Silvius to his two sons, "the loan or the throne?" Amulius took the loan, hired mercenaries to boot Numitor out, and took the throne too, thus getting both the gold and the Silvia. "Numitor's daughter, Rhea Silvia, is a Vestal virgin," he declared, "so she can't have any children to murder me!"

Unfortunately, she did have children, but at last they weren't born in the forest like everyone else, but in jail. "I was raped by the god Mars, who entered through my keyhole!" she explained, which is certainly better than admitting she slept with her Greek slave boy.

It was also rumored that Amulius himself had dressed up in kinky Martian armor to bed the gullible Rhea. The Father of the Roman race remains a mystery - as Mars, Uncle Amulius, or Rhea's slave boy (but my money's on the Greek).

"Even if it's not true, nobody laughs when we say we're descended from the war god Mars," wrote the Roman historian Livy, "just like they don't laugh at our army!"

Says the Vestal Rhea Silvia
I'm gonna be Rome's Mama Mia
by Mars I was rort
he'll pay child support
and Amulius caught goner Rhea!

Right: A Roman relief of magic Mars leaping into bed with ready Rhea.

Roman bites wolf

"Drown the two babes," Amulius ordered, but the flooded Tiber washed them back up, so they were borne in the forest after all, stuck in a fig tree. A she-wolf annoyed by their howling gave them her teats to suck, so they'd shut up. The Latin word for tits is *rumis*, so they were named Romulus and Remus since they were a pair of boobs. Picus the woodpecker fed *Remus* (Big-boob) and *Romulus* (Little-boob) on worms and tasty bugs.

Right: A tender fresco of a Greek baby suckled and tongue-bathed by a deer (Herculaneum).

In the original Greek myth, a mare suckled the boys. "Horse nipple? Oh, I thought you said a whore's nipple," explained the dopey shepherd *Faustulus* (Little-lucky) who took them to the local prostitute. *Faula* (Whore) was a bit of a dog, so the shepherds had nicknamed her *Lupa* (Wolf), and she suckled the boys. The prissy Romans however, decided to pretend they were descended from a real animal, rather than adopted by a lowly harlot.

Romulus and Remus, washed up in a ditch
suckled by Lupa, but we'll switch:
If I'm a son of a whore
folks will guffaw -
so call me a son of a bitch!

MIGHT AS WELL FATTEN 'EM UP BEFORE I EAT 'EM!

The boys grew up sharing sheep, and then graduated on to rustling. One day Remus was busy celebrating the *Lupercalia* (Wolf-festival), which entailed getting drunk and running about naked beating girls with a thong dipped in blood, when the shepherds caught him. Dragged before Amulius, he was charged with "Robbing Numitor's farm, indecent exposure, being a public nuisance, and making howling noises!" Unable to find that on the law code, Amulius decreed, "Oh, take him away and let Numitor sort it out!" Studying the terrified Remus, Numitor mused, "Hmm, you look kind of familiar?" Remus wailed, "Fear mars my face!" "Well, it's not fair, but you do have Mars' face, I'd recognize that big Roman nose anywhere," Numitor decided, "you must be my grandson!" "Let's kill Amulius to celebrate," cheered the reunited family, "and crown Numitor as king again!"

Numitor's beat by Amulius
who newly rules unduly us
But his twin kin
did him in
and truly rules unruly us!

ROYAL FAMILY

SIGH!

GRRRR

REM

ROM

RAISED BY A WOLF...

62

Romulus remiss

The twins decided to found a new city, but found themselves fighting over whether to call it Rome or Reme, instead of doing the sensible thing and calling it Romrem. They agreed to observe the heavens for omens, so Remus sat on the Aventine hill, and Romulus sat drinking on the Palatine. Remus saw six vultures, and jubilantly demanded the kingship, but by then Romulus was seeing double. "O yeah?" he boasted, "well, I saw twelve, so sod off!"

Let's call the whole thing off (as sung by Louis Armstrong)

You say Rome, I say Reme
You say Palatine, I say Aventine
Rome, Reme, Palatine, Aventine
Let's call the whole thing off!
You say six, I say double
You say tricks, I say trouble
Six, double, tricks, trouble
Let's call the whole thing off!

They didn't call the city Off of course, and Romulus began by plowing the sacred pomerium boundary around Rome. "Any enemy could jump over this ditch," Remus laughed, leaping over. "And anybody could kill this enemy," retorted Romulus, hitting the cultivated clodhopper on the head with his spade. "Anyone raids," he warned, "They get it in spades!" With Remus reamed, Romulus roamed, but to show that he could share, kept Remus' empty chair beside his throne.

Rap of the Sabine Women

He'd had omens, now Romulus needed Romans, so he gathered a gang of runaway slaves from the neighboring states. "Everyone who knows who their father was is a patre," he ordered, "so your descendants will be *patricians* (nobs) and claim that they're better than those other bastards, the *plebeians* (mobs)!" Unfortunately, before they could be *patres* (fathers), they needed some Patricias (Rowomans), so Romulus sent marriage proposals to the surrounding tribes. "The only way you'll get any of our women," they indignantly replied, furious that half their slaves were hiding out there, "is if Rome's made an asylum for runaway harlots too!"

Smarting from this rebuke, Romulus schemed. "Come to my big festival in Rome," he smilingly invited, "the Consualia, in honor of Consus the god of secrets!" Too late, the Sabines discovered the secret of the god 'Cons-us' when their women were suddenly abducted from the party. Each Roman grabbed as many virgins as he could carry, although some beauties had been picked out before hand. Romulus *raped* (kidnapped) Hersilia, while one klutz took somebody's wife. "She picked me up," he protested, "what could I do?" "I'm silly," Hersilia snorted, "- her sillier!"

The Romans raped the women of Sabine
by grabbing them and saying "Mine!"
but then to woo
cooed "I love you!"
it always works, that pick-up line!

A gang of men snatched a real stunner, crying out "Thalassius, Thalassius!" as they ran through the crowd, meaning she was reserved for the important senator Thalassius. It became a Roman custom to shout that out at weddings, while parting the bride's hair with a spear.

We're crying out "Thalassius!"
so that you won't mess with us
but she's so fair
we're gonna share
and really mean "The lassie - us!"

The outraged men of *Caenina* (Dirt) considered the rest of the Sabines way too slow to avenge this insult, and foolishly attacked on their own. Romulus beat them, killed King Acron and stripped his armor, which didn't fit him as wore spoils, so were renamed Royal Spoils. There wasn't a temple yet, so he nailed the armor to a sacred oak in Jove's grove, declaring, "From a little Acron does the mighty oak tree grow!" This didn't happen very often, or the tree would've looked like a second hand junk stall. This early on, wine was so precious that libations to the gods were poured out drop by drop, and often Romulus substituted milk during worship, explaining, "I don't serve drunks!"

Rome was attacked by Caenina
wanting their women back keener
fleeing their foes
their king lost his clothes
demean - but the Romans demeanor!

"I'll secretly let you into Rome's Capitol," Tarpeia promised the Sabines, "if you give me what you wear on your left arms!" She wanted their gold bracelets, but they instead piled their shields on top of her to play squash. Future Roman traitors would be hurled off the adjacent Tarpeian rock, named in her honor, so they could be flattened without having to bother with shields. "She's a heroine," decided the worshipers at Tarpeia's tomb, "who cleverly disarmed the Sabines by trickery!"

The Sabines didn't mind their *p*'s and *q*'s, so pronounced *Tarqeia* as Tarpeia, *Quinquillius* as Pompilius, and *quoquo* as poopoo.

The Sabine champion Mettius *Curtius* (Shorty) killed Rome's champion Hostius Hostilius, chasing the terrified Romans before him. "Rape our women, eh?" he bawled, "We'd rape your women - if they weren't really ours!" Dismayed, Romulus prayed to Jupiter *Stator* (Stayer), the aspect of the god that stops men wetting their armor.

When Romulus' men fled from the fray
he cried "O I wish that they'd stay
for Jupiter Stator
a temple, but later
turn round, the fight's that-a-way!"

The Romans religiously u-turned, and routed the surprised Sabines. Their big hero lost his horse, and fell into a filthy swamp, which was named Curtius Lake in his honor. The spot is still marked in the Roman forum today, by a muddy puddle.

The Sabine hero's mistake
of hiding in Curtius Lake
left him all wet
named not to forget
it's a swamp that dirty us make!

"We're pregnant," wailed the Sabine women, waddling between the two armies to expose their breasts and bellies as proof. "This makes us like family," they decided, so all kissed and made up. A treaty was signed, and the wily Sabine women inserted a clause: "We don't have to do any cooking." The in-laws moved in, doubling the size of Rome, with some forming the *Rapta* (Raped) family tribe. "You'll get Tit for Tat," tittered King Titus Tatius, who became titular co-king with Romulus, "because I'm naming my new tribe of women the Tities!" "So you won't get homesick, I'll call you Quirites," Romulus suggested, "after your Sabine hometown of Cures." "The cure's worse than the curse," the Sabines swore, "since we're better off in Rome and sick of Cures!" Romulus wasn't titillated for long however. "The new co-king did nothing about his old friends murdering us," the citizens of Lavinium complained, "so we gave Titus Tatius it for that!"

We're mad at Titus Tatius
because a tight-ass, that-he-is
favoring his friends
and not making amends
no more he'll spite-us, splat-he-is!

The poet Ennius wrote the first Latin tongue twister: *"Tite tute Tati tibi tanta tyranne tulisti!"* (Titus twixt Tatius trails tyrannical trouble!)

"Why aren't our kids born yet?" demanded the Romans, who were tired of waiting, and the Goddess of Childbirth answered, "First a shaggy goat must enter your wives!" The Romans weren't too keen on that idea, until an auger suggested, "I know! Let's kill a shaggy goat, cut its hide into strips, and whip our wives with it until their skin's cut!" This ritual brought on labor.

The Etruscan League attacks

The Etruscan towns, alarmed at Rome's growing power, lined up to attack. First up was Fidenae. Romulus feigned retreat, laid an ambush, and chased them all the way back to their city, straight through the gate behind them, taking it by storm. "In this battle 14,000 enemy were killed," boasts an ancient historian, who probably exaggerates, since he adds, "and Romulus killed half of them himself!"

Attacked by the Fidenate
uninvited raiding party
we chased our mates
through their city gates
how's that for a ready repartee?

Second up was *Veii* (Village). Being more civilized, they only sent a pack of pillagers to plunder, rather than fight a bloody silly war. Defeated, they diplomatically arranged a 100 year truce with Romulus, planning on coming back in a century, when he'd forgotten about it.

We are canny Veientes
here to plunder your plenties
but we don't want war
with all that gore
we're very cultured gentries!

Romulus rose

Romulus formed a bodyguard called the *celeres* (speedy), to protect him from his greedy *senate* (old men). While admiring his army on the *Campus Martius* (Field of Mars), a storm burst, enveloping him in a thick cloud, and he was never seen again. His 300 speedsters didn't get there quick enough, because they kept tripping over each other.

"Romulus flew up to heaven," the senators claimed, but it was believed that they'd actually torn him to bits, hiding the pieces in their togas, which may be how they got purple borders. The oldest monument in the forum is the *lapis niger* (black rock), marking his grave, which isn't there. The enraged people were about to rip the senate to pieces, when the ancestor of Julius Caesar, known as Julius *Proculus* (Far-out) cried, "Quirites! Romulus appeared to me to say it's real cool up there in heaven and Rome's going to rule the world! He wants you to worship him as the god Quirinus, so don't go all queer on us!"

Appeased by this news, the people performed queer rites as Quirites, while the senate got down to the serious business of fighting over which of them should be the new king. "Pick me!" Julius suggested. "No, we'll all be king," the senate agreed, "by taking turns as *interrex* (between-king)." "Oh no, you won't," the plebs warned, "We'll accept one king, but not one hundred!"

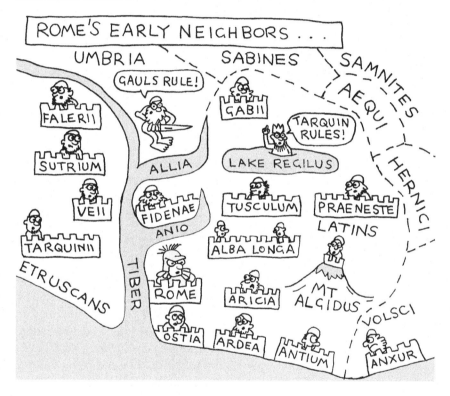

5 KIN KING CLAN KING THINKING WAN KING (715-509 BC)

Pompous Numa Pompilius (715-673 BC)

"Let's give the crown to a Sabine, Numa Pompilius," the senate agreed, "that way none of you others will get it!" Numa was said to be wise, because Pythagoras had taught him, which was pretty clever since Pythagoras hadn't been born yet. "Gods, approve me as king by sending a secret sign," Numa asked, and they did, but he wouldn't say what it was. His first act was to sack Romulus' lifeguards.

"To stop you fighting, I'm building the temple of Janus," Numa announced, "When its doors are shut, the Romans are at peace!" "It's too hot and stuffy with them shut," complained the priests, so the Romans were at war for the next 400 years. "War's doors are like a whore's drawers," Virgil lamented, "always open!"

"My slave girl's a goddess, the water nymph *Egeria* (Carried-away)," Numa bragged, "who wets my bed every night while ordering me what to do," since that was the only way to get the pigheadedly stubborn but gullibly superstitious Romans to obey his wet dreams.

I rule by superstition
but Egeria's position
leaves me squashed
and then washed
by her nocturnal emission!

"I'll set the calendar at ten months," Romulus had decided, "because that's how long it takes a baby to be born, which is quite enough trouble for one year. We'll name the months Mars (*March*), and Venus (*April*, after the Greek goddess *Aphrodite*), since they're our Dad and Mom, even if not with each other. Then we'll have Major (*May*), and Junior (*June*), so you'll remember that venerable elders like me, should come before you snotty youngsters!" Suddenly bereft of ideas, since he was a shepherd, not a poet, he added, "Oh, and the rest can just be Five, Six, Seven, Eight, Nine, and Ten (*Quintilis, Sextilis, September, October, November*, and *December*), okay?" Numa amended this idiotic dating system by adding *January* for Janus the *Janitor* (Doorman) of Heaven, and *February* for Februus (god of ghosts) onto the front of the year, so *December* (Ten) now became twelfth. An extra month

Mercedinus (Wages) was sometimes added to fix any shortfall, which was when the workers got paid. This erratic calendar was soon out of kilter, taking 20 years to return to the start, so the distraught Romans were celebrating summer festivals in winter and sunbathing in the snow.

The Calendar works by stealth
'cos the tenth month's now the twelfth
I do remember
October's December
and the change has ruined my health!

The 30-day *month* (moon) was marked by the *fasti* (right) days of the Kalends (new moon), Nones (half moon) and Ides (full moon). "That's too easy, so we're changing the months to alternate 29 or 31 days," the priests announced, "so we have the important job of yelling out on the *Kalends* (Calling) whether the *Nones* (Ninth) will be on the ninth or seventh day!" So he could take a break, Numa made the *nefasti* (not-right) days on which no one could do any business, and also the nefasti half-days, when he either slept in or had an afternoon siesta.

A head priest, the pontifex maximus, was employed to fix bridges while he prayed, *pont* being Latin for *bridge*, and still has his job today, as the Pope, although he's given up the useful repair work.

Permanent priests named *flamines* (blusterers), for their flamin' funny pointy apex hats, were appointed, and because one was dishonorably discharged when his hat blew off, the rest kept theirs firmly tied on with string. Their chief, the flamen Dialis, even kept his hat on inside.

The *flamen Dialis* (priest of Jove) wasn't very jovial, since he had to bury his toenail clippings under a fruit tree, and wasn't allowed to pat, or even mention by name a she-goat, raw flesh, or beans. He had to smear mud on the end of his bed, couldn't leave it for more than three days, and nobody could share it. He kept a box of bedside sacrificial cakes in case he felt like a midnight snack, and changed his underclothes indoors so Jupiter couldn't look down and see him naked. His wife, the flaminica, had to wear a stern look and wasn't allowed adornment, to bathe, or climb more than three rungs up a ladder in case somebody looked up her dress. The Tiber River god, deprived of victims by the bridge the *pontiffs* (bridge-builders) built over him, was propitiated in May by the flaminica pushing old men off the Tiber Bridge to drown.

The new Colleges of Priests, Augurs, and Coppersmiths prayed to the gods for help, and if that failed, could provide pointy bronze swords as backup.

A magic shield fell to earth, so Numa ordered Mamurius to make a dozen copies. These were so good that they couldn't tell which was the magic one, so Mamurius was beaten with rods and driven out of the city. To entertain the people, Numa commissioned the 12 *salii* (jumpers) as leaping priests of Mars, who danced about the city waving these magic shields like maniacs. If war was impending, the shields were said to rattle on the wall like an ancient early-warning system. Like modern pop songs, the words to the salii-songs were even incomprehensible to the priests themselves.

After scouring the city Numa managed to find four virgins to be Vestals, who kept the sacred fire of *Vesta* (Hearth) burning, in case anyone asked, "Hey buddy, got a light?" The Vestal virgin motto: "Logs tossed, legs crossed."

After 43 years Numa peacefully died, so for a while everybody thought he was only dozing. "Numa made so many new gods," St Augustine joked, "that there was no room left to deify him when he died!" But he had no shortage of priests to dance about his grave or fix a bridge over it.

A flood exposed Numa's stone coffin containing his holy books 400 years later. "They're unfit for public viewing," testified a praetor who'd read them, "and should be burnt!" "What did they say?" he was later asked. "They predicted that I'd declare them unfit for public viewing," he retorted, "since they revealed some secret wrongdoing of mine!"

"So who am I," he shrugged, "to mess with fate?"

Hostile Tullus Hostilius (673-641 BC)

The senate wanted to be kings again. "We vote for Tullus *Hostilius* (Enemy)," the plebs insisted, "since he's the grandson of our defeated champion Hostius, and we want to give him another chance!"

Tullus built the first senate house, the *Curia* (Men-meet) Hostilia, so they could fight even when not at war. "I'll give you more gods too," he growled, "*Pavor* (Trembling) and *Pallor* (Paleface)!"

"Rome is way too soft, with too many dancing priests," Tullus chided, "so to toughen you all up I've declared war on Alba Longa!" "Rather than just mindlessly killing each other," the Albans suggested, "why don't your Roman Horatii triplets fight our Alban Curiatii triplets to decide the outcome?" Rome agreed, so a solemn treaty was made by rubbing a handful of grass on the priest's head.

The two sets of three brothers all charged at each other and after a hard fought fight, two of the Romans were killed, while all three Albans merely wounded. The remaining Roman saw he was outnumbered, so bravely ran away. As the wounded Alban triplets chased him, he picked them off one by one. "For killing my brothers, I killed the first two," Horatius boasted to the Albans, "I kill this last one, to rule over you!"

Two brothers die of Horatii
and two more lie of Curiatii
said the last brother
to the other
let's call this horror-a-tie?
Nay, he said
me brothers dead
so there's no cure-a-tie!

HORATIUS KILLS THE PURSUING ALBANS ONE BY ONE!

Lugging the bloody Alban cloaks, Horatius met his sister who'd been engaged to marry one of the Curiatii triplets, but couldn't tell the threesome apart without checking their name tags. Bursting into tears, she tore out her hair and howled her lover's name. Annoyed that she wasn't cheering for him, Horatius drew his sword and slew her. "Forget your brother, and join your lover!" he growled, "So die all Roman women who lay with the enemy 'till mourning!" This horrifically bad deed entailed the death penalty, but his poor old father griped, "I'll have no children at all left!" Instead, Horatius was made to walk under the "Sister's Beam" with his head covered, hoping to bang some sense into it.

The 100-year truce was finally up, so Veii and Fidenae attacked Rome right on time. King Tullus now had the Albans for backup, but just as the battle began, they ran away. "No worries," he shouted, "I ordered them to attack from the rear!" The Etruscans lost, since they kept nervously looking behind. The furious Tullus shipped all the Albans to Rome and razed their city to the ground, leaving it Alba no Longa. He tied their king, Mettius Fufetius, to four horses and tore him apart.

Insidious Mettius Fufetius
now full of regret he is
as he departs
into four parts:
Met - Fufe - and duet Tius!

War broke out against the Sabines, and plague against the Romans. "Keep fighting!" Tullus insisted, until he caught it too, and tried an old religious cure given to Numa by Jupiter:

Jove said, "Cut off a head!"
I cut an onion. He said, "A man's top instead!"
I cut a man's hair. He said, "It must be dead!"
I killed a fish. Jove fainted, red.

Unfortunately, Tullus got the rite wrong, since onions, hair and sardines are the recipe to ward off thunder, and a lightning bolt fried him. Or at least that's what Ancus said, who'd murdered him and burnt the palace down to cover up.

Anchorite Ancus Marcius (641-616 BC)

Sick of war, the Romans elected King Marcius, the grandson of peace loving Numa. Nicknamed Ancus due to the abnormal stiffening of his arm, he was no good at holding a sword, but great at praying. The Latins attacked, assuming that Ancus would be busy praying in some temple somewhere. He was, but to their surprise, he'd divined new war rituals, and smote them.

Rome was built on seven hills (actually 13 hills, but the ancients loved the number 7, so we have 7 wonders, 7 wise men, 7 virgins, 7 vultures etc). The original settlement was on the Palatine, the Sabine women were captured on the Capitoline, and the Albans were caged on the Caelian. Ancus dumped the defeated Latins on the Aventine, leaving three hills to fill. Later, an eighth hill was added. Mount *Testaccio* (Broken-pottery) was formed from a pile of imported amphorae (and still stands today at 50 m high), since the Romans had a no-return policy on their empties.

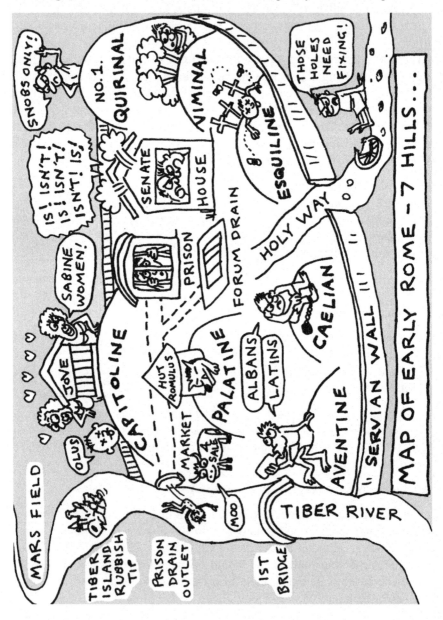

Seven Hills of Rome Song

If you'll be a pal o' mine
we'll settle on the Palatine
and rape the women of Sabine
captive on the Capitoline.
The Albans are all alien
so lock 'em on the Caelian
Latins just here for the wine
drunk upon the Aventine.

Posh snobs on the Quirinal
don't queue for the urinal
while trees grow on the Viminal
to hide if you're a criminal.
And buried on the Esquiline
are those that finally finished
- dyin'!

Ancus built the *Sublician* (Wood) bridge across the Tiber, so enemies would find it easier to attack, the port-city of *Ostia* (Rivermouth) so pirates would sack that instead of Rome, and the *Tullianum* (Prison), conveniently situated over the sewer for flushing away bodies.

A Greek refugee fled from Corinth to the Etruscan city of Tarquinii, where his son was laughed at for being foreign, despite disguising himself with the name Tarquin. "Let's move to Rome," nagged Tarquin's wife, "they're all foreign there!" "An eagle snatched off my hat," Tarquin reported, "then returned it." "That means you'll be king," his know-all wife explained (although maybe it was too small for a nest). Ancus died, leaving Tarquin to look after his kids who called him *Priscus* (Oldie).

Prissy Tarquinius Priscus (616-579 BC)

Tarquin Priscus sent Ancus' young lads off hunting for chimeras, and then elected himself as the first Etruscan king, by creating 100 new senators to get the extra votes, with his winning smile and catchy campaign slogan: "Etruscan? Ye trust can!" Defeating the Latins, he brought back enough booty to build the *Circus Maximus* (Fat Circe; named after the witch Circe who turned men into pigs) for horseracing,
but then was forced back to war for more money to pay his gambling debts. The Circus became a favorite pickup spot for prostitutes, and this ancient Roman tradition still endures nowadays.

The swamp in the *forum* (outside) was drained with the world's first sewer, the *Cloaca Maxima* (Big Pooper), still in use today, which is why Rome always floods in heavy rain. During its construction, the plebs hung themselves to get out of work, until Priscus threatened, "Anyone committing suicide will be crucified!"

A surprise attack by the Sabines wiped out half his army, so Priscus needed new centuries to even the score. "No change can be made," insisted Attus Navius, his Etruscan augur, "unless the birds give a favorable omen!" The Etruscans were famous soothsayers who'd

73

received their amazing powers from a baby with a long gray beard they'd found in a ditch one day. The tot's utterances were recorded in the *Book of Wails, Entrails and Gales* that interpreted sacrificed animal guts and thunderbolts. "We think lightning happens because clouds collide," wrote Seneca, "but Etruscans think clouds collide to make lightning, so their *fulguriator* (flasher) can read the future!" Roman augurs could only answer "Yes-No" questions, so deferred to the Etruscans who could also answer "Maybe."

Priscus wasn't used to running things by the birds. "Will the birds allow to be done," he demanded, "what I'm at this moment thinking?" Taking a chance, Attus said, "Yes." "I'm thinking," Priscus announced-ed smugly, "of cutting a stone in half with a razor!" Nothing daunted, Attus snatched up the razor, and with a dramatic slash cut the stone in half, or at least the hand of the poor sod holding the stone. That shows how much birds know. However, not wanting to push his luck with the gods, Priscus simply doubled the size of his existing centuries, and afraid for his stones, Attus agreed. Using an augur's staff, Attus recovered his reputation by finding his lost pig in a vineyard. "I shifted a fig tree from the Palatine to the forum," Attus added, "just to prove that if the need arises, I can perform miracles!"

Heed the augur's words
and don't mess with the birds
do as they say
or you will pay
beware of falling turds! (*Turdus* is Latin for *thrush*)

The Sabines demanded a rematch, so the Romans sailed flaming logs down the river, which burnt the bridges, and the panicked enemy drowned. The Sabine shields floated on down the Tiber to Rome and so announced the victory before the messenger arrived.

"I had sex," bragged a pregnant slave girl, "with a penis-shaped flame in the fireplace," which sounds marginally better than saying the chimneysweep did it. She birthed *Servius* (Slave), whose hair caught on fire, but didn't burn him. "Told you so," she crowed, "It just gave him dried-locks." Awed by this omen, Priscus married Servius to his daughter, who declared, "He's hot in bed too!"

Ancus' two sons, now back from hunting, realized they'd been duped. They hired two shepherd assassins who were dragged before Priscus for pretending to fight in the palace. "I'll resolve your dispute," he told the county bumpkins, who couldn't understand his Etruscan accent, "just axe me, I'm the king!" So they did, killing him. Priscus' wife summoned Servius and urged the hot head to seize the throne. "The King's got a bit of a headache," she shouted down to the plebs from the *fenestella* (little-window), "so Servius is in charge until he feels better!" Priscus was the only king who continued ruling after he was dead.

Servile Servius Tullius (579-534 BC)

Considered lucky to be king, Servius bragged, "The goddess *Fortuna* (Luck) sneaks into my bed each night through my lucky little window!" He declared war on Veii, to take the wrangle away from Rome.

The census was imposed to work out who the soldiers were, since amazingly enough, only the rich were allowed to fight. The first class sported a helmet, breastplate, shield, greaves, sword and spear. The second class couldn't afford the breastplate, the third class couldn't afford the greaves either, and the fourth class could only afford the spear. The fifth class threw stones or blew trumpets. The headcount had no property at all so couldn't have fun fighting, but had to stay home with all the women, which doesn't sound so bad. Eventually the poor were sent to form colonies in the conquered territories so they could earn enough to join the army. The first class also controlled half the assembly votes, so always got their way.

The Romans were farmers not fighters, and their first battle standard was a stick with a *manipulus* (handful) of hay tied to it, followed by a handful of soldiers called maniples. When they proudly marched into battle, the snooty sophisticated Etruscans laughed, "What the hay kind of stupid standard is that?" The embarrassed Romans quickly killed them to cover up and swapped the straw for various barnyard animal figures, like pigs or donkeys, which were eventually replaced by impressive silver eagles. To lose the eagles in battle was worse than dying. The commander appointed the most psychotic soldier as *aquilifer* (eagle-bearer) so the lunatic would charge into the midst of the enemy, and his dismayed fellows would have to fight to get him back. The richest citizens formed the knights, and stayed rich by voting that wealthy widows should pay for their horse feed.

"The Temple of Diana at Ephesus is one of the Seven Wonders of the World," announced Servius, "so I'm building her a shrine on the Aventine to be Number Eight!" "The witch said if I sacrifice this," bragged a Sabine, dragging a fat white cow into Diana's sacred grove, "we'll win the war!" "You stink," the Roman priest sniffed, "go wash yourself in the Tiber first!" While the dopey Sabine bathed, the cunning priest sacrificed the cow in the name of Rome, so not only won the war, but also had a first-class supper.

Servius married Tarquin's sons to his own daughters, the two Tullias, thinking that'd stop them killing him. "My husband's not ambitious enough," complained Tullia Jr, so poisoned him and her sister, to marry the other brother. "I'm ambitious, I want to be king," he told her, "but let's not drink to it!"

Said Arruns to Tullia Servilius
I think we're dying, silly us
we're dead drunk
goodbye (ker-plunk!)
that drink your sis serve - illy us!

Lucius Tarquin and Tullia celebrated their double bereavement with a wedding, and won the senate over with awful Servius slave jokes: "Servius don't dribble, he slavers!" "What d'ya call a slave at the dinner table? Servy-us!" "How's a slave get into his kingdom? Kinky!" "Did ya hear about the slave whose convictions included thinking he's king?"

Tarquin boldly claimed the throne, and Servius cried, "Hey, that's my seat!" Playing a musical chair, they fought until poor old Servius was tossed down the senate steps, and Tarquin explained, "He wanted to be throne!" As Servius crawled along the street, Tullia rode her new chariot across him in the world's first fit of road rage. Tarquin refused him burial, declaring, "Romulus wasn't buried, and what's good enough for a god, is good enough for a slave!" Rome often flooded so it was common to leave humps across the street so people could cross without getting their feet wet.

Doddering old emperor Claudius, who became a scholar by hiding in the library to avoid being abused at the mad emperor Caligula's drinking parties, claimed that King Servius was really called *Mastarna* (Leader). An intriguing Etruscan tomb painting depicts Mastarna's adventures grappling with various foes, but because he's always shown stark naked it could be just another drunken Etruscan orgy that got out of hand.

Superb Tarquinius Superbus (534-509 BC)

Tarquin the Arrogant didn't rule by election, but by fear, slaying most of the senate so they couldn't vote against him. He summoned the Latins to the Grove of Ferentina. "Murdering his father-in-law is bad enough," they muttered, "but keeping us waiting is too much!" "Sorry I'm late,"

Tarquin explained, "I was resolving a father-son squabble." "Ha, that's easy to settle," scoffed Turnus, "The son obeys his father - or else!" "I can't kill Turnus simply for being cheeky," Tarquin complained, so planted weapons under his bed, and accused him of plotting an orgy of violence. "Turn us free," the Latins begged, but he was weighted with stones and drowned in the fountain.

Unable to capture *Gabii* (The Pits) by direct assault, Tarquin sent them his youngest son Sextus. "I'm going through my rebellious teenage phase," Sextus told them, "I hate my father, so I've run away from home!" The gullible Gabinians put him in charge of their army, and Sextus sent a secret messenger asking, "Now what?" Tarquin didn't reply, but simply knocked the heads off all the tallest poppies. Baffled, the messenger told Sextus, "Tarquin's weeding the garden!" Fortunately Sextus had read the Greek historian Herodotus' *The Histories*, which is where the Romans stole this story from, and understood he was meant to assassinate all the top men, although just to be sure, he tore up their flower beds too. Gabii was handed over to Tarquin without a fight. Herodotus is known as the Father of History, and also the Father of Lies, since the two are pretty interchangeable. Tarquin is the Father of Lice, since he had such lousy children.

"Give the gods their eviction notices," Tarquin ordered, "I'm demolishing their shrines to build a gigantic temple of Jupiter on Capitol Hill." "They all agreed except *Juventas* (Teenager), so we'll have to build it around him," the augers replied, since it's hard to make most kids leave home. Plowing ahead on the foundations the workmen uncovered a still bleeding human face. "This means Rome will be head of the world," the soothsayers decreed, although the ignorant plebs thought it meant, "Tarquin's murdered poor old Olus!" (*Capitol* means *Caput Oli* or Olus' Head).

A Roman embassy sent to the chief Etruscan seer asked what the prodigy meant. The seer drew a plan of Rome on the ground and pointed, "The head was found here?" "No, not here, but at Rome," the Romans replied, since the seer's son Argus had warned them about this trick to transfer the good omen to Etruria. The outsmarted outraged seer chased his son all the way to Rome and killed him, which is how *Argiletum* (Kill-Argus Street) got its name. Like Priscus, Tarquin is also credited with building the *Cloaca Maxima* (Great Sewer), so scholars argue that they must be the same king, but more probably ancient drainage and road works took as long as they do today.

A barking snake slithered out of Tarquin's bed, so he sent two of his sons to Greece to ask the oracle of Delphi, "What's it mean?" Their cousin, who'd adopted the name *Brutus* (Stupid), when he saw clever Romans being murdered, carried their cases. Brutus had completed his disguise as a fool by eating little unripe figs dipped in honey. [Clever Odysseus often pretended to be a bumbling fool, which may have given the Romans the idea for Brutus' silly story. According to Greek legend, *Battus* (Stammerer) asked the oracle of Delphi, "C-c-can you c-c-cure my speech impediment?" "Move to Libya!" the oracle answered, "Because *Battus* is the Libyan word for *King*!" Battus did, and founded Cyrene (630 BC).]

The delegation arrived in Delphi and asked the oracle the question they were all anxious to have answered, "Who'll be the next ruler of Rome?"

The sly Greek priestess retorted, "The first to kiss his mother!" Fighting over who was going to kiss Mom, they agreed only not to tell their other brother back in Rome, in case he got in first. Brutus was tripped, fell flat on his face, and kissed the dirt, "Mudder Earth."

A sex scandal caused the expulsion of Hippias, the tyrant of Athens in 510 BC, so the impressionable Romans decided to copy his story into their own history. Of course, the Greek love affair had the tyrant chasing a boy, but the less open-minded Romans changed this part to a girl, as follows:

To resolve a silly quarrel at a drinking party over who had the "best wife," the disputants decided to surprise each spouse. The royal wives were caught dancing on the tables, while Collatinus' wife, Lucretia, was caught weaving wool. She won, since wives weren't supposed to have fun. Sextus Tarquin sneaked back to her bedroom and displayed his naked sword. "Lucretia, I love you," he whispered, "make love to me!" "Nope!" "I just can't live without you!" "Nope!" "You're the most beautiful women I've ever seen!" "Hmph!" "Just one little kissy-wissy?" "Gag!" "Your eyes are like stars, your lips are like honey!" "Haw!" "I'll buy you a big diamond ring!" "Ptshw!" "I won't tell anybody, you know you want to too!" "Nope!" "Grr! I'll kill you!" "Double-Nope!" "Double-Grr! I'll kill you, and then lay a naked slave's body on top!" "Ack, I'd rather be raped than have everyone think I sleep with the hired help!" After Sextus had his wicked way, Lucretia told Collatinus, then killed herself. "I don't want other women using me as an excuse," she explained, "for having illicit sex!" This was *mors voluntaria* (voluntary death), not *suicide* which in Latin means "the killing of a pig." Brutus pulled the knife from her heart and held it up, crying:

This villain Tarquin Sextus
has most sorely vexed us
let's remove these kings
and his other things
so he no longer over-sexed is!

"If you're playing Lucretia," the latter-day poet Petronius joked, when a slave-boy resisted sex, "I'm your Tarquin!" "Lucretia must have enjoyed being raped," reasoned the lust-prone monk Saint Augustine, "or

78

she wouldn't have killed herself!" Shakespeare's romantic poem *The Rape of Lucrece* recalls how "the Rape of Helen destroyed Troy," Lucretia's death meant "Tarquin pierced her Twice," and "Collatinus was to blame for bragging about her so much!" Tarquin's military-like assault begins when "his hand scales her bare breast, the nipple like a round turret flanked by ranks of blue veins."

Tarquin like a thievish dog creeps sadly thence
He scowls and hates himself for his offence
She like a wearied lamb lies panting there
He faintly flies, sneaking with guilty fear
Having not paid the common harlot's sixpence!
- After Shakespeare (1594)

Nudity in Medieval art was confined to Biblical events, such as David and Bathsheba (he spied her naked), Susannah and the Elders (they spied her naked), or Adam and Eve (god spied them not naked). The discovery of ancient nude statues led to Renaissance paintings of risqué mythological subjects. "Epic poetry would be banned from my ideal city," the philosopher Plato wrote in *The Republic*, "because the depraved sexual antics of the gods are a bad moral example!" Painting Roman history became popular, to illustrate good moral examples, so many artists painted several Lucretias, looking for the best-looking models. Here Cranach (left two pics), Durer, Tosini, and Artemisia use nudes and knives to promote chastity. Cranach obviously just liked painting sexy women, but Artemisia was raped by her painting tutor (or at least, as she said at the trial, she only had sex because she thought he'd marry her) so her violent paintings may represent repressed vengeance. Or else she shrewdly played on her rape-trial fame to sell ribald art to repressed male patrons.

Tarquin the Proud's pride was booted out of Rome, which wasn't so difficult since the king was away besieging Ardea, and when he returned, Brutus refused to open the door. "When you can't punish them," Tarquin complained, "you find out who your friends are!"

Sextus slunk back to Gabii where they lopped the head off his tall poppy. "Tarquin sacrificed boys to Mania at the crossroads," Brutus declared, "but we'll offer poppies!" The senate had duped the people, gotten rid of the king and were now firmly back in charge.

Seven kings of Rome Song

Romulus, sliced and diced
departed in a toga heist!
Dear old Numa, dozing dolt
Hostilius met a thunderbolt!

Ancus' crown was frisked by Priscus
until an axe whisked his whiskers!
Servius road-kill, Tarquin rotten
(Titus Tatius is forgotten!)

Modern scholars complain that only seven kings in 250 years are unrealistic, but since the Romans had already made-up 12 kings for the previous 400 years, they probably weren't keen on adding more.

6 ROMANA BE PUBLIC (509 BC)

The Roman Republic began with the election of two *consuls* (consultants), Brutus and Collatinus, along with a new priest, the *rex sacrificulus* (king sacrificer) who fooled the gods by pretending he was the king when making the traditional sacrifices.

The consuls didn't sit on the top couch like the king at drinking parties, but at the last place on the middle couch, to show that they weren't above themselves. Learning that Collatinus' middle name was Tarquin, the plebs were so horrified that Brutus had to fire him, since they'd accept "Stupid" as leader, but not "King." His replacement, *Poplicola*, which means "Suck-up to the people," proved that if you want to get elected, get a catchy name. "Instead of firing Tarquin," wondered the latter day Saint Augustine, "why didn't Brutus just rename him?!"

The new SPQR stood for *Senatus Populusque Romanus* (Senate and People of Rome) which modern Italians translate as *Sono Porchi Questi Romani* (What pigs these Romans are). SPQR survives today as the proud stamp on all Roman public drain covers.

The senators fought to be elected consul because it meant that the year would be named after them, and recorded in important events such as: "This wine was bottled in the year of the consulship of so and so," whose name was marked on the cork. You could only be consul once, so as not to confuse vintage dates. In later centuries, the priests in charge of the consul list (a *fasti*) added their own family names to it (a swifty), in order to brag, "Look! We're descended from an old, noble ancestor too!" "Some years have got five consuls," they baldly lied, "because the other guys got sick or died, okay?"

I've got a lovely bunch of co-consuls
(To the tune of *I've got a lovely bunch of coconuts*)

Down at the forum square
the *fasti* appear queer
when I hear a Roman
shouting of his grand forebear:
"Oh, I've got a lovely bunch of co-consuls
there they are all written in a row (Wife: *unus, duo, tres!*)
Collatinus, Poplicola, one called Stupid-head
an historical list, a flick of the wrist
will edit my name instead!

Oi, I've got a lovely bunch of co-consuls
adding my family name will make me rich (Wife: *et me amor!*)
and there stands me wife, I wrote her a new life, singing
roll a consul scroll add any which!
Roll a consul scroll add any which

roll a consul scroll add any which
roll a consul scroll
roll a consul scroll
rolling a consul scroll may add a glitch!

Oh, I've got a lovely bunch of co-consuls
wouldn't you like your name to make a switch? (Wife: *et tu nomen?*)
just pay me wife, and I'll write you a new life, singing
roll a consul scroll add any snitch!"

Brutus discovered a secret conspiracy to "Bring back the King," since the young nobles liked partying with the princes, including his own sons who thought, "Dad's way too strict." He ordered them beaten with rods and beheaded, so they may've had a point.

"We don't want to return Tarquin's legal property, or unlawfully confiscate it," Brutus decided, "so we'll let the plebs loot it - that way they're sure not to want the king back!" Tarquin's farm was consecrated as the *Campus Martius* (Field of Mars) and his crops tossed in the river. This caused all the rubbish to bank up, and formed the Tiber Island. Market days on the *Nones* (7th) of the month were declared unlucky, so there was none, since that had been Tarquin's birthday and the senate feared that any gathering of the plebs could see them start talking about restoring the monarchy, instead of the high price of fish.

The *Regifugium* (King-runaway) festival celebrated the expulsion of King Tarquin by having the priest suddenly stop praying in mid-ritual, then sprint away as fast as he could through the forum. The *Poplifugia* (People-runaway) festival on the other hand saw the population themselves flee through the streets, who sheepishly explained, "We're imitating our rout fighting the Latin army!"

King Tarquin returned at the head of an Etruscan army, and when Arruns Tarquin spied Brutus, he charged. Brutus had forgotten to stop acting stupid, so charged too, and ramming their spears through each other, they uttered identical dying words, "Hah! I killed you!" The battle was fairly evenly matched, but afterward the finicky Romans counted up all the bodies:

Now the fight is done
we say us Romans won
we counted score
and we killed more
so we beat you by one!

Pulvillus (Wee-pillow) succeeded Brutus. He won the coin-toss in a fight with popular Poplicola over who was going to dedicate Tarquin's new Temple of Jupiter by hammering the last nail in. Not yet beaten, Poplicola interrupted the ceremony, announcing, "Your son's dead!"

Wise to his tricks, Pulvillus replied, "Well go bury him then, I'm busy!" hitting the nail right on the head.

Annoyed at the size of Poplicola's house, the plebs made him pull it down, and rebuild a smaller one. They then relented and decided to give him more space, by letting him have his front door open outwards. It was the only door in Rome that did, so put a few noses out of joint. Poplicola was buried in the hole where his first house once stood, and so his descendants claimed the right to be buried there too. However, their elaborate funeral ritual always ended with them announcing, "Just kidding!" The deceased was then pulled up and buried outside Rome with everyone else.

Ejecting Etruscans (505 BC)

Returning with the even bigger Etruscan army of King Lars *Porsena* (Big-winner), Tarquin threatened, "If I don't reign, it Pors!" Everyone fled, except Horatius *Cocles* (One-eyed), who single-handedly held the Tiber Bridge, since he couldn't see how many there were. The Romans broke the bridge behind him, then he dived into the river and swum to safety in full armor (then found a fish in his helmet for supper, if you believe that). The bridge was later ordered rebuilt without the nails, to make it easier to pull down.

Pons Sublicius battle begun
when Cocles didn't run
loot there was none
nor captives a one
but by losing the bridge - we won!

Swimming the Tiber with a sword hidden up his cloak, Mucius Scaevola sneaked into the enemy camp. Observing that it was payday, with the soldiers all gathered around the king, he leapt out and stabbed him, then discovered he'd only killed some poor old sod doling out the money. "All these Etruscans look the same to me," he cursed, making a run for it. Dragged before the king, he tried bluffing his way out. "There's a secret suicide-squad sworn to kill you," he crowed, "and I'm just the first of many!" Porsena angrily demanded that he explain himself, before he was roasted alive. Thinking to outsmart the king, Scaevola stuck his own right hand into the fire and let it burn. Amazed at this stupidity, Porsena let him go. "You're a bigger danger to yourself," he gasped, "than to me!" Porsena didn't know that *Scaevola* means Lefty, so he never used his right hand anyway.

"I didn't believe that old story about Scaevola, but I just saw a criminal burn his own hand off in the circus," wrote the enthused poet Martial, "Wow, he was brave!" "I just found out that his alternative was being burnt alive," Martial later churlishly spat, "so the criminal would've been braver to *not* burn his hand off!"

When Mucius Scaevola swum
to the camp of the Etruscan
he killed the wrong man
and burnt off his hand
but what the heck - he still won!
- Martial, *Epigram* 1.21

Next, Porsena's female hostages all escape by swimming across the Tiber, led by the naked minx Cloelia. Her father knew what trouble she was, so handed her straight back again. Porsena let Cloelia choose some hostages to free, and she picked the good-looking underage boys. "Me and my girlfriends quite fancy those handsome Etruscan soldiers, but they like boys," she smirked, "and we don't want any competition!" "That statue is Cloelia," Seneca later said, of a bronze woman mounted on a horse in the forum, "and she's taunting the fat senators who ride past on their cushioned sedan chairs!"

"Rome agrees to let Porsena adjudicate our dispute," announced Poplicola, but King Tarquin refused, declaring, "A judge can't judge a king!" This was all too much for Porsena, who bawled, "I'm making peace with these crazy Romans!" He even left his wine supply behind so Rome could have a party.

The truth was that Porsena captured Rome, proven by the fact that the embarrassed Romans made up all these silly stories to hide their shame. However, his useless son was defeated at Aricia by the tyrant of Cumae, Aristodemus the *Effeminate* (Girly). "To make sure no one grows up to overthrow me," Aristodemus the Effeminate ordered, "all boys are to wear girls' clothes, perfume, and flowers in their hair. The schools will teach poetry, dancing and flute playing. Governesses will bathe, fan and shade the boys with parasols to keep their skin scented, soft and white." Proverbial for their cowardice, the Cumaeans were once terrorized by a fierce lion. "I'll save you," laughed a visiting Roman who pulled the lion-skin cover off of a braying, cavorting donkey.

Proof that the Greek city of Cumae gave Rome the alphabet comes from a drinking cup found inscribed: "Drink from me and Venus will make you bed my owner, but steal me - and you'll go blind!"

Rap of the Sabine Men (500 BC)

Some drunken Sabine youths carried off a few courtesans from the Roman games, so Rome declared war. "Look, you once raped the Sabine women" they complained, "so this only makes us even!"

Hey, we didn't attack them
you've got it wrong again
they grabbed us
your women lust
"The Rape of the Sabine Men"!

Observing that the Romans had no sentries or watch-fires, the Sabines launched a sneak night attack, and tiptoed through the unguarded defenses. As the sun rose, they were dismayed to view a huge pile of bodies. A Roman had been waiting in the darkness to kill them, one by one, as they crept in.

A Sabine refugee, Attius Clausus, was chased to Rome, and disguised himself as *Appius Claudius*. The Romans made him a senator, little suspecting the trouble that his same-named descendants would cause.

Flattened Latins (496 BC)

Ex-rex Tarquin moved into Tusculum with his son-in-law, Mamilius. "Looks like the only way I'll get rid of the Ex," Mamilius sighed, "is to talk the 30 Latin towns into attacking Rome for him!" Rome decided to appoint a single *dictator* (talker), so the two consuls couldn't simply blame each other for losing. Appointed at midnight, the dictator was forbidden to mount a horse, which is hard to do in the dark, so his *horse master* (knight-watchman) did that. Tarquin was now a feeble silly old codger, and at Lake Regillus he spurred his horse against the dictator, Postumius, but ingloriously fell off. A cohort of Roman exiles led by Lucius Tarquin, who were keen to get back to Rome to party, drove Postumius back. "Kill any Roman," Postumius ordered his bodyguard, "that turns to flee!" The Roman cavalry dismounted to fight beside the now exhausted infantry, and since this wasn't fair, the Latins left in disgust. Relieved, the cavalry leapt back onto their horses to chase them like they're supposed to do. "The heavenly twins, Castor and Pollux, fought by our side," the Romans bragged, but it seems highly unlikely that the *Dioscuri* (God-sons) would dismount their horses. "We saw them drinking in the forum afterwards," swore others, which sounds more like it, so *"Ecastor"* and *"Edepol"* became common swear words. Made-up miracles like this probably mean that the Romans really lost, but at least Tarquin was finally dead, at age one-hundred-and-something if you go by the dates. Arriving to help the Latins, the Volscian army found them already beaten, so turned around for home again. They indignantly complained when the Romans followed and thrashed them:

Yes, we sent the Volscian might
but it still just isn't right
to surprise us
and chastise us
when we didn't even fight!

Rome formed a triple alliance with the Latins and Hernici, proudly led by their respective mascots, the wolf, bull, and pig. The wolf ate the pig first.

A sick man carried into the senate announced, "In my dream Jupiter said to tell you we have to hold the Great Games again, because he didn't like the leading dancer! I ignored him, and my son died, then I got sick, so here I am!" He then got up and walked out, completely cured. The amazed senate asked, "Who was the lead dancer?" "Nobody," they were told, "unless he means that slave who was whipped across the field before the ceremony began?" "Okay, let's hold the games again," the senate decided, "Any excuse for a party!"

"I think we should ban Volscians from the games," advised Tullius the Volscian, who wanted to stir up a pretext for war, "You know how drunk and rowdy we get, eh?" The senate agreed, and Tullius told his countrymen, "Look, the Roman snobs are afraid we'll ruin their games, so let's attack to teach them a lesson!"

Coriolanus shakes spear (490 BC)

Impressed by a Greek tale about the ungrateful Athenian expulsion of their general Themistocles (who then joined Persia against Athens, disguised as a girl), Rome and Shakespeare copied this story as follows:

The besieged townsfolk of Corioli made an unexpected sortie to thrash their Roman attackers, when ugly Roman Marcius inadvertently strolled in through their city gates behind them. The silly Corioli women took one look at him, and screamed so loudly that their men-folk tossed down their weapons in surrender, believing the town was taken. Since the dumbfounded Marcius had captured Corioli single-handedly, he was nicknamed *Coriolanus* (Town-bum). Tired of his boasting, the plebs eventually drove him into exile, and he fled to his old enemies the Volscians.

I despise the plebeian crowd
who complain that I'm too proud
but they'll pay
and rue the day
I make their women scream loud!

"Rome always wins because of its leaders, not its troops," the Volscians reasoned, "and now we've got a genuine Roman general of our own!" Coriolanus led the Volsci army to conquer city after city, until he stood before the gates of Rome. The terrified senate sent official envoys, then priests to beg for mercy, but all to no avail. Finally, they sent the women. "Haw, if I didn't respect the majesty of Roman envoys, or the sanctity of priests," Coriolanus guffawed, "do you think I'll care for the bleating of a few women?"

He was surprised to find his mother and wife at the head of the delegation. "Ever since you were born you've been no good," scolded his mother, who severely berated him for all the trouble he'd caused her, and demanded, "Am I your mom or prisoner?" She bared her breasts and belly, bawling, "I wish I'd never had you!" "When are you going to get a proper job," his wife demanded, "instead of fighting with your crummy enemy friends all day?" His numerous snotty-nosed children howled behind her, and she too bared her breasts and belly, shrieking, "I wish I'd never had you, too!" Coriolanus remembered the real reason he'd left Rome, to get some peace and quiet, and retreated into retirement again.

I don't listen to diplomats
or silly priests in funny hats
but it's me wife
she'll give me strife
I'm gone, goodbye, you win - congrats!

Shakespeare decided this ending wasn't good enough, so in his play has Coriolanus bloodily stabbed to death like Julius Caesar.

Newly leaderless, the combined Volsci-Aequi army decided to have a battle to see who would choose their new general, and completely wiped themselves out. The Roman priests searched for the cause of the war by inspecting animal entrails, and the flights of birds. "The problem must be," they finally decided, "that the Vestal virgin, Oppia, isn't!" so buried her alive.

We divine religious lore
studying livers, guts and gore
by taking terns
we soon discern
our virgin ain't no more!

Fabulous family Fabii! (480 BC)

In this year, the 300 Spartans made their heroic last stand at Thermopylae against the gigantic Persian army invading Greece. Greatly impressed, the Romans copied this tale, but since no one's as tough as the Spartans, they added six soldiers extra. The Fabii family was originally called *Favi* (Pit) because they descended from a woman whom

Hercules had raped in a pit (Hercules was the first to teach how wild animals could be caught in pit traps). They now offered to fight Veii all on their own, all for free, and 306 of them marched off, as the smallest Roman army ever. They fought numerous running battles, and to Veii's great mortification, the most powerful city in Etruria was badly beat up by a single Roman household. Having no luck in honest warfare, Veii set a cunning ambush, and trapped the entire Fabii clan on a hill, where they fought bravely until treacherously attacked up the rear, just like the Spartans had been. Only a single pimply boy survived, who'd slept in that day.

> We're the fabulous family Fabii
> wiped out by the Veii
> but one didn't die
> so we'll re-multiply
> we just hope he isn't gay!

That sinking feeling (474 BC)

The Greeks fought the Etruscans in a sea battle off Cumae. "Fight with few," ordered their oracle, so the Greeks reluctantly sailed only five ships into battle. The haughty Etruscans were offended by this apparent mockery of their abilities, so sent only five too. The Greeks sunk them, then another five, then another five and so on, until finally the Etruscans had no navy left. This gave Rome the chance to conquer Etruria, and they later marched south to thank the Greeks by conquering them too.

7 PATRICIAN ATTRITION (494-440 BC)

The Romans fought each other, and their petty neighbors in between times. The plebeians preferred war to peace, since on the battlefield they were free to rob others, but back in Rome were themselves debt-slaves to the patricians.

The Romans were still fighting each other 400 years later, and since the first historians didn't really know what had happened way back here, they padded it out with a few of their own conflicts, figuring that one punch-up's pretty much like another.

A crazed old man appeared in the forum, dropped his filthy toga to display whip marks, and was recognized as an ex-centurion. "What vile enemy did this to you?" demanded the angry crowd, and he sobbed, "While I was away fighting in the Sabine War, they burnt down my farm, then the senate charged a war-tax and sold me in debt-slavery to an underground workshop!" Enraged, the mob chased the senators through the streets, baying for justice. The senate convened, and began a fierce debate. "How should we," they argued, "punish the mob?"

The senate tries to ignore 'em
then haven't got a quorum
but the plebs demand
you make a stand
are you agin or forum?!

At that moment, a Volscian army arrived, announcing, "Salve! We're here to attack you!" The plebs were overjoyed at this news, and joking, "Let's see the senate fight by themselves, haw!" "All debt-slaves shall be freed immediately," the senate decreed, "and set on the poor unsuspecting Volscians!" who they chased all the way back to Suessa Pometia, which was pillaged to pay their debts off. A new war-tax was imposed, and the plebs were all sold back into slavery again.

The Sabine War was declared. "Let's cancel our oath to fight for the consul," the plebs agreed, "by murdering him!" To their chagrin, the priests advised that a religious obligation couldn't be voided by a criminal act. Instead, the Plebs Union voted to strike, marching out of Rome to camp on Sacer Mons, called the Mount of Cursing, because they were so angry.

Nothing secedes like secession
against senatorial aggression
senile senators scold
alas we're too old
to join in your sex session!

"We're the belly," the senate explained to the people's assembly, "and you're the limbs, but if you don't feed the belly, then we all die, okay?"

The plebs glared at the senators' bellies, then advised them to cut out wine and go on a diet. The plebs set up their own cult of the threesome *Ceres*, *Liber* and *Libera* (Food, Wine and more Wine).

The plebs returned, but only after being given two tribunes of the plebs who could veto any idiotic new laws, by crying, "I forbid!" "The tribune's job is to stand at the senate house door," the senate reckoned, "and stop the plebs yelling abuse at us!"

Pleb's tribune (To the tune of Strawb's *Part of the Union*)

Now I'm a pleb's tribune, empowered to impugn
I say what I think, that the senate stinks
because I am immune.
When we meet on the local hill, to secede from the senate's will
with a hell of a shout, it's "Out, brothers, out!"
and the consuls both look ill.
Oh, you don't get me I'm a pleb's tribune, you don't get me I'm a pleb's tribune, you don't get me I'm a pleb's tribune, because I am immune, because I am immune.
When I spy poor plebeian sods, threatened by the lictor's rods
I set them free, and they can't touch me
'cos I'm sacrosanct like the gods.
And I always get my way, because I disobey
when they pass a law, on the senate floor, this is what I say:
Oh, you don't get me "I veto!", you don't get me "I veto!", you don't get me "I veto!", because I'm a pleb's tribune, because I'm a pleb's tribune.
Before the plebs elected me, I wasn't even free
but a debtor-slave, now the money I've saved
by accepting bribery.
And though a lowly working man, I can ruin the patricians' plan
they blow their lid, when "I forbid!"
like I'm the Roman superman.
Oh, you don't get me I'm a pleb's tribune, you don't get me I'm a pleb's tribune, you don't get me I'm a pleb's tribune, unless you're a dictator, in that case, see you later!

The Sabine war was a false alarm, announced and concluded in one night, since their raiding party had pillaged wine, and were caught dead drunk.

Peaceful campaign of military disobedience

The plebeians began a peaceful campaign of military disobedience. They routed the Veientes with a single cavalry charge, and then refused to chase and kill them. The puzzled enemy noticed this, stopped running away, and confident that they were in no danger, returned to yell taunts.

Thinking quickly, the Roman generals ordered, "Retreat!" The belligerent soldiers immediately charged, giving the startled Etruscans the biggest thrashing of their lives.

We'll do no battle today
unless our generals say
"Not to fight"
and then we might
'cos we always disobey!

The Volscians attacked, hoping the plebs would not only strike again, but also join them in a protest march. The Roman army hated the consul Claudius Appius, who hated them right back. They deliberately fought badly to blame Appius' leadership, and wore bandages to pretend they'd suffered enemy wounds. If he ordered, "Work," they slept, and when he ordered, "Sleep," they worked to keep him awake. When he ordered, "March faster," they walked slower, and if he ordered, "Retreat slower," they ran faster. He ordered, "Charge!" so they fled back to camp. "Well," Appius spat, totally exasperated, "let them sack your baggage then!" so they turned to defend themselves. Appius cursed this small victory, while the troops cheerfully celebrated their defeat:

I'm not ashamed to race
from the Volsci in disgrace
spear my behind
but I draw the line
at stealing my suitcase!

Marching home to Rome, the Volscians fell on the Roman column. "Fight!" Appius shrieked, but they disobediently died. "Stand fast!" he squawked, but they scrambled over bodies to flee. "Stop running!" he screeched, but they kept going, even though the Volsci had long given up chasing them. "I'm killing the rest of you myself!" Appius howled, "Execute anyone who's lost their sword, standard or bugle, every centurion, and for good measure, decimate the leftovers by killing every tenth man!"

In contrast, the other consul, *Barbatus* (Bushy-beard), was exceedingly nice to his soldiers. They were fighting the Aequi, who preferred to fight an army like Appius had, which wouldn't fight back, so left Barbatus alone as he plundered their lands. "Men," Barbatus beamed, "you carry the booty so well!"

"We're impeaching Appius," the tribunes clamored, "not for killing his army, but for opposing our petty Agrarian land law!" It was traditional at trials to wear sackcloth and ashes, while begging for mercy, but Appius arrogantly appeared in his best toga. "You ungrateful plebeian scum!" he bellowed, so that some thought he was actually prosecuting them.

Pigheaded to the end, Appius died of an illness rather than let the idiot plebs get him. "We love him much more dead," the plebs sobbed at his funeral, "than we ever hated him alive!"

"The Romans might run away again," fretted the Volscians, who were very keen to fight, and so maintained a night watch on their camp. The Romans also hired a gang of Hernici to ride around the Volsci camp blowing their bugles and yelling taunts, while the Romans got a good night's slumber. At daybreak, the Volscians lent against their spears half-asleep, fled at the first charge, and were caught crawling into their beds at Antium. "We'll get rid of the plebs," the senate decided, "by letting them settle in Antium," but so few applied, they had to let the Volsci back.

Fabius, the only survivor of the Fabian family funeral, fought the Aequi. "This isn't war," they growled, when he took too long to order his army up, "it's line-dancing!" "We don't fight after hours," they complained, pointing at the setting sun, "and we sure don't want to sleep with you!" "We'll be back," Fabius snapped, "and we won't respect you in the morning!"

"Of course we were beaten in a battle," the Aequi army told their generals the next day, "since that's what the Romans are good at, but we're much better at raiding!" The surprised Romans hadn't expected a raid from a beaten foe. They caught the Aequi lugging their stolen loot, so walloped them again. The Aequi begged the Volscians of Ecetra for help, and together they defeated the outnumbered Romans.

We're the boastful men of Ecetra
and we're going to upset ya
we are the best
better than the rest
etcetera, etcetera, etcetera!

Fearing more raids, the farmers herded their livestock into Rome, turning the forum into a barnyard. The stink of animals, with their constant lows, bleats, and cluckings, let no one sleep. A plague swept through the city, and the superstitious Volscians were disconcerted to encounter an eerily deserted countryside. Spitting over their shoulders for luck, they hurried off to attack *Tusculum* (Etruscan-town) instead. The Roman matrons managed to lift the plague by sweeping the temple floors with their hair, and the recovered Romans surprised the Volsci, as they returned loaded with plunder.

"All slaves," screeched Herdonius the Sabine, who seized the Capitol citadel by night, "revolt!" The brainless plebs ran through the streets wailing, "The city's under attack!" "It's just a senatorial trick," shrilled the tribunes, "to prevent the passing of our Agrarian land law, so nobody fight!" "It's the gods' house that's been captured," the senate sighed, "not ours!"

While the Romans were busy fighting each other in the streets, an allied army from Tusculum arrived. They charged up the hill, freed the gods, and sacrificed the renegade slaves in their honor.

Curly Cincinnatus (458 BC)

Cincinnatus (Curly-hair) put up bail for his hotheaded son, hard *Caeso* (Cut-up), who was charged with murdering a pleb. "Caeso is an angry young man," his lawyer told the judge, "but if you wait a while he won't be young anymore!" The minute he was released from court, Caeso fled, thereby bankrupting Cincinnatus, who was forced to retire to a little farm across the Tiber.

"You Aequi have broken the peace treaty!" complained the Roman envoys. "Give the senate's message to that old oak tree over there," their general snorted, "I'm busy!" The Aequi surrounded the Roman army at Mt Algidus, and things looked grim.

The senate sent for Cincinnatus, who was busy plowing his field. Donning his best toga, he hurried into Rome and was saluted as dictator. Running his rustic eye over the situation, he thoughtfully chewed on a corn stalk, then ordered, "All Romans of military age assemble on the Campus Martius, armed with twelve palisades!" Marching his men at double speed through the night, he encircled the Aequians encircling the first Roman army. Each man gave a shout, dug a trench and stuck his posts in the ground, fencing the Aequi in. Attacked from both sides, they begged for mercy.

"Damn fool," Cincinnatus told the sheepish Roman general, "I've lost 15 days farming!" "Good fences make good neighbors," he added, eying up the loot, "especially when you've got stolen property to sell!" His job done, Cincinnatus used his new power to convict his runaway son's accusers, then resigned and went back to his plow. The happy army sung triumphal songs:

Cincinnatus makes no sense
'cos twelve posts orders hence
we wood take
playing with high stakes
as an attack of-fence!

Elected consul, Cincinnatus blocked the tribunes' Agrarian land law. "No worry, we'll reelect the same tribunes again next year!" laughed the plebs, so the senate retorted, "Then we'll reelect the same consul!" "No you won't," growled Cincinnatus, "to imitate the plebs is disgraceful!"

"I'm supported by nine of the ten tribunes," boasted Spurius Cassius, "so I'll bribe the plebs to illegally reelect them!" Unfortunately, his power base crumbled when the tenth tribune burnt the other nine alive for acting illegally.

12 laws on tables (450 BC)

The Romans decided to copy the Greek law code, and so appointed ten *decemvirs* (tenners), nicknamed the Ten Tarquins because they were so arrogant and corrupt. "Siccius, a soldier who mocked us," they announced, "has been ambushed and killed by a *sicarius* (cutthroat)!" The search party found Siccius' body covered by the decemvirs' dead assassins he'd valiantly fought off, without a real enemy in sight.

The *Laws of the Twelve Tables* were publicly exhibited, so the senate could no longer make it up as they went, or pass judgments after sunset. Written in clear legal language, the *Tables* called a farm a garden, a garden an inheritance, and an inheritance a farm. Some examples:

Table 1. If you owe money, the plaintiff can drag you to court, but if you're sick, he's got to carry you.

Table 2. If you can't find your witness, you can stand outside his house screaming at him.

Table 3. If you don't pay up, you'll be sold into debt-slavery, or split up proportionately between the plaintiffs. If they cut you into the wrong sized pieces, too bad. It's illegal to cast a magic spell against them.

Table 4. A child born more than ten months after his father's death should not get the inheritance. A father, as *paterfamilias* (household head), has the right to kill or sell his family, but can't sell the same son more than three times.

Table 5. If the paterfamilias dies, guardians shall be appointed for all lunatics, spendthrifts, and women that were under his control.

Table 6. If you can keep a thing for a year, you own it. If a woman doesn't want to be owned, she must keep to herself for three nights every year.

Table 8. Anyone breaking someone else's limb shall have their own limb broken in like manner. Anyone inflicting minor harm shall be fined 25 coins. (One arrogant senator liked to strut about the forum, slapping freedmen across the face, while his following slave paid them the 25 coins, to save going to court.) It is illegal to curse someone else's crops. You can kill a thief at night, but if you catch him during the day, you have to keep him as your slave. When entering another's house to search for stolen property, you must be naked, so that you can't plant any evidence, but you may hold a dish before your face, so that women won't recognize you. Any one caught composing or singing rude songs shall be clubbed to death (the law that most concerns us!).

Table 9. Judges shouldn't be caught accepting bribes.

Table 10. Gold mustn't be burned on a funeral pyre, unless the deceased has gold teeth. All bodies must be buried or burned outside town, so Rome isn't accidentally burnt down. All parts of the cadaver must be buried - no keeping of souvenirs! Women mustn't wail or scratch their cheeks at funerals, and no sprinkling - don't waste expensive perfume or good wine on a dead loss.

Table 11. Plebs can't marry patricians.

Table 12. Miscellaneous stuff added to give the decemvirs another year in office.

Malefactors could also be punished for forming an abusive gathering outside a complainant's house, stalking underage children, malicious wearing of mourning-dress, or beating another person's slave, which was regarded as an insult to their master.

Aricia and Ardea were exhausted from fighting over some land, so asked Rome to adjudicate, due to the fame of their new laws. This was the first legal case where the judge awarded itself the disputed property.

"I'm madly in lust with beautiful young Virginia," lamented evil Appius Claudius the Decemvir, "but can't marry her because of my own stupid law forbidding marriage between patricians and plebeians!" The frustrated Appius soon thought of a cunning plan to bed her without getting married. "I'll pretend Virginia was the daughter of one of my slaves," he cackled, "and so therefore she belongs to me!" Appius' thugs dragged young Virginia out of her school, but her cries attracted an angry mob who demanded that the matter be settled in court. Unfortunately, Appius was the judge. "Your father, Virginius, must appear," he ruled, then sent off an order forbidding him army leave. Thwarted, when her father appeared in court next morning, Appius ruled, "She's a slave anyway!" "I meant my daughter for a marriage-bed, not a brothel," Virginius cried, "Are we to copulate like apes?" "I'd rather be father to a dead virgin," he snorted, as he stabbed her, "than a live slut!" The horrified plebs revolted, and chased Appius out of Rome.

The deceiver Claudius Appius
has abhorred unhappy us
we chased him out
without a doubt:
Clawed-he-is Ape-he-is!

Waving his bloody dagger, Virginius paraded the army out of Rome, and up Mt. Curses. "Are you going to give laws," the senate inquired, when the decemvirs refused to step down from the deserted forum, "to the walls and roofs?" Reluctantly they resigned, and the plebs asked that they all be burnt alive. The senate objected, but Appius killed himself anyway. "You're not sending me to the Palace of the Plebs," he snarled, meaning prison.

Pat the plebs

The plebs asked to marry patricians. "That's like a skunk mating with a monkey," the senate objected, "with the children born all confused!"

Plebs cannot marry a patrician
because of the offspring's condition:
Would we call a plebpat?
Or a patpleb, begat?
We just couldn't make a decision!

Finally, some poor patricians decided it was a good idea to pat the plebs by marrying the rich ones.

Patricians began calling themselves plebs to get elected as tribunes, so plebs demanded to be elected as consuls. The senate called them consular tribunes, to distinguish them as riff-raff. The plebs wouldn't vote for themselves, since they knew what their candidates were really like, but blamed this on the patricians being better looking, so banned them from whitening their togas at election time.

A severe famine struck Rome, the slaves' rations were halved, and starving plebs jumped into the drink. Spurius Maelius distributed free corn to the poor. Outraged, the senate charged him with: "Trying to be king." They sent for the now 80-year-old Cincinnatus, who was busy teasing his hair. He donned his best toga, hurried into Rome, and was saluted as dictator. Running his rustic eye over the situation, he thoughtfully chewed on a corn stalk, then ordered, "Post guards around the forum, and summon Spurius!" Spurius made a run for it and was killed by *Ahala* (Armpit), so named because he kept a dagger hidden up his sleeve. "He wasn't killed for treason," Cincinnatus explained to the rioting plebs, "but for not coming when he was called!" His job done, Cincinnatus resigned, and headed home to finish doing his curls. Do-gooders always came to a sticky end in Rome.

Another of Cincinnatus' guilty sons was tried for military incompetence. "Which one of you will tell his father?" asked his clever lawyer, and the terrified jury decided, "We'd rather set him free!"

War wares on (438-407 BC)

Revolting from Rome, Fidenae joined King Lars Tolumnius of Veii. Rome sent envoys to complain, who had to wait while Lars lounged on his bed playing dice. "I'm making a killing!" he cried at a lucky throw, and his idiot guards took this as an order to murder the Roman envoys. In the ensuing battle, King Toly was killed by Cossus, who claimed his armor as the Royal Spoils. Toly's head was paraded on a spear, and the happy soldiers sang rude songs about Cossus, instead of their dictator:

Aulus Cornelius Cossus	King Tolumnius Lars
taught Toly not to cross us	don't hang around in bars
he laid in bed	'cos us and Cossus
then gave his head	dealt him losses
and after dice he'll toss us!	and buried there he lars!

"Hey, I found Cossus' old trophy, which someone has written that he was actually a consul across," the spoilsport emperor Augustus claimed 400 years later, "so only I can win Royal Spoils, and not my annoying commanders!" (The historian Livy is criticized for not confirming this finding - but only a fool would dare to contradict the emperor.)

The Romans decided to try government by six military tribunes, instead of two consuls, thinking that then they wouldn't be bossed around so much. Three generals were appointed to fight Veii. They gave conflicting orders for an advance, a retreat, and a parade, which resulted in a rout. "We beat three Roman generals," the Veientes bragged, "in one battle!" Attacking Fidenae, the Romans were surprised by troops who ran out waving blazing torches. These didn't stab as well as swords, so Fidenae was recaptured for the seventh time. The next battle was more even, since the Romans fought worse, and the Volsci better, than usual. Each army fled, so they called it a draw.

Rome again appointed three generals to fight the Aequi. Their fierce quarrel over who's in charge was cut short, when much to his chagrin, one's Dad said, "You can stay home!" The other two ruled on alternate days, and always gave the same order, "Cancel all yesterday's orders!" Observing this, the enemy feigned a retreat. Sergius, eager to win the victory for himself, tried to storm their camp. Bursting forth with a sudden charge, the Aequi drove the startled Romans over a steep bank, where they fell, rather than fled.

The dictator *Priscus* (Severe) took over. "Standard-bearers advance at double-pace," he ordered, and himself killed one that marched too slow, to show he meant business. The Aequi fled, and the annoyed Priscus found himself unemployed after only one week on the job.

"I've changed my mind about letting you sack an Aequian town," Postumius warned his troops, "So shut up, or else!" "Or else what?" they demanded, and he ordered, "Crush them under a hurdle!" The mob freed them, stoned Postumius, and then complained when they were let off by the senate.

Sacking Carventum, Valerius sold the entire spoils for the treasury, depriving the soldiers of their share. The soldiers exercised their traditional right to sing songs about their general, as he marched into Rome with them:

Gaius Valerius Potitus
took the loot allotted us
of carved up Carventum
to the senate sent 'em
so he's really knotted us!

Victory Veii (407-396 BC)

Rome sacked Anxur with great slaughter. "We'll die fighting!" the desperate Anxurians howled, and noting their fury, the general ordered, "Harm no one unarmed!" so they laid their swords down again. "Our soldiers should be paid for fighting," the senate decreed, "so we'll levy a new tax on our soldiers to pay for this!"

"Scram," *Veii* (Village) told the Roman envoys, "before you get what Lars Tolumnius gave you!" War begun and Veii elected a king. Rome elected eight military tribunes, who began fighting each other more vigorously than the enemy. Etruscan backup arrived for Veii, and the Romans were surrounded. "I'm not helping Sergius," Virginius snarled, "because he hasn't asked!" "I'd rather die," spat Sergius, "than ask him for anything!" The army was massacred, while Sergius and Virginius raced back to Rome to fight over who was to blame.

Camillus (Altar-boy) became famous when he was wounded in battle, but kept on charging at the enemy. He was appointed dictator, and either dug a secret tunnel into Veii, or crawled in through the drainpipe. "How do you want to  divide up the spoils?" Camillus asked the senate. "A soldier gets more pleasure from some small thing that he steals himself," the senate decided, "than from a larger treasury payout!" All of Rome rolled up, intent on sacking the city, much to the puzzlement of the watching Veientes. To their surprise, soldiers broke in behind them, and set fire to the houses from which desperate women were hurling stones. The city gates were flung open, and after a ten-year siege (since that was how long the Trojan War took) Rome's old enemy fell. More Romans were injured fighting over the plunder than in the battle, and the senate decreed a four-day party to recover.

"Do you want to go to Rome?" the statue of Queen Juno (the Greek goddess Hera) at Veii was asked, since it was sacrilege to despoil enemy temples, and she shyly nodded. Just to make sure it really was consensual, she was asked again, "What's a nice goddess like you doing in a place like this?" "Take me," she cried, "I'm yours!" At least, that's what the temple robbers told the outraged Roman priests who demanded, "Why are you lifting Juno's bust?"

I'm just the statue's bearer
but if you listen nearer
she said, "I want to go"
did Juno?
Didn't you Hera?

"Can we move to Veii and get free houses?" the plebs asked, but the patricians refused, "No! Then who would pay our exorbitant rents in Rome?" "A city abandoned by the gods," Camillus decreed, "should not be inhabited by men!"

During the siege of Falerii, a Greek teacher led the schoolchildren out of the city, handed them to Camillus, and demanded his due for the betrayal. "We Romans are murderers," gasped the tightwad Camillus, "not blackmailers!" He handed the delighted children sticks to beat their teacher, and they drove him naked and bleeding back into the city. "If the Romans are that tough on teachers," the Falerians fretted, "we'd better surrender!"

"Oops, I forgot to mention that I promised to build my mother a temple out of the spoils of Veii," Camillus told Rome, "and I've already spent my share, so you'll have to give half back to pay for it!" The dedication rites for the temple of Mother Matuta comprised of the matrons taking their slave-girls into the secret place, then driving them out again with blows and slaps, which shows just how mad they were.

"If the gods are angry at Rome's great victories," prayed Camillus, "take it out on me!" Immediately he slipped onto his backside, his son died, and he was prosecuted for having bronze doors on his house. "We won't help defend you in court," his friends told him, "but we'll help you pay the fine!" Camillus went into exile, and decided his first prayer had been a bit too hasty. "If the people are angry at my great victories," he prayed to the gods, "take it out on Rome!"

8 APPALLING GAUL (390 BC)

The Gallic Italy tour

To get revenge on his wife for sleeping around, Arruns of *Clusium* (Famous-town) sent a jar of wine to the wild Gauls across the Alps, with an invasion invitation. The Gauls were fierce beer-drinking warriors who laughed at death, since they didn't get jokes. They got drunk to fight and fought nude, although the more modest covered up with paint. Their hair was washed in a lime solution and combed into threatening shapes, like early punk rockers. They sported handy bushy moustaches that acted as food-mixers and drink-strainers. Due to their strong belief in an afterlife, letters addressed to their dead relatives were tossed onto funeral pyres in the expectation that the newly deceased would act as postman.

O we don't wear pants
on the southern side of France
so present a fearsome stance
excepting when we dance!
- *Gallic war song*

Delighted by the gift of wine, the Gallic Senones from Sens arrived in Italy on a wine-tasting tour, looking for Sens satiation. King Brennus, the menace, asked for land, and the Etruscans foolishly retorted, "We'll give you a graveyard!"

"Why should we help you?" Rome demanded when their Etruscan enemies begged for aid, who replied, "Because we didn't send help to our friends in Veii when you attacked them!" "What right've you got to be here?" the Roman envoys demanded, and the barbarian Gauls grunted, "Our right's held with our swords, except the left-handers!" *Ambustus* (Burnt-out) killed a Gaul, so the Gallic army immediately left off Etruria, marching against Rome instead. The Etruscans waved goodbye, cheering, "Thank you very much!"

"Look out, the Gauls are coming!" warned a mysterious voice, so the Romans erected an altar to *Aius Locutius* (Public Announcements). "You got us into this mess," screamed the senate at Ambustus, "you get us out!" "Am bust us!" the terrified Roman army cried, as they turned to flee the screaming horde of Gauls at the Allia River. Most Romans were stabbed in the back by their own comrades trying to get past them to escape. "Shh," whispered the survivors, hiding out in newly captured Veii, "they'll never think of looking for us here!" A fleeing peasant, *Albinius* (Pale-face), booted his own family off his cart, so that the nubile Vestal virgins could ride snuggled up with him, and has ever since been honored for this pious deed.

PIOUS ALBINUS

Rolling up at Rome, the Gauls saw the city gates standing wide open, since the priests had forgotten to shut them as they fled, although they hadn't forgotten to take the treasure. "A trap!" they grunted, and lay down to sleep on the ground outside. Waking next morning to find the gates still open, they cautiously entered, looking about for breakfast. Draped in dazzling white togas, the old senators sat proudly on ivory chairs in the porticoes of their respective mansions. The Gauls gazed in wonder at the ancient relics of the forum, and one barbarian carefully pulled a senator's flowing white beard, wondering if he was a statue. Springing to life, the old man angrily rapped the astonished Gaul on the head with his ivory stick, which incited a bloody massacre. The enraged barbarians stormed the citadel by clambering up the steep sides, only to be casually pushed off as they gained the top, by the unperturbed Romans. Crestfallen, they began a siege, and spread out in search of beer.

GAULS IN THE FORUM

INSPECTING THE OLD RELICS...

Still in exile, Camillus led the Ardeans out during the night, and butchered the unguarded Gauls who lay sprawled about, snoring in drunken slumber. He also caught the ungrateful Etruscans raiding Roman territory, and thrashed them, warning, "Don't ask for our help again!"

Back in Rome, *Dorso* (Humpty-back) pulled his toga over his head, boldly marched down from the citadel, through the middle of the Gallic army, and up to a temple on the Quirinal hill. He sacrificed a pig, then marched back again, unmolested. "Why didn't they stop you?" asked the incredulous senators, to whom Dorso shrugged, "They didn't recognize me!" "No, it's because we're a very religious people," the Gauls explained, "and it's against our custom to kill a half-naked crazy man!"

"Can the senate pass a resolution declaring the exiled Camillus dictator," panted a runner from Veii, who sneaked into the citadel, "so that he doesn't commit an illegal act by saving you?" Noticing the runner's footprints, the Gauls tried a surprise night attack, climbing up the same route. Awoken by the warning quacks of the sacred geese, the Romans hurled the Gauls back down the cliff, as well as the sentry who'd been asleep on duty. The sacred geese's good work became commemorated with an annual festival, which consisted of parading a crucified guard dog through the streets of Rome for failing to bark that night.

To conceal the food shortage, the citadel holdouts hurled their last hard loaves onto the barbarians' heads, warning, "And there's plenty more where that came from!" The Gauls had camped in a swamp, so began dying of disease, as unwitting victims of early germ warfare. "We'll set Rome free," they offered, sick of burning corpses, "for a payment of gold." "The weights are rigged," the Romans complained, and Brennus tossed his sword onto the scales, growling, "*Vae victis!*" (Losers ain't choosers!)

Brennus' sword prick tricked us
of our gold he nicked us
"*Veni vidi vici!*" said he (I came over, I saw, I overcame)
said we "*Vae victis!*" (I'm sore, I'm overcome)

"We'll buy back Rome with steel," announced Camillus, pricking Brennus' backside, "not gold!" The Gauls were beaten, then provided with as much wine as they could drink, and farewell boats across the Tiber.

Camillus paraded through Rome in triumph, hailed as Romulus Jr, and The Second Founder of Rome, since it'd been lost. "All unmarried boys will marry the old war widows," Camillus decreed, to replenish Rome, "and all orphans will pay tax!"

The senate was voting to pack up and move to Veii, when a centurion outside yelled, "Halt men! This looks a good place to stop," and they decided to stay, so the soldiers couldn't sleep in their senate house. "That was a very close shave," the senate decreed, so dedicated a new temple to Venus the Bald in honor of the matrons who'd cut off their hair for bowstrings during the siege. The matrons who'd donated their gold jewelry to help buy off the Gauls demanded it back, but unfortunately it was now sacrosanct, so the senate passed them a vote of thanks. The priests dug up the treasure they'd hidden beside the flamen's house, and deciding this land was now holy, decreed it a "No Spitting" zone.

Rome was quickly rebuilt, rather haphazardly, which is why it looks like a squatters' settlement instead of a properly planned city. The first addition was a higher wall, built from the remains of Veii.

Rome wasn't built in a day
after the Gauls went away
due to sheer fright
it was built in a night
with muddled disarray!

The truth is that the Gauls heard about some other barbarians invading their homeland, so charged Rome tribute, then charged home to fight the back-stabbers. They embalmed the heads of distinguished Romans in cedar oil, which were kept in a chest and proudly displayed to visitors.

The Library records had been torched, so the Romans had to make up everything that happened in their History so far, which was why they've copied so many dopey Greek stories. The boast of beating the Gauls was patriotic fantasy, and it took 50 years for Roman power to recover.

They'd learnt a lesson however, and amended the law, "The priests don't have to fight," by adding, "unless the Gauls attack again!" The new *Lucaria* (Grove) festival was celebrated in the thicket where the Romans had hidden from the Gauls. Rome is also first mentioned historically at this time, when the Greek philosopher Aristotle wrote: "The barbarians sacked it!"

The Latins rolled up to negotiate a peace treaty. "We'll rape your wives," they offered, "the way you did to the Sabines!" The perplexed Romans were in a quandary until a maidservant advised, "Why don't you send me and the other slave-girls disguised as free women to sleep with those handsome Latins?" The dubious Romans accepted this plan, and the eager slave-girls soon exhausted the gullible Latins with unremitting sex. The shagged Latins fell asleep, a slave-girl lit a signal fire in a fig tree, and the Romans launched their victorious surprise attack. Thus originated Handmaiden's Day, which the girls celebrated by throwing stones at each other in fond memory of how they joined in to help with the battle, before accosting passersby.

Gone Gaul (389-360 BC)

"The Gauls wiped out the Roman army," the Volscian generals insisted, "so it's safe to attack!" "Then why," asked their soldiers, "has Camillus been appointed dictator for the third time?" Terrified, they barricaded their camp with impenetrable logs, which Camillus simply torched into a funeral pyre. As the drunken Etruscans sacked Sutrium, Camillus surprised them too, so that the town was captured twice in the same day.

The Volscians returned with the Latins and Hernicans. "We're going to fight," the Roman soldiers wailed, "a hundred to one!" "The troops are flagging," observed Camillus, now a silly old man, "but I've thought of a new tactic." He threw a standard into the middle of the enemy, and ordered, "Get it back!" The barbarians were packed together so tightly, that they could be killed three at a time, which evened the odds. "Where the heck," asked the Roman historian Livy, who usually believed anything, "did all these enemies we killed keep coming from?!"

Soldiers from Tusculum were discovered amongst the enemy, so Rome declared war. However, when Camillus marched the army there, he found everyone working, playing and carrying on as normal, with no soldiers to fight anywhere. Bamboozled, he marched home again, and this has been the only tactic that's ever worked against the Roman army.

"We'll fight at Allia where the Gauls beat you," Praeneste told Rome, thinking, "Then they'll be too scared to show up!" This plan didn't work, and the Romans sacked Praeneste.

Camillus prosecuted Manlius Capitolinus for trying to outdo him. "I saved Rome," Capitolinus sobbed at his trial, pointing up at the Capitol, "by hurling down the falling Gauls!" The plebs demanded his release, so Camillus held a retrial where the Capitol couldn't be seen, making it pointless. Capitolinus was condemned, and himself hurled from the very Capitol he'd been named after.

"To close the new hole in the forum," declared the priests, after an earthquake, "the most precious thing in Rome must be dropped in!" None too keen on tossing their gold in, when Curtius boasted, "That'll be me!" the Romans let the loony leap in, horse and all. This is another tale of how Curtius Lake got its name, but the only way to be sure is for some archaeologists to dig it up and see who's really in there.

CURTIUS AND HIS HORSE FILL THE HOLE IN THE FORUM

Rome had two seasons: war (Mar-Oct) and winter. The Italian cities fought annual wars, but didn't destroy or annex competing towns, so that there'd be somebody to fight again next year. Rome now decided to change these rules (368 BC), took over the Latin League, and overturned their upstart allies into underlings. The new policy of assimilation converted all rivals into Romans, thereby gaining more territory and army recruits, in an ever-increasing expansion toward world conquest.

Consul the plebs (376-366 BC)

Lictors were the lackeys employed to parade in front of anyone important, and carried an axe wrapped in a bundle of rods (*fasces*), which symbolized that they could beat you, then cut your head off. They wore red coats like early flashing lights and screamed at everyone to clear the way, except Vestal virgins and matrons, since consuls didn't mind bumping into them.

One happened to bang on a door, terrifying Stolo's dopey wife out of her wits. Her sister, along with the other women present, guffawed and made fun of her as an ignoramus, since this was normal practice. Enraged, she berated *Stolo* (Useless-sucker) to become a tribune and pass his veto, so nobody could bang on anybody's door. Rome was placed in turmoil for ten years (this anarchy was invented to explain a missing piece of Roman history) until Stolo was elected as the first plebeian consul, so somebody could bang on everybody's doors again.

When a door knock tricked her and her sis' laugh pricked her Stolo said
I put my wife to bed
and to comfort her, banged her lictor!

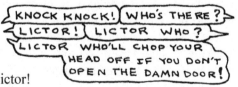

KNOCK KNOCK! WHO'S THERE? LICTOR! LICTOR WHO? LICTOR WHO'LL CHOP YOUR HEAD OFF IF YOU DON'T OPEN THE DAMN DOOR!

The rich plebs ganged up with the patricians, and called themselves nobility, while the poor plebs agreed, "They've no-ability!" The Romans worked on an unofficial system of patronage, where a rich man (*patron*) fed the poor men (*clients*), and gave them favors in exchange for their votes. "My patron knows it's cheaper to act miffed," the poet Martial griped, "so he can avoid giving me a gift!" Since Rome had no police force, a large gang of clients was handy for beating up your enemies or protesting outside your court case. The richer you were, the more clients you had, and some had whole countries. Veils before an entrance symbolized the dignity of the patron beyond it. The higher the rank, the more veils to pass to gain access, with each being guarded. Clients were classified on how far they could approach their patron. "I do the dance of the seven veils," bragged one client, while another was told, "*Vale* (Goodbye)!" The poor weren't inclined to topple this setup, for fear of losing their own patron and the free handouts, but did complain about getting out of bed early to queue up to pay their respects.

My toga's muddied by my heel
or so hot it leaves a weal
but I'm reliant
as a client
to wear it for one lousy meal!
- Martial, *Epigram* 12.26

Martial was outraged to find that after dragging his toga through the heat and mud, his patron wasn't even home, but had gone to pay respects to his *own* patron! "It's hardly worth it to see you, but I could've stayed home and *not* seen you!" he griped, "If you want to be my patron - stay in bed!" Many clients did the rounds with a sick or pregnant wife in tow to elicit sympathy, or else pretended that they had a wife in order to claim for two. Martial describes a client's duties in *Epigram* 3.46: "Why did you send me your slave," my patron complains, "instead of yourself?" "Because," I retort, "I can't keep up with your litter, but he can carry it. I'm knocked over by a crowd, but he can barge through it. I'm silent at your court case, but he'll roar support. I'm polite to your enemies, but he'll spit foul abuse!" "Then exactly what can you do?" my patron demands. "Everything," I answer, "my slave can't!"

Publilius owed Papirius money, so sold him his son to discharge the debt. Papirius pestered the lad for sex, but was rebuffed. Hades has no fury like a Roman scorned, so Papirius flogged the naked boy through the streets. "Buying our kids is one thing," complained the outraged plebs, "but bedding them is another!" The sheepish senate was forced to pass a law finally outlawing debt-slavery (*nexi*).

Papirius told Publilius
don't be so supercilious
it's illegal to *nexi*
but kiss me sexy -
and I'll pay punctilious!

The long Pleb-Pat cold war ended in 287 BC when another secession of the plebs extorted the appointment of the plebeian dictator Hortensius, who passed the lex Hortensia, giving resolutions of the people's assembly the force of law. "It isn't fair," the senate protested, "Now everybody can make laws for anybody!" But the senate still had their *dignitas* (rank in society, since every Roman had a number), *auctoritas* (moral authority), *gravitas* (seriousness), *gloria* (fame), *fama* (gossip), and *ambitus* (bribery).

Gall of the Gauls (360 BC)

A plague struck Rome and the priests tried every ritual they could think of to appease the gods, even inviting the enemy Etruscan actors to sing and dance. Young Romans imitated their performance by substituting ribald verses and crude gestures, so beginning Roman theater, and were called *histriones* for their histrionics. Professional acting companies derogatorily known as *grex* (herd of sheep) were debarred from military service, but the amateur Roman performers were considered so bad that they were allowed to join the army as if they had no connection with the stage. The gods expressed their displeasure by overflowing the Tiber in the middle of a show, causing a complete washout.

The priests decided to recall an old custom of appointing a dictator to hammer a nail into a wall to lift the plague. *Imperiosus* (Bossy) was elected, and eager not to miss a chance at glory immediately declared war and enforced a rigorous levy. To his chagrin, the tribunes vetoed, so he sadly hammered the nail and retired again.

"Imperiosus, I charge you," announced a tribune, "with making your son stupid by keeping him locked up with dumb animals on a farm!" Titus Manlius, the son, visited the tribune, who eagerly let him in, assuming he wanted to testify against his father. To his surprise Titus pulled out a knife, and holding it to the tribune's throat, demanded, "Don't you no charge me with being stupid by my Dad!" Terrified out of his wits, the tribune agreed, even though he now had conclusive evidence. The plebs praised Titus for defending his father, who in turn agreed, "I'll let him out of his pen more often, okay?"

The Gallic raiding party returned, camped by the Anio River, and a naked Gaul of tremendous size poked his tongue out, bellowing, "I challenge you!" Everyone took a step backwards, except our thick Titus, who found himself volunteered. Traditional Gallic pre-fight preliminaries saw the Gaul sing songs of his martial prowess, whilst mocking his puny opponent. The battle was fierce, as the huge Gaul swung with crashing brute strength, but the smaller Roman inadvertently stabbed up under the taller Gaul's shield, hitting him in the groin, "Ouch!" Titus took the Gaul's necklace torque, as a rather nice belt, and was dubbed Torquatus since he was all talk.

My secret for fighting a Gaul
when he's nude, and he's mean, and he's tall
is to stab under his shield
which makes him yield
and shows that I'm right on the ball!

The Gauls plundered Alba, and guzzled so much wine that they saw the approaching Roman army double, so drunkenly staggered off. Surrounded on Mt. *Haemus* (Blood), a Gallic gang chopped down all the trees to build a rampart. To their surprise, the grove was fed by a spring, which now gushed forth unabated, and they were washed away in a landslide.

Torquatus demanded the Etruscan king's daughter, Clusia, and laid siege to the city when refused. To end it all, Clusia decided to leap off the battlements, but the wind caught her skirt like a parachute, and she landed safely through the roof of Torquatus' tent. The surprised Torquatus thought his dreams had come true, ravished her, and the senate banished him to Corsica.

The Etruscan League strikes back

Marching in their army's front line, the Tarquinian priests wore live snakes twisted in their hair, and waved flaming torches like furies. The terror-struck Romans fled, until halted by the consul guffawing at their folly. Enraged, they turned to thrash the Tarquinian tricksters:

Okay, first I ran away
like a chicken from the fray -
now I don't dread
snaky head's
bad-hair-day toupee!

This led to the whole of Etruria rising, since no priest likes being laughed at. "Burn the Roman prisoners alive!" the priests ordered, while Rome retorted, "We're too civilized to burn people!" "Humanely scourge and behead the Etruscan prisoners," they added, "please!"

"They're scared," the Gauls thought, observing the Romans dig a trench around their camp, so charged uphill to attack. The Romans gave them a shove, and they crushed each other falling down backwards into a messy heap.

"I challenge you," another giant Gaul howled at Pomptinum, poking out his tongue, "and I hold my shield low!" When *Corvus* (Crow) stepped forward, a crow landed on his helmet, and pecked the Gaul's eyes out. It seems the Romans had stopped copying Greek stories, and begun copying kiddies' fairytales.

As the nude Gaul came to attack
and the raven sat on my hat
it's not fair, he cries
as it pecked out his eyes
because your pecker fights back!

The invading Gauls settled in the Po Valley, pushing the Etruscans out, and moved on down the Adriatic coast, which became known to Rome as the *Ager Gallicus* (Gaul Land).

Below: An Etruscan warrior's horse defeats five naked Gauls, supported by two topless goddesses (Volterra cinerary urn).

Left: An Etruscan tombstone featuring a trendily dressed warrior with fancy boots charging at a gigantic naked Gaul.
If the Etruscans were really so good at killing Gauls, why are they the ones who are dead?

9 ROAMING ITALY (343-290 BC)

1st damn Samnite War (343-341 BC)

Whenever a Sabine town became overpopulated, the priests declared a Sacred Spring by dedicating the surplus to the gods, which in layman's terms meant they booted the riffraff out to go form a new town. Thus originated the *Picentes* (Woodpeckers), *Mamertines* (Mars-men), and *Samnites* (Sabines who can't spell) who fought Rome for control of central Italy.

The Samnites attacked Sidicini, who begged Capua, "Help!" who in turn begged Rome, "Help!" "Sorry, can't," Rome replied, "We've got a Samnite alliance!" "We're giving you our city," Capua declared. That was different. "Hands off Capua," Rome told the outraged Samnites, "it's ours!" "We don't think it's fair," chided the Samnites, "to get a city without fighting for it!"

War began, and the Samnites trapped a few Romans. They tried to sneak away under cover of darkness, but one klutz tripped over a Samnite guard, which triggered a night-fight. The confused Samnites spent the entire night chasing each other about, while the escapees returned to the main Roman army. "Launch a surprise attack," they urged, which struck the stunned Samnites just as they were hopping back into bed: "This is your wake-up call, Argh!"

Making peace with Rome, the Samnites returned to the original plan of attacking Sidicini. The Sidicunes tried to give their city to Rome too, but were turned down, so begged the Latins, "Help!" They sent a huge army that smashed the Sam-

nites. "We suffer more as your allies," the Samnites complained to Rome, "than we ever did as your enemies!"

Right: A naked Samnite chieftain leads his rather hesitant looking warriors into battle (Old Paestum tomb painting).

Flattened Latins again (340 BC)

Rome made a treaty with Carthage: "Don't raid our Roman towns, but help yourselves to all the Latin slaves you can catch." The Latins demanded equal rights, insisting, "Call us Romans too!" The outraged senate declared war. "Don't call them Romans," they ordered, "or even call them!" The consul Torquatus' son, Titus, accepted a challenge from a loudmouthed Latin, and killed him. "Crown his head with a garland for valor," his father ordered, "and then chop it off for disobeying orders!" No one else talked to the Latins after that.

"That's what their army will get too," boasted Torquatus, when the Latin envoy slipped on the top step and landed on his backside.

Down the stairs with a splat
the Latin envoy fell flat
lying like dead
Torquatus said
I'll flatten the Latins like that!

"To win the war, one of the consuls must kill himself," the soothsayers decreed, so *Mus* (Mouse) rode into battle wearing his toga pulled over his head. The Latins killed the naked crazy man, and then fled. "I've heard my fellow consul's been awarded a triumph," gasped the jealous Mamercinus, who broke off the fighting and raced back to Rome shouting, "Gimme one as well!" "Okay," the senate decided, "the Latins are Romans too," which was all they'd wanted in the first place, and the Latin League was dissolved. Rome signed individual treaties with every town, in a new policy known as divide and rule. Knowing nothing about sailing, the Romans stupidly broke the ramming prows off the Latin warships, and proudly mounted them in the forum. This is why the speakers' platform is called the *rostra* (beaks), not because they've got big noses. Torquatus refused to be consul again. "I couldn't stand your blunders," he spat, "nor you my punishments!"

A mysterious plague broke out among the leading men, which a slave-girl promised to cure. She led the magistrates to surprise their wives concocting a brew. "It's only a herbal remedy," they vehemently swore, then taking a swig to prove it, dropped dead, since suicide seemed preferable to torture. The Court of Poisonings was opened, and over 170 wives were convicted. "The only way to halt this lunacy," the priests decreed, "is to appoint a dictator to hammer a nail into the temple wall!" Which they did.

2nd son of Samnite War (327-304 BC)

The consul Philo was about to sack Naples when his consulship expired, leaving the relieved Greeks to yell taunts at his overly legalistic retiring army. The enraged Romans voted Philo as the first *proconsul* (consultant-consultant) which extended his power in office so they could return to thrash the surprised Greeks.

"The keeper of the sacred chickens says the auspices are in a peck of trouble," growled the dictator, Papirius *Cursor* (Run-around), "so I'm racing back to Rome to redo them. Don't attack the Samnites until I get back!" The minute he was gone, Fabius attacked, won a splendid victory, and burnt all the booty so that Cursor couldn't parade it in his triumph.

"Chop Fabius' head off for disobedience," Cursor ordered, "but even worse, for grabbing the glory!" The army begged, "Don't," but he refused. The senate begged, "Don't," but he refused. The plebs begged, "Don't," and he relented, pleased to see the whole of Rome groveling at his feet, which was better than any silly old triumph. The cavalry asked to be excused from some onerous chores, and Cursor replied, "I release you from the duty of rubbing your back when you dismount."

Ignoring the 'Slow soldiers at work' sign, the Roman army marched into a tight pass called the Caudine Forks. The Samnites had undertaken road works, upgrading it to a 'No-exit.' Retreating, they found it was also a 'No u-turn.' The Romans were trapped, so resorted to digging trenches, while the Samnites laughed at them from above, hurling taunts.

Into a trap we walked
and the Samnites got us corked
at the Caudine Forks
the consul gawks
sorry lads, we're forked!

"What'll we do with 'em?" wondered the Samnites, and their wise man grunted, "Let 'em go!" Indignant at that answer, they asked again, and he spat, "Kill 'em all!" "We're not renowned for our wise men," they sighed. "Make peace," they ordered the Romans, "then strip naked, and march under the *yoke* (three spears tied together)!" Disgusted by the sight, the Capuans threw secondhand clothing at the Romans to help them recover. No sooner had the Samnites let them go, when they returned. "The guaranteed peace isn't binding," the Romans claimed, "because the senate didn't vote for it, so we're returning the hostages for a refund!" They handed over the consul Spurius, declaring, "He's all yours! And to make it look good, you can also have the boy who held the sacrificial pig while the treaty was made." "That makes me a Samnite now," insisted Spurius, and kicked the Roman envoy in the leg. "Yeow!" he shrieked, and Spurius announced, "Now Rome has just cause to fight us Samnites!" "You're kidding, right?" asked the astonished Samnites, "You dumb Romans kick each other, and claim that we broke the peace? Sheesh, I thought you were stupid when you let us fork you!" "Good," the Romans agreed, "so it's war then?"

Roman history alleges that they won this battle, and evened the score by making the enemy march under the yoke too, boasting, "You can't break a Samnite without making a few yokes!"

Surely the Romans joke
when they claim the peace is broke
they get their kicks
by playing tricks
but themselves can't take a yoke!

Below: A parade of Samnite warriors who have remembered their flags, but forgotten their pants. The Romans derided the Samnites for allowing barbers to shave their pubic hair in public (Paestum, 350 BC).

"I'm charged with being drunk in charge of a Roman army," hiccupped Papirius, "but I only drink to help me sleep better, by passing out!" "Lictors, prepare the beheading axe!" he growled, as his terrified troops looked on, expecting the worst. Then he pointed, "Trim those tree roots, so the soldiers won't trip over on the way back to their tents!"

"Set our camp on fire," the dictator commanded, gleefully pointing, "Look men, now there's no retreat!" Furious that all their booty had been burnt, the troops fought twice as hard, taking it out on the poor Samnites. Returning, loaded down with Samnite loot, they saw that the camp wasn't burnt after all. "The dictator lied," they gasped indignantly, "now we have twice as much junk to lug!"

The Samnites returned with high hopes of victory, because they had dressed in brilliant silver-gold armor. "Men, if you want booty," the Roman general pointed, "they're wearing it!" The Roman silversmiths used the captured shields to decorate their shop-fronts around the forum.

Senseless censors

Two censors were created to enforce the *mos majorum* (moral majority). Usually they just fought with each other: "I accuse Crassus of losing his favorite pet fish," charged Demetrius, "and going into mourning!" "I accuse Demetrius of losing three wives," spat Crassus, "and not mourning any of them!"

But occasionally they did really stupid things, like now. "We forbid the guild of flute-players," the censors ordered, "to hold their yearly party in the temple of Jupiter." Outraged, the flute-players blew raspberries, packed up and left for Tibur. "Who'll play at the sacrifices?" asked the alarmed senate. The sacrifices required strict silence, so blowing the *tibia* (shin-bone) was necessary to drown out any ill-omened noises, like someone passing wind. Tibur was begged to return them and obliged by getting the flute-players blotto-drunk, tossing them onto carts and dumping them back in the middle of the Roman forum. "You can't have a one day party in the temple of Jupiter," the senate ordered, when they woke up, "it has to be three, okay?" The flute-players got so drunk that they dressed in women's clothes, and this became a proud annual tradition.

"I'm closing down the music hall," another censor decreed, "because I can't help dancing to the beat whenever I go pass!" Upon his second appointment as censor, Censorinus decreed that you could only be censor once, and although legally elected for five years, it became customary to sack the censors after only 18 months.

The Etruscan League strikes back (310 BC)

"*Sutrium* (Stay-put) is the Roman door to Etruria," growled the Etruscans, laying siege to the city, "so let's close it!" They glared at the Roman relief army until sunset, and then charged so that they wouldn't waste the day. The Romans won, but stopped fighting first, because it was too dark to see whom they were killing. More Romans died of their wounds after the battle than from it. The Etruscan peasants attacked the plundering Roman army to get back their spoils, and became spoils themselves.

Another huge Etruscan army arrived, and dropping their javelins to run faster, charged uphill with drawn swords at the outnumbered Romans. The Romans pelted them with a hail of rocks that handily covered the hillside. Cursing that they had nothing to throw back, the Etruscans turned tail and fled.

They returned with a new army, marched right up to the gates of the Roman fort, knocked, and asked, "Fight?" "Don't feel like it," yelled the Romans. "We ain't going anywhere," the Etruscans growled, "until you chicken Romans come out!" They stood waiting. "Slaves," they ordered, after a while, "bring our dinner up!" "Slaves," they belched, after dinner, "bring our bedrolls up!" "Slaves," they yawned, lying down for the night, "tuck us in!" Ignoring the rules of civilized warfare, the Romans charged out of their camp and chopped the sleeping enemy to bits.

The Etruscans raised yet another huge army by using a pyramid scheme where every soldier picked another. At Lake Vadimo both sides were so keen to fight that they didn't bother with the preliminaries of throwing javelins, but just charged with drawn swords. The defeated Etruscans were ordered to provide two tunics for each Roman soldier.

Spurius laid siege to Troilum and charged the Etruscans huge exit-fees to escape, before killing everyone who hadn't paid up. The soft fun loving Etruscans of *Orvieto* (Old-town) decided it was easier to let their slaves fight the Romans. However, the slaves soon took over and Orvieto was forced to appeal to Rome for help. The Romans sacked the place and returned the cheeky slaves to their rightful masters.

3rd play it again Samnite War (298-290 BC)

"Hey," yelled a cowherd outside the Roman fort, "I reckon we could herd our cows straight through the middle of those cowards' camp!" "Grr," raged the soldiers, "let's thrash those cheeky cowboys!" "Wait," the consul chided, "Notice their funny accents?" Suspiciously peering about, he hollered, "Stop hiding!" To his soldiers' surprise, the disguised Etruscan army sheepishly emerged from their ambush concealment. Forced to fight fairly, the incensed Romans spanked them as cheats.

The Etruscans employed a huge Gallic army to fight Rome. "No, no, that gold wasn't paid to fight Rome," the Gauls insisted, as they tramped off home again, "but for us *not* to fight *you!*"

Volumnius marched through Samnium, sacking the cities one by one, and made his soldiers march light, by selling their booty to a gaggle of following traders. He received a letter from Appius Claudius, begging, "Help!" so marched to Etruria. "Letter! What letter?" Appius asked, "I didn't send any letter!" Volumnius shrugged, and turned to march away again. "Please," begged Appius' army, "stay!" "Volumnius is the best general," they agreed, after a heated dispute, "but Appius is the best orator!" Volumnius led the armies out to battle, and Appius hurriedly followed, so that it looked like his troops were obeying him. The combined Samnite-Etruscan army was defeated, with Volumnius leading by example, while Appius boasted, "What'd I tell you? I said we'd win, eh!" "Volumnius learnt speaking from me," Appius added, who retorted, "Pity you didn't learn fighting from me!"

Ganged-up Samnite, Etruscan, Umbrian, and hired Gauls War

The Samnites, Etruscans, Umbrians, and hired Gauls, united to fight Rome at Sentinum (295 BC). "I'll only need a small army," bragged dictator Fabius, "so it's easier to divide up the loot!"

Approaching Appius' camp, Fabius found the terrified Romans out scrounging about for wood. "Pull down your camp walls," he ordered, "then you'll have plenty of timber!" The Gauls cut off a legion, and rode about waving the Roman heads on spears. As the battle began, a wolf chased a deer between the two armies. The wolf ran to the Roman side, which they thought was lucky, while the deer ran to the Gallic side, which they thought was lucky too, since they ate it for supper. Fabius fought slowly, to tire the Gauls out. Mus' loopy cavalry raced in all directions, terrified by the Gallic chariots. "To save the day, I'll kill myself as a sacrifice," Mus announced, "just like my Dad did!" He then did a kamikaze belly flop onto a spear. The triumphant Romans sang victory songs:

We drink to Mus's health
for he's increased our wealth
he won the day
we're pleased to say
by going and killing himself!

The Roman matrons celebrating Patrician Chastity banned Virginia from attending because she'd married a pleb, so she summoned all the plebeian women and converted her bedroom into a shrine for Plebeian Chastity. "We'll show those patricians," she screeched, "that we're chaster than them!" "Our soldiers are away too long," griped several married women, who were fined for adultery. The money collected was used to build a new temple of Venus, rather ironically, since she was the goddess of love.

Out in the field, both armies had fought each other to a standstill. Neither wanted to continue, but the Samnites had to march past the Roman camp to escape, which they thought was a new attack.

Nobody wants to fight today
we'd all just like to march away
if you don't tell
we won't as well
and both say that we won, okay?

"We won," crowed the Romans, "by marching 8,000 naked Samnites under the yoke!" "Wait a minute," cried the Roman scribe, "I've counted up our bodies, and we've got 8,000 Roman dead!"

The Samnite priests forced their soldiers to swear a terrible oath to kill all Romans, and sacrificed any dissenters on the altar. Dressed in fabulous crested helmets, the Samnites now appeared way taller than anybody.

The Romans were keen to fight, but the sacred chickens refused to eat. "They're eating so fast that the corn's falling out of their beaks," the chief priest lied, "Nothing succeeds like a toothless chicken!" "No, they chickened out," reported Papirius' annoying nephew. "Thank you for being so diligent," Papirius retorted through gritted teeth, "- but I wanted a good omen!" "I'll avert this fowl play," he grumbled, "by putting the chicken-keepers in the front line!" "Look, the gods were pleased with my offering," he nodded, as the battle began, "They killed them first!"

SACRED CHICKEN KEEPER FIGHTING IN FRONT ROW...

Getting the worst of it, Papirius pointed at a monstrous dust cloud approaching. "We're saved," he yelled, "another Roman army's coming!" The Samnites fled, and some old mules Papirius had arranged to drag dust-raising branches behind them slowly ambled up.

The Roman generals often vowed to build an expensive temple for the gods out of the enemy booty if they won a battle, and some of their promises became so extravagant that it was actually cheaper to lose. *Scipio* (Stick-waver) was highly praised for instead vowing a libation to the gods. After the battle, he poured the dregs into a cup, flung it in the air, and then poured the good stuff for himself. He awoke with a bad hangover, rubbed his forehead, and groaned, "I didn't build them one - so the wine gods demolished *my* temple!"

The Samnites decided that the only way to win was to bribe the Roman generals. Their ambassadors found *Dentatus* (Tough-teeth) in his rundown shack, boiling his rancid turnips for supper. They made him a fabulous offer. Slapping his ears, eyes, mouth, and crotch, Dentatus announced, "So long as these work, I'm happy! I really can't take money I don't need from you who do!" He generously passed the stunned Samnites the single wooden bowl he'd kept as war booty and offered, "Would you like to feast with me?"

The Samnites sighed, gave up and gave Rome control of central Italy. "Better dead," Dentatus also said, "than living dead!" He died so poor that the senate had to pay for his daughters' dowries.

"Well, the Samnite War's over," decided the general Megellus, "so the army can work on my farm." He was fined for sowing disorder.

Culpable Aesculapius (293 BC)

A blabbermouth white raven once told Apollo, "Your pregnant girlfriend is sleeping with mortals!" Angry Apollo burned the girl (the smoke turned the raven black) but saved the unborn baby to be raised by a herd of goats. Baby Aesculapius grew up to be such a good doctor that he even made dead people well again. "The dead now live after I've killed them," complained Jove, who blasted Aesculapius with a thunderbolt, "but he can't cure himself!" Apollo got even by killing the Thunderbolt-makers, and reviving Aesculapius as the healing god. Jove got even by making Apollo into a Greek king's slave for a year.

"To cure the plague in Rome," read the *Sibylline Books*, "get the Greek god of healing, Aesculapius."

The Romans stumbled all about Greece asking, "Have you seen Aesculapius?" "Yeah," nodded a wily local, "that stone you just tripped over is him!" The Romans paid an extravagant price for the pebble, and then proudly carried it back to their boat. "You've been duped," laughed another Greek, pulling out his pet snake, "this is really him!" After some fierce haggling, the Romans bought the snake. "Aesculapius," they muttered, sailing away before another Greek could talk them into buying his pet gerbil, "he scalps us!"

They pompously led the snake into Rome, where the shrieks of the terrified matrons caused it to flee. Its temple was built on Tiber Island, the last place it was seen. Saint Bartholomew later took it over as a church hospital that still functions there today. Aesculapius was the first doctor to make bedside house calls, since he often visited patients in their dreams.

Aesculapius' snake wrapped around a stick became the symbol of doctors, but is often confused with Mercury's Caduceus (two copulating snakes wrapped around a stick) symbol of thieves.

Above: Poynter's painting *Visit to Aesculapius* (AD 1880) suggests why Aesculapius might have become a doctor. Sacred dogs kept in the temple were employed to lick patient's wounds.

10 SATIRIC PYRRHIC VICTORY (280-275 BC)

On the instep of Italy lies the Greater Greek town of Tarentum, which was founded (700 BC) by Sparta's exiled "sons of virgins," who were sired while her warriors were away fighting a 20-year war.
"You'll reign when a clear sky rains," the oracle of Delphi told their leader, but after several defeats he cursed, "That's impossible!" As his wife *Aithra* (Clear-sky) picked the lice from his hair, she wept on his head. With a whoop, he realized the tricky oracle was fulfilled, and charged off to thrash the local barbarians.

In 331 BC, the Tarentines hired Alexander the Great's uncle to fight the local Samnites, who surrounded him in a surprise attack. "That was a lucky escape," boasted Uncle Alex, when he broke out with some Samnite exiles. "It was for us," they replied, "because we made a secret deal with the enemy to be set free in return for handing you over!"

Right: The local coinage depicts Neptune's son Taras riding on a *dolphin* (womb-fish) to found Tarentum.

Tarentum tantrum

"Other men worry about working today so they can have fun tomorrow," boasted the fun-loving Tarentines, "But we have fun today and don't worry about working tomorrow!" In 282 BC, while they were celebrating the festival of the wine god Bacchus by getting drunk, the Tarentines observed a Roman fleet sail past and for a joke, sunk it. The humorless Roman envoy arrived, demanding, "Sober up!" A drunk nicknamed Piss-pot turned his back, lifted his skirt to fart, and then wiped his backside on the ambassador's toga. The Greeks mocked the Roman's quaint speech and dress by singing songs to capering steps. "Laugh now," he fumed, "but I'll be back to wash my toga with your blood!" They roared with mirth since that wouldn't get it clean. The envoy marched back to Rome and sadly displayed his soiled toga to the dismayed senate. "We don't think," they advised, "we can get a stain like that out!"

"We better send for help," Tarentum decided, after sobering up, "to our Uncle Pyrrhus and his rent-an-army!" King Pyrrhus of Epirus was a ferocious looking warrior, because his upper jaw was one continuous bone with slight notches resembling the gaps of teeth.

As a baby, Pyrrhus fled for his life because the royal family was assassinated in a palace coup. Trapped at a river, with soldiers in close pursuit, Pyrrhus seemed doomed. "Help!" his guardian cried to the peasants on the far bank, who replied, "What?" After some time shouting, the guardian finally thought to write "Help!" on a piece of bark tied to a rock, and threw it across the river. The peasants read it and built an escape bridge. A neighboring king laughed when Pyrrhus pulled on his robe, causing Pyrrhus to burst into tears. The guilty king decided to accept Pyrrhus as a refugee so it wouldn't look like he was teasing a baby. Pyrrhus grew up getting into so many fights, that when asked who was his best soldier, the king answered, "Pyrrhus - when he grows up!" Pyrrhus returned to share the throne of Epirus. "I'm going to poison Pyrrhus!" boasted his drunken co-king, but Pyrrhus thought to switch cups and so became sole ruler. Pyrrhus' consummated his power by marrying the daughters of Epirus' three neighboring enemy kings.

Old Pliny tells the tall tale that the tall *Pyrrhus* (Redhead) bred a herd of red cows like himself, which were so tall that you could only milk them standing up. Pyrrhus also had a magic foot, with which he would walk on his patients' backs to cure inflamed spleens, so long as they asked him nicely.

All Pyrrhus thought about was war. When asked, "Do you think Python or Caphisias is the best musician?" he growled, "Polysperchon is the best soldier!" Pyrrhus believed he was descended from Achilles, and liked the idea of sacking Rome, as the new Troy, just like his ancestor had done. "The Trojans can run," he warned, "but they can't hide!"

"What'll you do after you've conquered Italy?" asked his advisor Cineas, and Pyrrhus snarled, "Conquer Sicily!" "And then?" "Conquer Carthage!" "And then?" "Conquer the rest!" "And then?" "Then we party!" "But majesty, we're doing that already," Cineas pointed out, "without the risk of being killed!"

Pyrrhus cheered up when the oracle of Apollo told him, "You the Roman army will defeat!" "Don't you think I look like Alexander the Great?" Pyrrhus boasted to an old woman, who squinted, then retorted, "No, you look like Batrachion the Cook!"

Pyrrhus found the Tarentines lolling in their baths, blowing bubbles, and expecting him to fight alone. To their dismay, he pulled the plug, and ordered, "Get yer armor on!" "You pick the big men," he told the recruiting officer, "and I'll make them brave!" "Only slaves," the Tarentines muttered, sneaking out of the city, "do what they're told!"

At his banquet, Pyrrhus was outraged by boys calling him rude names. "You should've been called worse," they scolded, "because the wine ran out!" "Better that I hear a badmouth," Pyrrhus explained, when they weren't exiled, "than the rest of the world does!"

The Roman method of declaring war entailed the priest hurling a spear into enemy territory. Pyrrhus was their first overseas foe, however, and try as he might, the priest couldn't reach Greece. "I'll build a bridge from Greece to Italy," Pyrrhus had boasted, "to save my army sailing," but the Romans gave up on waiting for him to do that. Finally, a captured Greek soldier was made to purchase a little patch of land outside the temple of Bellona, the goddess of war, in Rome. The exhausted priest thankfully hurled his spear into that.

The Romans caught a Greek spy in their camp at Heraclea, so gave him a guided tour, and then sent him back. "The barbarians," Pyrrhus snorted, "have a very polite way of conducting war!" "You couldn't mistake that for a barbarian camp," exclaimed Pyrrhus, when he saw the neat rows of Roman tents, "but do they fight as prettily?"

The battle began, Pyrrhus fell off his horse in the first charge, and his troops fled, believing him dead. A soldier was quickly dressed in the royal cloak, and rode about the field. "I'm Pyrrhus, I'm Pyrrhus," he shrieked, rallying the troops, "I'm not dead!" Unfortunately the imposter was struck down, so the army fled again. "Look, look," the recovered Pyrrhus screeched, uncovering his head, and running about his army waving, "I'm the real me!"

"Ride the Indian war elephants forward," he commanded, "before the Romans kill me again!" The elephants charged and made a big impression on the Romans, stomping them flat. They'd never seen such huge ugly oxen.

Above: A marble bust identified as either Pyrrhus or his cook, but definitely not Alexander the Great.

Right: Pyrrhus begins in the Tarentum baths, ready to fight Rome. He won at Heraclea, drew at Ausculum and lost at Beneventum where run-away pigs scared his elephants off. Naples made money, Mus tried to kill himself, and regal Rhegium just partied on.

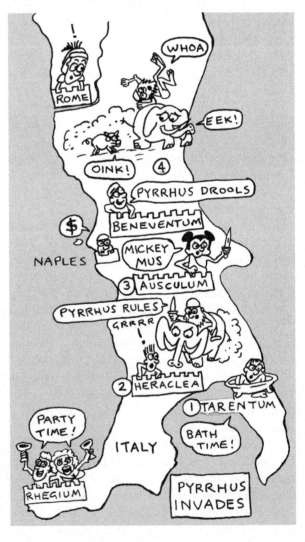

Elegant elephants

"Elephants are the common enemy of mankind," wrote Appian, "since in warfare, they flatten everyone!" Their mahouts carried mallets and spikes that they hammered into the elephant's spine when it ran amok, so that most were killed by their own drivers. "Elephants are almost like men," wrote Pliny, "except they are honest, wise and just. They are pleased by honors, and revere the heavens."

"When a keeper mixed gravel into his elephant's grain," wrote Plutarch, describing their habits, "it scooped up ashes, and flung them into the keeper's dinner pot as revenge. Another keeper used to steal half his elephant's grain ration for himself. When the owner arrived, and the keeper poured out the full ration in front of him, the elephant nodded to the owner, and then neatly split it into two with his trunk, thus indicating in the clearest way how he'd been cheated.

Another elephant picked up a boy who'd teased it, and trumpeted as if to dash him to the ground. Then it gently put him down again, deciding that making him soil his toga was punishment enough. Yet another elephant was often beaten for being a slow learner, so could be seen practicing alone in the moonlight, rehearsing all the tricks it'd been taught that day.

An Alexandrian elephant fell in love with Aristophanes the Grammarian's girlfriend. Whenever he passed the market, the elephant would give her gifts of fruit, and if Aristophanes wasn't looking, sneakily put its trunk inside her dress like a hand, to gently stroke her lovely breasts."

"An elephant's breath is good for curing headaches," wrote Tatius, "you just have to stick your head in its mouth!" "However, the elephant knows this, so like a quack doctor demands payment in advance," Tatius added, "For a handful of peanuts he'll let you keep your head in his mouth all day!"

"Elephants are so common in Africa that we build fences out of their tusks," King Juba told the gullible Romans, "We catch them by sawing through their favorite tree. When they lean against it, the tree snaps, the elephant falls, and can't get up again!" In warfare, the Indian elephant was preferred to the smaller African bush elephant, now extinct due to its losses.

Dis dress

"Pyrrhus defeated our general," insisted Luscinus, the Roman ambassador, "but the Greeks didn't defeat the Romans!" Pyrrhus tried to scare him by having an elephant poke its head into his tent, but didn't know *Luscinus* means "One-eyed," so he never noticed. Greatly impressed, Pyrrhus offered to make Luscinus his second-in-command, who declined by boasting, "If you do, your men will make me first-in-command!" "The Greek philosophy of *Epicurus* (Helper)," bragged

Cineas, "tells us to not worry, and be happy!" "Ye gods! May you Greeks always think so," Luscinus retorted, "so long as you fight us!"

Rufinus thanked his sworn enemy Luscinus for getting him elected, who replied, "I chose to be robbed by a Roman, rather than sold into slavery by the enemy!" since as a corrupt judge, Rufinus would steal, but as a general, he could lose the whole army.

"Bang your shields and howl the war-cry," Pyrrhus ordered, meeting another army on the way to Rome, "to scare them off!" The Romans raised an even louder din, so at least won the shouting match. However, they'd cheated by letting their camp-followers join in banging pots. "With soldiers like those," Pyrrhus marveled, "I could rule the world!" "Or at least they could," he sighed, "if they had me as their general!"

Changing tactics, Pyrrhus sent Cineas to Rome. "Your Roman grape vines grow so tall," Cineas simpered, admiring the vineyards. Then he tasted the wine, spat it out, and squawked, "The parents of this deserve to be hung on such a high gibbet!"

"I've pretty dresses for you," Cineas told the ladies, remembering his mission, "if you talk your husbands into making peace." This was working fine, until cranky old Appius Claudius *Caecus* (Blindman) decided he didn't like his. Carried to the senate in his litter, he was dumped in the forum. "I'm in distress," he shrieked, "so unless Pyrrhus changes a dress, it'll stay wore!" "Yes, it'll stay war," the senate agreed, "unless Pyrrhus leaves Italy!"

"When I made my Samnite prisoners build the very first Roman road, the Appian Way," the blind Appius shrilled (who'd had to check the road workmanship by feeling with his feet), "I never meant it for our enemies to be more comfortable marching against us!" "I was angry when I went blind, but now I wish I was deaf too," he screeched, "so I knew nothing about Pyrrhus beating Rome!" "Pyrrhus didn't come here to help the Greeks," he added, "but to escape his enemies at home!"

This was such a great speech that it was written down to become the very first Latin prose. Appius shouldn't be confused with the later historian Appian who also had a way with words: the Appian way.

Encouraged by this, Appius went on to pen rhyming aphorisms, like: "We're all the master, of our own disaster!"

"Anyone pronouncing z (*zeta*) screws back their lips to show their teeth like a corpse," Appius declared, giving a demonstration, "so I'm removing z from the Latin alphabet! All Greek poets be, a chimp-and-zee!" When Rome later conquered Greece they had to reintroduce z, since translating Greek into Latin was Zeus-less without it, which is why it's now our last letter.

"Blind old Appius is only bold," the senate muttered, "because he can't see how big Pyrrhus' army is!" Appius only pretended to be blind in any case, so he could take advantage of everyone else. "I didn't march on his stupid road either," Pyrrhus complained, "but used the via Latina!"

Appius was elected censor. "We're not mad because Appius has created new senators who are all his supporters," the outraged senate declared, "but because they're freedmen's sons!"

"Call me Hunter," boasted Appius' co-censor, "because I discovered the source of the spring water for our new aqueduct by falling in it!" "Appius tricked me into retiring," Hunter later lamented, "in order to name my new aqueduct after himself!"

Loose change (280 BC)

The original Roman cash was cows (*pecus*; hence *pecuniary*) until they changed to the *as*, a heavy one pound 100mm bronze disc which didn't require feeding. The Romans decided to get off their *asses*, because they were too unwieldy to lug around in a toga, and issued silver *denarii* coins. The face of the coin portraying the braggart moneyer who'd coined it was the *obverse*, the other side displaying one of Rome's gods was the *reverse*, and the edge of the coin when cheats scraped silver off was perverse. These coins were minted by the Greek city of *Naples* (New-city) inscribed: "For those Romans" in Greek. The Romans copied the fancy Greek coins, but instead patriotically inscribed: "For us Romans" in Latin.

The first Roman coin depicted a beardless Janus (god of beginnings) and Mercury (god of thieves). A bit later Janus grew a beard and the Romans discovered ships, which were depicted on a 'gambling' coin you could flip to bet on "Heads or Sails."

The first mint was located in the temple of Juno *Moneta* (Nagger), which was why it's called *money*, because the wife always nagged for some. Saving in a *fiscus* (basket) was sound fiscal policy before banks. Coins spread news, stamped with such propaganda as military victories or such slogans as "*Felix tempus reparatia*" (Happy days are here again). Money was also useful to pay (*pacare*; pacify) troublemakers.

The money supply was increased by steadily debasing the *denarii* silver content (inflation) and shrinking the *as* from the largest Roman coin to the smallest (deflation). Upon world conquest, the Romans ceased putting their name *ROMA* on coins, since they considered all money was theirs anyway.

Pyrrhic valedictory

"Hah," Rome warned Pyrrhus, "now you can't buy us off!" "I'll poison Pyrrhus," his private physician offered, "if Rome pays the right price." The shocked Roman senate refused to part with their newly minted money, so reported the traitorous doctor to Pyrrhus. "Make him into a rocking chair," Pyrrhus ordered his executioners, "out of doc skin!"

At Ausculum, the Romans were afraid to fight. "I'll sacrifice myself for victory," cried the loopy Mus, "just like my Dad did, and his Dad before him - *sum summus mus*!" (I'm the mightiest mouse!) "How in heck," the army wondered, "does his family manage to keep on breeding?!" "Don't kill any naked crazy men," Pyrrhus ordered, "just mus them up!"

His elephants trampled the Romans, but Pyrrhus found his tent had been looted by his Samnite allies behind his back, with his suitcase and slaves stolen. "Another win like this," whined Pyrrhus, when congratulated on his victory, "and I'm lost!" A "Pyrrhic victory" became known as a win not worth winning. As a gesture of goodwill, he released his Roman prisoners. "You'll sleep outside," the senate told them, "until you bring back two enemy heads!"

Sicily asked Pyrrhus for help against Carthage, which seemed easier to beat, so he sailed there. "I'm not relieving Rome," he explained, "but killing Carthage!" After he'd won, Sicily asked Carthage for help against him, and Pyrrhus sailed back to Italy in disgust. "I'm not ceding Sicily," he growled, "but regaining Rome!" By now he was so mad, that when an insolent barbarian blocked his way, demanding single combat, Pyrrhus strode forward and cleaved him in half with one blow, growling, "Split!"

At *Malventum* (Bad-wind) his elephants marched over a mountain pass by night to trick the Romans, but were too slow, and arrived just after breakfast. No longer surprised by the weird fat gray oxen, the Romans shot them with flaming arrows up the hindquarters, and then released squealing pigs, the one animal that elephants fear. To make sure they squealed, the pigs were set on fire, and the terrified pachyderms turned to trample their own side. The battlefield confusion was compounded by a lost baby elephant crying for its mother, since all the other elephants chipped in to help look, which is why you shouldn't field under-age fighters.

Rome won, and took four elephants prisoner, which Dentatus proudly marched as suppliant slaves in his triumph. He sold a series of souvenir plates depicting the grand event, with the baby holding its mother's tail. "The holes aren't for hanging the plates up," he explained, "but to honor me by you pouring out wine libations!"

Commemorative coins were stamped showing the Roman swine beating the Greek elephants, with the logo: "We'll win when pigs fry!" The Romans were so impressed by Pyrrhus' captured camp that they instituted imitation entrenched camps in their army from then on. Pyrrhus packed his trunks and left, leaving Rome in control of Italy. "I'm not relinquishing Rome," he explained, "but mashing Macedonia!"

The pachyderms at *Malventum* (Bad-wind)
didn't do as Pyrrhus sent 'em
so an elephant's fart
was his farewell depart
which we renamed *Beneventum*! (Good-event)

Pyrrhus adopted a dog he'd found guarding its murdered master's body. As he sat on his throne reviewing the troops, his dog pricked up its ears and began incessantly barking at a group of guilty looking soldiers. Accepting the dog's testimony, Pyrrhus ordered the soldiers executed for murder. The next day Pyrrhus wondered if he mightn't have been a bit hasty, when the happy dog began barking at yet another group of soldiers, after having chewed the previous case over.

In need of loot to pay his remaining troops, Pyrrhus attacked King Antigonus of Macedonia. He hung the captured enemy shields in his temple, inscribed: "The Gauls bled and Antigonus fled." His own hired Gauls dug up the Macedonian graves looking for gold and insolently scattered the bones about. "I beat Antigonus," Pyrrhus fumed indignantly, "but still he wears his purple cloak!"

"Come fight Sparta," invited the Spartan king's uncle, clownish old Cleonymus. "I've got a hot new young wife," he wailed, "but the King's son beds her behind my back, while everyone laughs to my face!" "I'm not missing Macedonia," Pyrrhus explained, taking up the offer, "but sparring Sparta!" The Spartan army was away, and to Pyrrhus' surprise, the Spartan women fought even harder. One boy fought so well that the Spartan elders yelled at him to stop fighting and, "Go bed your girlfriend to make some sons!" Held off just long enough to get bored, Pyrrhus instead marched against Argos.

"I'm not sparing Sparta," he explained, "but are-going Argos!" Fighting in the city, a dead elephant blocked the gates, causing a pachyderm jam. A mahout fell off his elephant, which proceeded to trample everyone in its fury to pick up its dead master. In the thick of the street brawl as usual, Pyrrhus swung to kill some poor Argive, whose old mother was watching from the roof. Argive women were so like men, that on their wedding night they even wore false beards. She saved her son by dropping a roof tile on Pyrrhus' helmet.

Antigonus' son tossed Pyrrhus' head at his father's feet, and Antigonus angrily beat him with his staff for showing such disrespect to a king. "Pyrrhus' proper place," Antigonus announced, lighting the fire, "a pyre is!" Pyrrhus' big toe refused to burn, so it was stored in a temple chest, and revered as a magic cure for inflamed spleens. "I conquered Italy, Sicily, Macedonia, Sparta and Argos," Pyrrhus epitaph read, "For a while, anyway!"

Fiery feats on papyrus
of the warrior Pyrrhus
who always departed
just as he got started
until he fought where his pyre is!

I GOT A TOE HOLD ON PYRRHUS!

Wrecking Rhegium (270 BC)

Perched on the toenail of Italy, the town of *Rhegium* (Broken-off) was well known for its sense of humor, like the time the tyrant Dionysius asked for a bride, and they sent him the public executioner's daughter. The humorless Dionysius sacked the place. The Roman garrison now guarding them, jealous of the great parties that the locals threw, decided to do the same. "The Rhegian men will get the blade," ordered Decius, as they gatecrashed, "and the drunken ladies laid!" After the massacre, Decius got blind drunk, then ordered something for a hangover. The foreign doctor gave him blister-beetle ointment to put on his eyes. When Decius washed it off, he found that his eyesight was gone, but did see that the doctor must've been an angry ex-Rhegian. "Kill the drunken Roman rebels," ordered the senate, on hearing the news, "it's against military regulations to have fun!" "Isn't it illegal," someone asked, "to kill Roman citizens without a trial?" "Alright, only kill 50 a day, hide the bodies," the senate muttered, "and keep it quiet!"

Rome Rules Okay! (265 BC)

Rome ravaged Etruria, sacked *Volsinii* (Hill), and looted the art works. "I can't believe you Romans have killed our men," complained *Miso-romaeus* (Roman-hater), "just to capture statues of them!" "I bought back a statue of the Etruscan god *Vortumnus* (Shape-shifter)," boasted the Roman consul, "by shifting his shape!" Another captured statue was nicknamed *Minerva capta* (Minerva the prisoner). The ignorant Romans adorned their forum with statues of great Greek thinkers like Pythagoras, who believed in reincarnation, so might've erected it himself. The conquest of the Etruscan League and Greater Greece left Rome in control of all Italy.

WE GOT RID OF THEM GREEKS EH!

126

11 ROME IN POEM

The defeat of Pyrrhus caused a sensation in the Greek world. "Who the heck are these upstart Romans?" they asked, and all things Roman suddenly became very trendy:

Poor Pyrrhus came to woe
so now we want to know
how the Romans came
to get their name
from our Greek letter *P*? (*Rho*, in Greek)

The Egyptians sent an embassy to Rome, who in turn sent three senators to Alexandria. Completely new to the diplomacy game, they were awkwardly embarrassed to be given expensive presents, after they'd already pinched the bed sheets for new togas. They then placed their gold gift-crowns on the king's statues, mistaken for the hat-stand. A soldier who accidentally ran over a cat was stoned to death by the mob, even though King Ptolemy himself tried to save him. "If they get that mad over cats," the shocked Romans whimpered, "I'm glad we didn't kill a person!" Consequently, Rome left off conquering Egypt until much later, after they'd conquered everything else.

Roman snobs adopted Greek names like *Sophus* (Philosopher) and *Philo* (Philosopher), to show that they were as clever as the Greeks. Callimachus wrote a poem about a Roman called Gaius:

There once was a Roman called Gaius
who arrived in Athens all pious
he then saw a Greek boy
he longed to enjoy
too bias to try us to buy us!

Roman nomen

Romans usually had three names, although the more pompous added extra names (*agnomen*) for some deed, like "*Africanus*" who destroyed Africa, and "*Achaicus*" who destroyed Greece, although Marcus Maecius Maemmius Furius Balburius Caecilianus Placidus had seven, and destroyed nothing, while Gaius Marius had none, but destroyed lots of things. By the late empire one pompous fellow labored under 40 names. Only a very few first names (*praenomen*) were used, repeatedly, so you wouldn't forget anybody:

Call us Aulus, Vibius, Gaius
mark us Marcus, Flavius, Gnaeus
mint us Quintus, Servius, Numerius
write us Titus, Publius, Tiberius!

These were normally abbreviated, so the foregoing should read:

Call us A., V., C.
mark us M., Fl., Cn.
mint us Q., Ser., N.
write us T., P., Ti.!

This was how the efficient Romans liked it, with none of that rhyming poetry nonsense. Notice how the letter *G* was made up to write Gaius, but was left as *C* on all inscriptions, since the stonemason charged for the extra stroke.

Manius meant born at breakfast, *Lucius* at lunch, *Marcus* by Mars' temple, *Tiberius* by the river, and *Gaius* on the earth. *Quintus, Sextus, Septimus, Octavius, Nonus*, and *Decimus*, were born respectively fifth to tenth, while *Numerius* is any number, for those that lost count. *Postumus, Spurius*, and *Agrippa*, were born late, illegitimately, and feet first. *Caeso* was cut free with a Caesarian, *Gnaeus* was born with a birthmark, and *Publius* with pubes.

The second name (*nomen*) was the clan, whose distinguishing feature was always "*us*." See if you can spot the imposter in the following Latin clan names: Julius, Tullius, Attila, and Sempronius. Particular families reused favorite names, which is why the troublemaker Appius Claudius kept the same name over the centuries, so to avoid confusion was often described as: "Claudius, son of Claudius and grandson of Claudius." (This was little help!)

The third name (*cognomen*) told them apart, such as big-nose *Naso*, buck-teeth *Brocchus*, knock-kneed *Vatia*, pot-belly *Galba*, fat-ankles *Scaurus*, slow *Lentulus*, big-head *Capito*, bushy-beard *Barbatus*, bleary-eyed *Luscus*, black *Niger*, baldy *Calvus*, stammering *Balbus*, limping *Claudius*, beastly *Bestia*, wasted *Nepos*, drunkard *Tricongius*, won't-shutup *Ravilla*, bad-news *Tubero*, small-penis *Pipinna*, little-twat *Porcella*, asshole-and-a-half *Sesquiculus*, and nice *Lepidus*, which was a joke-name since he was really nasty.

Scrofa (Sow) earned his nickname by hiding a stolen pig in his wife's bed. "I swear that there is no old sow in this house," he truthfully told the soldiers who questioned him, as he pointed at his wife, "except for the one lying in those blankets!"

Sonless senators often adopted a full-grown male from another clan to continue their family name. When a rich woman died, having adopted Cicero's son-in-law in her will, he advised, "We'll decide if it's legal, when we find out how much money she's left you!"

Women didn't have names, but were called after the family nomen, like a bag-tag, so Julius' daughter was *Julia*, Antony's *Antonia*, and Silius' *Silia*. To tell several daughters apart they were called *Prima, Secunda, Tertia* (1, 2, 3), so in the public baths you would hear the cry, "Number three, your time is up!" To tell a young Julia from an old Julia, she was called *Julilla*, a young Livia, *Livilla*, a young Vania, *Vanilla*, or a young Godzia, *Godzilla*. When women got more rights, like names, these were their father's ridiculous cognomens, making Caesar's daughter, *Caesonia* (Hairier), even worse off.

Laws (*lex*) passed by the senate were all feminine, so a law passed by Julius was a *lex Julia*, by Livius a *lex Livia*, but by Dysius a *dys Lexia*.

Slaves were simply called *Statius* (Waiter) until they became too numerous. Then they were given their master's name, so you'd know who they belonged to, added to either *-por* (Boy), so Verus' slave was *Veripor* (Very-poor), or barbarian-king-joke-names like Perseus Publius. "The freed slave Cinnamus Furius wants to be addressed as Cinna," snorted Martial, "but I'd rather call him *Fur* (Thief)!" Dwarves were named "Hercules," Africans as "Snowball," and ugly girls "Miss Rome." Slaves freed by women weren't named after their mistress, but backward *C*, which sounded better than a boy named Sue. A *nomenclator* was a slave employed to whisper names in your ear, so you could remember your friends and not forget your enemies. "Often the nomenclator couldn't remember either," Seneca complains, "so cunningly invented any name to whisper in his witless master's ear!"

Barmy Roman army

The size of a Roman army depended on how many escaped the draft, and then how many got killed, so tended to vary wildly. A *legion* (levy, of about 5,000 men) fought in three lines. The *hastati* (spear men) were the new boys in front who wore plumed helmets, trying to look taller, the *principes* (first men) were the men pushing this javelin-fodder forward, and the *triarii* (third men) were the wily old codgers who'd survived being in the first two, sitting in reserve to watch the show. The *velites* (cloak-wearers) were poor skirmishers who opened the fight by flinging their javelins or rocks at the enemy, then ran back to hide with the triarii. An old Roman adage, "It's reached the triarii," meant you were in deep doo-doo.

The centurions were picked from the meanest troops, who beat the others, and one broke so many canes over backs that his nickname was *Cedo Alterum* (Hand-me-another). "The army should fear their leaders," he growled, "more than the enemy!" The soldiers bribed their officers for exemption from duty, so that nearly a quarter of the troops could be found lounging about the barracks, or missing altogether. Some performed slave's chores to earn the money to pay the kickbacks to get out of working, whereas the rest robbed the locals. If a soldier came into money, his centurion beat him harder and piled on more duties until he was paid off.

Cavalry attended each legion, until the Romans realized that their knights were useless riders. "It's only because," they protested, "we've got such short legs!" They became junior officers in charge of allied Numidian or Gallic horsemen.

As the Romans conquered the world, their allied armies expanded, obtaining specialist fighters like Balearic slingers, Indian mahouts, Arab camel-jockeys, and Ethiopian archers who didn't use quivers, but wore their arrows in headbands. A slinger had further range than a bowman (350 m), and their inscribed pellets struck with a force which left imprints on the victim's flesh, such as: "pig," "dgo" (some couldn't spell too good), "scumbag," and such pleasantries as: "catch," "didn't duck," "take that," "I got it coming," "an unpleasant present," "have this one on me," or "I went to war and all I got was this lousy pellet shot!"

The army practiced with heavy iron weapons, so in combat their real swords felt light, and it was said: "Their maneuvers are bloodless battles, and their battles just bloody maneuvers!" "The *tortoise* is a formation of overlapping shields that looks like a Roman tiled roof," reported Livy, since they were also quite rickety. The Latin word for soldiers is *miles* (probably due to how far they marched) and they were renowned for their toughness. "I intend to fight," retorted one soldier, who'd been chided for advancing into battle lame, "not run away!"

Every night the Romans laid out a camp, with a trench and palisade to keep their booty, usually captured cows, from wandering off. The camp was always square, with the tents always in the same place, to stop everyone getting lost. Those caught asleep on duty, sleeping with another man on duty, or running away from battle were clubbed to death. If the whole army ran away, every tenth man drawn by lot was clubbed to death by the other nine, in a *decimation*, and the survivors had to sleep outside, eating horsefeed.

The first soldier over an enemy wall got a gold crown, whoever saved a life got a wood crown, and whoever saved the whole army got a grass crown, so not many bothered doing that. Depending on the period, these crowns were easier or harder to win. "Nobilior hands out gold crowns," complained old Cato, "not for sacking cities or burning enemy camps, but for building fences and digging latrines!" Other rewards for the troops consisted of gold bracelets, necklets and medallions, or the pointless *hasta pura* (headless spear).

Rome coming parade

Generals who killed more than 5,000 enemies in one battle were entitled to a *triumph* (parade), and a law had to be enacted to stop them lying about this. The triumph began with a victory banquet, and it was traditional to invite the consuls, then send them a note saying: "Sorry, changed my mind, you can't come," so that no one outranked the victorious general at the dinner table.

The proud general paraded through the streets with his face painted in red mud so he looked like the statue of Jupiter. A slave held Jupiter's huge gold crown over his head, which was too heavy to be supported by a mortal's puny neck, and whispered in his ear, "You ain't that good, you know!" His children rode in the chariot beside him, entertained by a crowd of rude *ludiones* (comic-actors), but he made the mother-in-law walk behind.

ROMAN TRIUMPH PARADE...

First were the trumpeters, followed by men dressed as walking sandwich-boards, written with the story of the war, so you'd know exactly who he'd robbed and beaten. All the enemy spoils were displayed, except for what he'd hidden for himself, along with wee models of the conquered cities. Next came flute-players, white bulls, the priests to sacrifice them, and weird animals brought from distant lands, like the *camel-leopard* (giraffe). Enemy weapons heaped into rickety carts clashed together with a noise that terrified spectators. The captured slaves were dragged along, usually kings of obscure tribes, before being strangled. A display of gifts the general had received from the allied tribes followed, if they knew what was good for them. His soldiers marched last, complaining about their small bounty, and singing rude songs in revenge. Last of all was a chained doddering old man, traditionally led by the town-crier who cried out: "Etruscans for sale!" This was in memory of Rome's ancient victory over Veii.

Honors rat race

If you had connections, you started public life in the Honors Race as one of 20 *quaestors* (seekers) at age 20-something, keeping the military financial accounts that might enable you to advance your career by prosecuting your own commander. You then hoped to get elected as one of the six *praetors* (preceders) at age 39, which entitled you to run as one of two *consuls* (counselors) at age 42, if you'd lived that long.

Competition was fierce, so the optional office of *aedile* (temple-sweeper) allowed you to cheat by putting on expensive games to make the voters love you. Finally, you were sent to govern a province, where you could rob the locals and recoup your losses. Returning to Rome, you were tried in the extortion court, condemned, and then exiled off to some well-deserved quiet *otiation* (leisure). Roman business was mostly *negotiation* (not-leisure).

The army assembly elected the officers, but the tribal assembly took over running the courts. The rich landowners kept control by using their 31 small rural tribes to outvote the 4 huge urban tribes containing the mass of poor Roman plebs.

Originally, senators took their young sons along to view senate proceedings, where they were sworn to secrecy, until a boy was forced by his mother to reveal what had been discussed. "They debated a new law to decide whether men should have two wives," he lied, "or women should have two husbands!" The next day a huge crowd of women thronged the senate house. "Please," they begged, clutching at the passing senators' togas, "Vote that women have two husbands!" When the cause of their distress was revealed, the lad was commended for not breaking his oath, but henceforth all boys were banned.

"Make sure you tell nobody," a senator told his wife, pressed about private senate business, "but a lark wearing a golden helmet was seen flying about with a spear!" Setting off for the senate, he arrived to hear a pleb shouting, "Have you heard the news? About the lark in the gold helmet?" "Praise be to my wife," the senator laughed, "the story reached the forum before me!" "Oh woe," he told his wife when he got home, just to teach her a lesson, "We've been exiled for revealing the secret!"

All senators wore a simple iron ring. "Zoilus made his chains into a ring," complained Martial, when a freed slave became a senator. "The greatest Roman criminal," wrote Pliny, "was whoever first wore a gold ring!" Eventually senators wore a gold ring on each finger, and then on each joint. "Charinus wears six rings on every finger and never takes them off in bed or bath," wrote Martial, "- because he can't afford a ring-case!" Sets of seasonal summer and winter rings were worn, the latter too heavy for hot weather, and one ring was so large that the owner was advised to wear it on his leg instead of his hand.

Everyday living it up

The early Roman house was merely an improved mud hut, being a series of windowless rooms built around a courtyard called an *atrium* (from *ater*, meaning *black*, for the original foul gloomy interior), designed to let smoke out, keep burglars out, and let rain in for watering your wine. The smell of the bedrooms was disguised by burning bread.

At first, the plastered walls were unimaginatively painted with scenes of the brick or stone that they covered up. Then, to open the enclosed space up, dummy windows were painted on the walls showing outside landscapes, along with false doors and balconies displaying attractive women lounging about. Rich Romans became so bored with luxurious surroundings that they had one room decorated as a 'pauper's hovel,' just for something different. Eventually the lazy Greek practice of lying down to eat was adopted and a *triclinium* (three-place-diner-recliner-room) added. "Slave, treat our guests well," commands one wall-inscription, "Wash their dirty feet first, and make sure to put a cloth over the good cushions before they lie down!" "When visitors are expected, the master cracks his whip, and all of the slaves run in circles looking for cobwebs, muddy prints, or a dog turd in the lobby," laughed Juvenal, "Things that one small slave-boy could fix with a bucket of sawdust!"

As the population burgeoned, high-rise *insulae* (islands) were knocked up to house the huddled masses, leaning on each other for support and prone to sudden collapse. "I've built tenement blocks," boasted one proud architect's CV, "some of which stayed up!"

The really poor holed up in temple corners and left their basket chained to a column while they went off scrounging. Rome had no numbered streets, nor very many street names, so your address might be: "Pass the crossroads, before the temple, after the statue, next to the tree with the beggar beneath it." Ordinary Romans had few possessions. "A flame, some water, the knife, the axe, the pestle and mortar, etc.," griped one neighbor, "are usually borrowed off of me!" Whereas the Greek historian Polybius complained, "In Rome nobody never gives nothing to no one!" Probably because they didn't get it back again.

Right: A silver service platter with a rather severe looking Roman ancestor's head mounted in the middle - probably as a reminder of table manners (From the Boscoreale Treasure).

Romans ate with their fingers and used slaves for napkins by wiping the fingers in their hair. Ghosts were believed to haunt the floor looking for food, so any dropped scraps were burnt in their honor, which saved paying for a proper sacrifice. For illumination, clay lamps burnt olive oil, so you had to stop the kids drinking it. Clothes were washed by a fuller, who jumped on them in a tub of urine to remove the grease and dirt. He was willing to pay you for good urine. For a lighter wash, he simply spat on your laundry.

Communal toilets allowed you to sit around with your friends discussing the latest gossip, although toilet paper was a shared stick with a sponge on the end, and naughty boys liked to float burning paper boats down the running water channel under your buttocks. At home, you used an old wine jar that was emptied out the window into the street, and many lawsuits arose from angry showered pedestrians. "Only a fool goes out in the streets of Rome," Juvenal advised, "without making their will first!" Despite Aelian's story of an octopus entering through a toilet to raid the jars of pickled fish, private houses weren't connected to the main sewer for fear of explosive gas buildup, which was blamed for causing many of Rome's fires.

Combing Rome

Mirrors were made of polished brass, so if you couldn't admire your image on the front, you could at least leer at the erotic engravings on the flip side. One brave husband, whose wife complained about the lewd etchings, instead gave her a mirror depicting the snake-haired Medusa on the reverse, whose hideous look turned viewers to stone.

Right: Copy of a bronze engraving depicting the perils of mirror gazing (From Praeneste, 300 BC).

Fashionable women's hairstyles became steadily taller, more elaborate and bizarre, so that today they can be used as a reliable guide for dating statues. Some women's statues even had detachable hair so that they could update to the latest fashion, even after death. "From the front, or the back?" answered Juvenal, when asked how tall his new girlfriend was, "Her hairdo rises like a multistory tenement block, but behind is a sawn-off pygmy who stands on tiptoe for a kiss!" The bald compensated by wearing caps cut from animal bladders, horse-mane wigs, and hairpins ready to prick any smirking maids. Blonde hair was prized, so the German slave was likely to have her locks shorn off to adorn her mistress' head.

"Fabulla swears her hair's her own, in case you never thought it," wrote Martial, "and she swears true, I can confirm - 'cos I know where she bought it!" "She also greatly improves her looks," Martial added, "by hanging out with a gang of hideous old crones!"

"Oh, you've changed your hairstyle?" Ovid politely asked, upon noticing that a woman he'd surprised had hastily donned her wig on reversed. Some easy-care wigs were carved from mess-proof solid marble. Others simply painted hair on their bald heads, so it was joked that they didn't need a barber, but a sponge.

Below: An engraved bronze Etruscan mirror depicting Pan blowing his pipes. A hairy-suited actor molests a maiden, while his companion brings a lighted torch, an amphora of wine, and his dancing shoes.

The maid put a pin out of place
so Lalage broke her face
shave your hair
so the mirror's stare
reflects your cracked grimace!
- Martial, *Epigram* 2.66

Street barbers armed with blunt quips and razors scraped the face, and Juvenal noted that the Billy goat was wise for growing a beard. Martial constantly complained about how rich his barber was, and so slow that by the time he'd finished a beard had grown on the other side of his chin again. "My chin scars weren't made by a boxer, or a fierce wife's sharp talons," he lamented, "but my cursed barber's razor!" "I tried a lady barber, but she didn't shave me - she peeled me!" Martial added (referring to his foreskin, since she also provided sexual services).

"A good barber has a simple pair of scissors," advised Lucian, "while a bad barber displays a bewildering array of tools - so get your hair cut by the first, and then peer in the second's fancy giant mirror to brush it!"

Only the Gauls had soap, made of goat fat and ashes, which the Romans thought they used to tint their hair red, observing the muck that came out of it as they washed. "Better to be bathed by being sweated and scraped with a strigil," Martial advised, "which will save your towels being worn out by the fuller jumping on them in the urine vat!" Doctors recommended soaking in the public baths as a good cure for weeping sores, runny ulcers, and any other mysterious bodily discharges.

"Anybody who smells nice all the time," wrote the fastidious poet Juvenal, in regards to the copious use of perfumes, "doesn't!" "Whenever I smell Gellia coming, I think the perfume-seller spilt his jar," sniffed Martial, "You're not fooling anybody - my dog could smell sweet the same way!" "Bassa pretends to like babies," he added, "so she has someone to blame when she farts!" Farting wasn't approved in polite company, as Ovid's *Art of Love* observes noble ladies at their toilet, doused in expensive perfumes, loudly farting - much to the amusement of the maids behind their backs, at least those that weren't gagging from the stench. The demented infirm emperor Claudius, on the other hand, often loudly belched and farted at his dinner parties. "My doctors say holding it in is bad for my health," he explained to guests who probably thought, "Yes, but letting it out is bad for ours!"

Lazy matrons swallowed idiotic diet fads, such as using dew soaked cloth to melt their excess fat away. "So great is the value of their jewelry," Plautus quipped, "that some women wear entire farms about their necks!" Cosmetic makeup comprised lead, flour and chalk to make the face lighter, or charcoal to make it darker. "A woman wearing her damp bread face-pack is almost as comical as she's repulsive," wrote Juvenal, "and her longsuffering husband kisses her greasy lips, which she wipes clean for her lover!" "Polla plasters her face with bean-meal," advised Martial, "but would better let her pimple show, since the hidden flaw's always presumed worse!" To the complaint that he himself painted his lips with white lead, Martial retorted, "To avoid kissing you!" The desperate covered blemishes with stick-on leather patches, especially ex-slaves hiding the brand mark on their foreheads.

Our proud peer sure does vex
sporting purple shoes like a *Rex*
his toga to match
but lift up the patch
on his brow and you'll read: X!
- Martial, *Epigram* 2.29

MY NEW PURPLE SHOES HIDE MY BRAND!

"Toupeed Spanius dreads wind, pearl-powdered Fabulla dreads rain, and white-leaded Sabella dreads sun," laughed Martial, "but Maximina should dread mimes - since her laugh shows three black teeth!"

"Thais' teeth are black and Laecania's white. Why? One set's original, the other bought!" he added, "And the fraud Aefulanus chews a tooth-pick in order to pretend that he's got teeth!" The Romans ridiculed the Spanish barbarians for using urine as toothpaste, whereas they used powdered mouse-brains, ground oyster-shells, dog-teeth ashes mixed with honey, or just licked their slave's fingers.

Egnatius smiles goofy-faced
since Spanish toothpaste
is his own pee
so he grins widely
because he hates the taste!
- Catullus, *Poem* 39

Sorely sexed

Many Roman men judged it acceptable to have sex with whomever they liked, provided they were the penetrator (*ooh*, active) and not penetrated (*ouch*, passive), except for freeborn boys whose father could take you to court. Fortunately not all males were Ro-men, so slaves, freedmen and foreigners were fair game, at least until they grew their first beard. Roman poets swing like confused pendulums between praising their girlfriends, or boyfriends: "Alas, I've lost my dearie, 'cos he grew too hairy!" Men were expected to sleep with their slaves simply because not using what you owned seemed odd, like not riding your chariot, although wives often complained about the cheaper models.

Whenever I'm feeling randy
and a maid or boy is handy
Do I hold back?
No! I attack!
Quick cheap sex is dandy!
- Horace, *Satire* 1.2

Female prostitutes were generally low class and inexpensive, whereas boys were the reverse and even took over *Volgivaga's* (Streetwalker) Feast as their own Male Prostitutes' Holiday, so they could get a day off. "Rome's become so decadent," Cato complained, "it now costs more to plow a pretty boy than a field!" Old Cato's problem wasn't with sex, but the expensive waste of money (he was so tight that the traditional wine press became known as a Cato Press). "But without prostitutes, society would collapse," pointed out St Augustine, "when everybody went crazy through unsatisfied lust!" "Lord, make me chaste," Augustine prayed, "but not just yet!"

"You pull Parthians, caress Cappadocians, suck Sarmatians, solicit Cilicians, indulge Indians, do Dacians, ejaculate Egyptians, lay Alans, shag shaggy Germans and serve circumcised Jews," Martial griped to the Roman prostitute Caelia, "You roam every man but a Roman!"

"The positions are all too complicated," complained Lucian of Philaenis' illustrated *Sex Manual*, while the monk Clement noted, "It's easier to buy pictures of her labors, than those of Hercules'!"

Cunnilingus was considered distasteful, for it involved oral pollution (*os impurum* or badmouth), and calling a Roman a *fellator* (sucker) was an even ruder insult than *pathicus* (rear-ended).

Masturbation on the other hand was a worse worry, since even the *dexterous* (right-handed) customarily performed it with the *sinister* (left) unlucky *manus* (in the fist). "Horatius begat triplets (Horatii), Mars begat twins (Romulus and Remus), but you beget nothing," complains Martial's *Epigram* 9.41, "Stop using your left hand as a mistress, Ponticus - you're wasting Romans!" "Outside the bedroom door, while Andromache rode Hector like a horse," he added in *Epigram* 11.104, "her Phrygian slaves saw - and pulled themselves off course!"

"The shoemaker *Kerdon* (Greedy) made me a nice *baubon* (soother) *olisbos* (slipper)," boasts Koritto, in Herodas' mime *The Dildo* (250 BC), "much firmer than any man's stand!" "Euboule begged to use my *baubon*," she angrily adds, "and now I find all of my friends have used it - before me!"

Right: A pleased looking woman carries a big *baubon*-shaped fish (Vase painting).

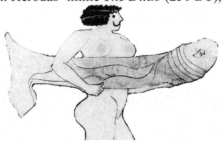

The god of the marriage-bed, symbolized by a house snake, was called *Genius*, since that's how good the men thought they were at making love. In answer to that, the women's deified sex power was *Iuno*, pronounced: "I? You? No!"

Loose women worshiped *Fortuna Virilis* (Man's Fortune) in the men's baths, since that's where the part of man that sought women's favor hung out. This ritual was supposed to blind men to their bodily defects (probably because they were underwater).

Women were required to parade naked on the first day of Venus (April Fools Day), but unlike shameless Greek prostitutes the Roman matrons wore myrtle crowns to modestly cover up.

Below: A Pompeii wall fresco of fat-bottomed lovers (AD 50).

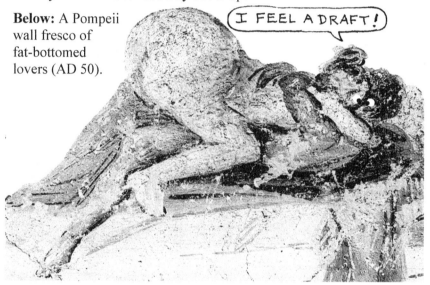

Wedded bliss

The father had absolute control over the household, killing or selling his children at will, but when he died his eldest son took over, unless he'd been sold already. A son could escape control, by either becoming a prisoner-of-war, or proving Dad was insane. The selling of married men was eventually banned, since it wasn't right for a freeborn woman to suddenly find she was married to a slave. The legal marriageable age was 12 for girls and 14 (or puberty) for boys, but in practice, the groom was about ten years older. Her father could break the marriage whenever he wanted to ally with someone else. "Your hymen's divided betwixt your parents and you," Catullus wrote in *Poem* 52, "so you're outvoted, one to two!" *Poem* 61 on *Hymen* (god of marriage) read, "O Hymeneal Hymen's wedded joys, your husband has to give up boys!"

Elite patricians, priests, and snobs who liked a fancy ceremony were married by *confarreatio* (wedding-cake). Marriage by *coemptio* (bride-purchase) saw the bride also pay three coins, two to the household gods, and one to her husband as a tip for carrying her over the threshold, which she'd rubbed with lard in order to give bad spirits the slip. "What's your first name?" the groom ritually asked, and not having one, she cleverly replied, "If you're Gajus, then I'm *Gaja* (gaga)!" During the ceremony she sacrificed her childhood toys, and then clung to her mother, as the groom roughly dragged her away in ritual imitation of the 'Rape of the Sabine Women.' The guests sang rude songs about the couple in order to ward off envy, by pretending they weren't really very happy: "She slept with his brother, and he hates her mother, but now they're married, they do both to each other!" The torchbearers shook their torches like loons, since a tall flame meant the husband was hot in bed, but a dim flicker meant a limp wick. The bride wore a flame-colored veil to show she was hot too.

Below: A Roman wedding frieze from an engraved bronze pot. Boy meets girl, boy rapes girl, boy marries girl.

Once he'd lugged her inside his house, the bride sat on the phallus of the fertility god Mutunus Tutunus and offered her virginity. Originally, the groom's friends slept with her first, but this was replaced by tossing nuts into the bedchamber, much to their chagrin.

The concerned groom followed the custom of not deflowering his timid wife on the first night, instead restraining himself by sodomy. Unable to wait any longer, it was traditional to make love the day after the wedding. This was the groom's only chance to see his wife naked, since from now on it would be lights out and clothes on. Even the prostitutes kept their brassieres on for modesty's sake. Used to forcing himself on the slaves, the husband was probably bewildered to finally have a willing partner. "Quirinalis has bedded so many slave-girls," wrote Martial, "he's got more children than if he'd married!"

Besides the slaves in attendance, the groom also had plenty of help from the bedroom gods: *Subigus* dragged the bride to the bed, *Virginensis* pulled off her clothes, *Prema* held down her struggles,

Pertunda performed the penetration, *Janus* opened the way, *Saturnus* made the sperm, and *Liber* did the ejaculation. "What the heck," whined the exasperated groom, "do I do?!" "Pertunda should be ashamed of herself," complained St Augustine, who was not much for equal rights, "she shouldn't be in the bedroom, and certainly not doing a man's job!" Afterwards a ritual bath was taken. This vase relief (right) has a slave hurrying to toss a holy pail of water over a couple caught *in flagrante delicto* (AD 50). So much for the ritual bath!

Marriage by *usus* (using) occurred if a couple simply slept together for a year. A wife could avoid her husband's authority by spending three nights of the year in someone else's bed, so long as he didn't catch someone else in it. "Women who're away for the last three nights of the year don't comply," argued one clever lawyer, "because half the last night belongs to the new year!" This allowed rich senatorial widows to cohabit with handsome freedmen, whom they couldn't officially marry.

"Let's compare whose husband makes love to them the most," agreed two girlfriends married on the same day. The next morning the first wife stood on her balcony and proudly held up ten fingers. Shamefaced, the other wife held up one finger. The following day the first smugly held up nine fingers, while the second again held up one. In successive days the first held up eight, then seven, then six fingers, and so on, while the downcast second wife continually held up only one. Finally, the furious first wife shook a clenched fist to show that she wasn't getting any, while the second still proudly held up one finger.

Guidance counselor

The biographer Plutarch (100 AD) wrote a famous letter of marriage advice to a bride and groom, which begins:

"Dear Pollianus and Eurydice,
Congratulations! My wedding present to you is some philosophical marriage advice. There's a song played on the flute called *Horny Horse*, because the music stimulates horses to mount each other, and I hope my words will do the same. However, weak men who are too effeminate to leap onto their horse, teach it to kneel down, and so some men try with their wives. Before hopping into bed, a wife should eat a quince so that she tastes nice. Many brides are annoyed with their husbands following their first experience, since they feel like beekeepers who've endured the stings, but haven't tasted the honey. The bride's chaplet of asparagus sports vicious thorns to symbolize that a husband should bear her tantrums patiently. Wives shouldn't use spells or love potions, which

might turn their husbands into crazy fools. Remember, the witch Circe turned her lovers into pigs, which are no good in bed at all.

Herodotus was wrong to say, "A woman takes off modesty with her underwear." A modest wife shouldn't be mad when she catches her husband with the maidservant, but think, "It's out of respect for me that he shares his drunkenness, debauchery and depravity with her!" A wife should have no feelings or friends of her own, but enjoy her husband's with him. Just as I call my drink wine, although the larger part is water, so should we regard all joint-property as the husband's, even though the wife contributes the larger share.

The Egyptian women aren't allowed to wear shoes, so they stay home. If you take a Roman woman's pearls, bracelets, anklets, purple dresses and gilded slippers, she'll stay home too. The statue of Venus with one foot on a tortoise symbolizes that loving wives stay home in silence. A woman's shoulders shouldn't be exposed in public, even if they say, "There's no 'arm in it!" Romans prohibit presents between man and wife, since they should share everything anyway. In Africa, the wedding custom is for the bride to send to her mother-in-law for a pot, who replies, "I haven't got one!" Thus, the bride knows she is disliked from day one, and won't be resentful when a worse incident occurs later on. Sometimes philosophy isn't enough. The best cure for an argument is sex - with each other!"

Divorced bliss

A wife could be divorced for adultery, poisoning the kids, copying the house keys, becoming ugly, or nagging too much. Any captured adulterer was tossed to the slaves, who laughingly inflicted sexual dishonor on him. "I wasn't trying to bed your wife," one culprit caught in the bedroom explained, "but your slave-boy!" He was let off.

"You say the smooth poof hanging around your wife does her jobs," Martial scoffed at another husband, "But I'll bet he's doing your job!"

The adulterer you propose
to cut off his ears and nose
but you're dense
since his offence
wasn't done by those!
- Martial, *Epigram* 2.83

Right: A bronze satyr with sex always on his mind – is this the original dick-head?

The law forbade prosecuting barmaids for adultery, since they were presumed to be prostitutes. "It's not for my wife bedding everyone," a childless husband declared, when he initiated the first Roman divorce in 235 BC, "but for not bedding anyone!" Wives were banned from drinking wine, and this was the origin of the homecoming kiss, when the husband sniffed her breath to check as an early breathalyzer test.

Egnatius Maetennus clubbed his wife to death for drinking wine straight out of the vat, while another matron was starved as punishment for breaking into the wine cellar to drink it dry. The cup painting (right) depicts a wine swilling matron followed by her longsuffering slave lugging the wineskin. One wife was divorced for pulling her dress over her head in public, another for not doing so, and yet another for sneaking into the circus games.

"I'd rather marry a noble woman than a rich woman," advised Old Cato, "since they're both insufferably arrogant, but at least a noble woman caught committing adultery will be ashamed of it!" It became customary for adulterous wives to be paid by their lovers, either in a lump sum or by installments, although some cads tried to reclaim these gifts when the affair was broken off. "She's not a prostitute who gave herself because she was paid," the jurors held, if the wrangle reached court, "No, she gave herself of her own free will and was rewarded for it!" Women chased the wages of adultery as eagerly as men chased their dowries. "Don't send her money, just send her a toga," joked Martial, which was the prescribed dress for convicted wives. "Your wife puts a eunuch to watch over you, Linus?" he added, since husbands usually set watchers over their wives, "She's wise - and spiteful!"

"Some noble women count their years, not by the number of consuls," Seneca complained, "but by the number of their husbands!" One wife had married 22 husbands before finally meeting her perfect match, a husband who'd married 20 wives. "Proculeia's husband has become praetor, yet she's leaving. Why?" asked Martial, "Because his purple robe will cost 20,000 and the festival 100,000? This isn't a divorce - it's good business!"

Seneca says: "It's so coarse
how women show no remorse
when they don't tarry
but divorce to marry
and then marry to divorce!"

Child hood

Childbirth was even riskier than warfare, since the mortality rate was higher, but women were assisted by the goddesses *Mena* (Menstruation), *Libera* (Orgasm), *Vitumnus* (Fetus), *Sentinus* (Kicking), *Lucina* (Labor), and *Ops* (Birth). The newly born *infant* (can't-talk) was ceremoniously dumped at their father's feet. Boys he bounced on his *genu* (knee; hence the word *genuine*), girls he nodded at, and the unwanted he kicked out for the daily slave-trader pickup. One husband's blunt letter to his pregnant wife reads: "Joy if boy, hurl if girl!" Of live births, about a quarter died by age one and another third by age ten.

Right: A funerary relief of a midwife looking for the baby (Ostia necropolis).

"Nothing is more important to a Roman than being a good father," advised the great statesman Cato, "apart from being a great statesman!" "I don't admire the Greek troublemaker Socrates for being a philosopher," he added, "but I do admire him as a father - for putting up with a nagging wife and retarded children!"

The nurse tried to shape the baby by kneading the head to make it round, tugging the nose, pinching the bum, and pulling the foreskin. "Don't let them sleep or they'll be stupid," Varro advised on childcare, "and eating stunts their growth!"

Right: Bath time for baby (Funerary relief, Rome).

"I need more help," the mother complained, to which the father retorted, "Why? The baby's got the goddesses *Vaticanus* (Wail), *Levana* (Cuddle), *Cunina* (Cradle), *Rumina* (Breast milk), *Statilinus* (Standing), *Adeona* (Walking), *Abeona* (Running away), *Iterduca* (Lost), *Domiduca* (Found), and *Mens* (Good behavior) helping out already!" Children were given toys, dolls, pets and slaves to play with.

Flaccus pets his long-eared lynx
ugly Cronius strokes his monkey
Publius' lapdog loves high jinks
as does Canius' Libyan flunky
Marius pats a mad mongoose
Lausus' talking birds annoy
Glaucilla's slimy snake is loose
Telesilla's songbird gives her joy
they love beasts, so my excuse
is why shouldn't I love a boy?
- Martial, *Epigram* 7.87

144

Right: A bronze mirror class-room parody has 'Schoolmaster' Silenus flogging a naughty nymph held by two winged-cupids, as another keeps count of the strokes behind.

Skooling

"A man who hasn't been flogged," read the Latin school motto, "hasn't been trained!" Boys were often taught at home so that they couldn't be seduced by strange men on the way to school, a constant risk in Rome, where even the Greek teachers were viewed with suspicion. Some teachers coaxed their pupils to learn their ABCs by rewarding them with biscuits and a kiss. "Avoid all teachers of grammar and rhetoric," Martial advised, "and if your son writes poetry, disinherit him! If you want to make money, teach him the flute, but if he's stupid, make him an auctioneer or architect!" "The teacher next door awakes me with his loud lecturing before the rooster has even crowed," Martial added, "I'll pay him his fee - to shut up!" Not especially interested in learning, if a Roman wanted to know something, he bought a Greek slave to do it. Instead of a library, one rich Roman owned a gang of slaves whom each knew an entire book by heart and were always handy to supply him with appropriate quotations - except he was such a fool that he always repeated them wrong.

The Egyptians fashioned their swamp-growing papyrus plant into sandals, baskets, ropes, boats, and even paper, which was handy for plugging holes in the others. Ink was mixed from soot, resin, cuttlefish and wine dregs. Books were published on papyrus rolls, and some over-long rolls (10 meters) had grammarians cursing: "A big book is a big nuisance!" Once finished, the roll had to be rewound to the beginning again, so many lazy authors just quoted other writers from memory, which is why so many ancient quotes are wrong. The scrolls had line numbers, not so it was easier to mark your place, but because the copy-scribes were paid by the line and wanted to keep count. Relaxing in his bath, the avid bookworm Pliny listened nonstop to his reading-slave recite, who eventually spat blood before collapsing exhausted.

BOOKS WERE WRITTEN IN BIG WRITING

since reading glasses hadn't been invented. Many ancient books only survive because they were the set texts for classroom study, and therefore every ancient student had a copy. Judging by how violent, sexy and bloodthirsty the surviving Greek plays are, we can only wonder at how shocking the other ancient texts must've been which weren't approved for school study! There was no Roman language, so they learnt Latin instead:

LATINWRITINGCRAFT
HASNOPUNCTUATION
ORPARAGRAPH
ALSONOSPACES
ANDNOLOWERCASES
SOREADINGITSALAUGH

Latin uses rather tricky *declensions*, so that the Roman Republic *falls*, but the Roman Empire *declines*, and students are forever regretfully declining. Conjugal verbs like love (*amo*) can be accusative (*ammo*) or dative (*armor*), depending whom you're hitting on. Latin also likes substituting *i* for *j* (jay: *iay*), *v* for *u* (you: *yov*), and dropping *h* (ache: *ace*), so *Ivlivs* was often blamed for what Julius did.

Latin maxims abound: *"Quod licet Jovi, non licet bovi!"* (What Jove can do, an ox cannot!) *"Malo malo malo malo!"* (I'd rather be, in an apple tree, than a bad boy, in adversity) *"Eo eo cum eo eo!"* (I go-go!) and *"Cave Canem!"* (Beware of the Dog!)

Saint Jerome deplored the way his students learnt pig Latin by laughing at the irreverent *Testamentum Porcelli* (Piggy's Testament) where a pig about to be slaughtered for the Saturnalia feast parodies a military will. "I, Cooked-leather, am dictating my will," says the piggy, "because I can't write with trotters. I leave 30 acorns to my family, my bristles to the barber, my ears to the shoemaker, my bladder to the schoolboys, my tail to the girls, and my muscles to the inverts. Write on my tomb in gold letters that I nearly lived to be 1000, and make sure I'm served with pepper and honey so I taste nice and am praised forever."

The Romans were so bad at math, that they used the alphabet for numbers: I (1), V (5), X (10), L (50), C (100), D (500), M (1000), O (10,000), Q (500,000) and nothing for zero, so MDCLXVI is 1666, and a 10% tax is X-rated. A smaller number before a larger one was supposed to be subtracted, but the only rule seems to be that there were no rules: 4 has been found written IV or IIII, 8 as VIII or IIX, 18 as XVIII or XIIX or even IIXX, 19 as XIX or XVIIII, 40 as XL or XXXX, 80 as LXXX or XXC, 90 as XC or LXXXX, and 400 as CCCC or CD. As you C (100), this COOL (20150) number IDIOM (11500) can MIMIC (2102) words in a COMIC MIX (11199 + 1009), so while 1549 + 153 might make you MILD and CIVIL, 557 + 99 could make you LIVID and ILL, which is really ODD (11000). A pupil may think 1501 makes them MID in the class, while their teacher says it really makes them DIM. Asked if you'd done your homework, you could answer DID (999), and brag that you also had an IQ of 499,999.

Slave power

Every Roman had at least one slave as a rent-a-friend, who was allowed to earn enough money to buy their freedom, which their master then used to purchase a newer, better model. "You can't judge a slave by their looks," advised Pliny, "but by what you hear about them!" At the sales, slaves danced a jig to display their sound physique, wore a note around their neck listing any defects, and came with a guarantee not to commit suicide or steal. "No one in my household is more trusted," Cicero said of a dishonest slave, "since nothing is barred or sealed to him!" Slaves were also allowed to own slaves, so you might find yourself as a slave's slave's slave, and if a free woman slept with your slave, she became your slave too. An auctioneer hoping for higher bids kissed a slave-girl to show that she was clean, but instead found all bids withdrawn since he

was so dirty. For seriously weird Romans, the Monster Market catered in abnormal and hideously deformed slaves. Morons were sold as curiosities, and Martial demanded his money back for one he bought, complaining, "He's got his wits!" Deaf slaves were dearer, since they couldn't eavesdrop. One Roman slave's job was to walk in front of his master and at every curb, warn, "Watch your step!" "You'd think Romans didn't know how to walk," complained Lucian, "They don't

need a slave's mouth to eat their food, but evidently require their eyes to see, suffering themselves to be given directions fit only for blind men!" "Riding in my sedan chair is such hard work, that I feel like I've walked the whole way!" retorted Seneca, "But at least the rattling cleared my blocked nose!" Running away was considered as theft, because the slave was stealing itself. "A runaway slave's also a thief," advised Martial, "because their feet teach their hands naughty tricks!" Slaves wore chalked feet, so you could try following a runaway's footprints, advertise a reward for their capture, or else hire a *fugitivarri* (slave-catcher) to

track them down. The freedom-ritual consisted of the master slapping their slave on the face, and the consul beating them on the back with a wand. After their head was shaved, they put on the funny red cap of liberty and were then free to be laughed at. They also traditionally touched the nude statue of old, fat, drunk Silenus because he wore a funny bonnet too (and reminded them of their master).

147

Freedmen still had to obey their old master however, or they'd be made a slave again. "If you were free like me," Martial told a rich man's slave, "you wouldn't dine out, you'd drink bad wine, laugh at gold dishes, wear a dirty toga, bed cheap harlots, and stoop to enter your dwelling. Do you still want to be free?"

The pubs entertained their customers with resident slave-girls, who celebrated the annual Slaves' Holiday by washing their hair, since that was about the only amusement that a slave had (apart from annoying the master by slacking, pilfering and sabotage).

Law caught

Originally, the lawyers kept the lawful days secret. "They act like Chaldean astrologers," grumbled one litigant, "predicting when the court will be open!" In 304 BC, a plebeian clerk published an unauthorized copy of Appius Claudius' stolen secret Court Calendar, and suddenly the public could conduct lawsuits without lawyers. Litigants weren't actually represented by lawyers, but by loudmouth orators who didn't require any legal training. Alarmed for their business, the lawyers proceeded to invent arcane secret rituals (legal technicalities), such as having disputants each bring a clod of dirt to court, go out, knock on the door, and come back in again if the dispute was over land, or fight a mock duel with sticks if the dispute was over property.

Rome went strictly by the letter of the law, so the jury voted with *A* for *Absolvo*, *C* for *Condemno*, and B for baffled, which meant a further hearing was held. One bribed jury declared it was baffled seven times, so a law was passed fining anybody who was undecided more than twice. *K* was branded on the foreheads of anyone convicted of false accusations, meaning *Kalumnia* (or klutz).

Romans swore oaths holding their private parts, hence the word *testify* (testicle), and so women couldn't testify, not having any. Once, when a bold woman appeared in court, representing herself, the amazed judges sent off to the oracle to ask what this prodigy meant. Slaves could testify so long as they were tortured, which was the only way to ensure that they were telling the truth.

Roman justice was hard, but fair. "You're guilty," the wily judge told a woman who'd killed her mother for poisoning the children, "so come back in 100 years for sentencing."

"Your honor, I don't know the accused, or his crime," testified an ex-consul, who'd simply strode into court off the street, "but when I met him on the via Laurentia he didn't get off his horse to let me past first!" This secured an immediate conviction.

Tricho appeared in court for beating his son to death, and was almost killed when the outraged jurors stabbed him with their pens. One lawyer who liked to strut up and down the court was asked, "How many miles have you talked?"

The jailers were perplexed when an old woman condemned to starvation, didn't die. Her daughter was strip-searched thoroughly before visits, so they were certain she wasn't smuggling food. Informed of the miraculous event, the judge ordered her released. "Guess what," gloated the daughter, as she led the old woman from jail, "I've been breast-feeding Mom! Nyah!"

For electoral bribery, a convicted offender could have his status restored, but not his fine repaid, if he himself managed to convict someone else, like a game of legal tag, so the courts always had a long queue.

Doctored Rome

The first line of defense against illness was wearing a magic amulet, which also covered you against witchcraft, accidents, robbery, and the evil eye. The best ones came from people who had suffered a violent death, so the body parts of gladiators were eagerly sought after.

Praying to the goddess Fever not to bother you also helped. Some resorted to trickery, with inscriptions over doors warning: "Get lost sickness - Hercules lives here!" If you did get sick, you submitted yourself for public inspection and took the advice of whoever's suggested remedy seemed least painful. Here's a sample of cures:

1. For runny eyes - write "ROURARBISAROURBARIASPHREN" on a piece of papyrus and attach it to an amulet.

2. For headache - take oil in hands and say, "Jupiter sowed a grape seed, we got grapes; he didn't sow it, we got no wine."

3. For coughs - write in black ink on hyena parchment, "THAPSATE STHRAITO." Hang it round your neck, and keep it dry.

4. For hardening of the breasts - write in black ink on a fine linen cloth, "@EPT@AP@P4."

5. For swollen testicles - take a cord from a coin bag and say with each knot: "Kastor" once, and "Thab" twice.

6. For fever - take oil in hands and say seven times, "SABAOTH," then rub the oil from the sacrum to the feet.

"You can't get cured by leaving your toe nail clippings on your front doorstep," scoffed skeptical Old Pliny about one remedy, "you have to wear them in an amulet around your neck!"

Votive offerings to the gods consisted of terra cotta models of the afflicted body part, such as a foot, penis, or even a womb if a woman was childless. Other votive statuettes depicted the sufferer clutching their

149

head or belly, to show the gods exactly where it hurt. The carved marble relief right depicts a suppliant determined to make sure that the gods notice his votive offering!

NOW THE GODS WILL FIX MY VARICOSE VEINS!

The first Greek doctor in Rome was known as the Butcher, due to his love for cutting and burning. Medicinal cures included gladiators' blood, cat pee, baby brains, and inhaling burning dog dung through a reed, as an early form of smoking. Wounds were smeared with honey antiseptic and bandaged with vinegar soaked cobwebs. Physicians recommended boxing as a good remedy for headache, or wearing a woman's breast-band on your head.

Below: Votive offerings consisting of genitals, wombs and breasts.

"Burning lignite will detect anyone faking either an illness," Old Pliny advised, "or virginity!" Asclepiades was a famous doctor because he knew nothing about medicine, so cured the sick not by inventing new remedies, but by not using the old ones. Nicknamed "Wine-giver" for getting his patients too drunk to worry, he himself was never ill, lived to a ripe old age and died by falling down the stairs.

"You stole my cup!" a patient complained to another doctor, who retorted, "You fool! My prescription was for you not to drink!"

In one celebrated case, a surgeon cut open a lady's cyst to reveal a penis. "I want double-fees," he demanded, "I've treated a woman - and a man!" The newly formed man had to give up her job as a priestess of Ceres, and was convicted of impiety for witnessing women-only rituals. He was lucky however, since hermaphrodites detected at birth were placed in a box and tossed into the sea (to avert the bad omen).

Below: Both sides of the same hermaphrodite.

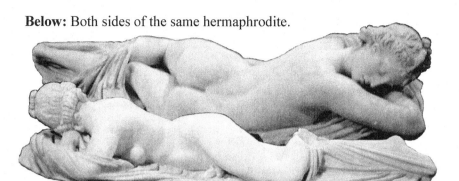

"I know a glutton who constantly coughs," wrote Martial, "because the doctor prescribes honey, nuts and sweet cakes!" "The fever won't leave gluttonous Laetinus," he added, "because he rides in a litter, eats oysters and drinks Falernian. Why should it shift to a beggar?" The rich got sick from overeating, and the poor from not eating. "Polycharmus is ill ten times a year and wants presents when he recovers," Martial griped, "He's making me ill!" "I didn't have a full blown fever when the doctor's apprentices began pawing me with their cold hands," he added, "but I do now!"

Doctors were renowned for their bedside squabbles, and many tombstones read: "Too many doctors killed me!" "If the doctors say I'll die, then I'll kill myself," announced Pliny's sick friend, "but if they think I'll live, then I won't!" The median age of death found inscribed on gravestones was 34 years for women and 46 for men.

Dialus-a-physician
is now Dialus-a-mortician
putting the dead
into bed
assuming the same old position!
- Martial, *Epigram* 1.30

Dead reckoning

Open pits on the Esquiline hill received all the filth that couldn't fit down the sewer, including dead animals and paupers. Left uncovered, even when full, the stench was so unbearable it finally became a danger to the whole city. The emperor Augustus finally thought to cover them over, forming awfully fertile gardens.

Everyone had to be buried outside the city walls, except for Greek couples buried alive in the forum to appease the gods, so in 97 BC a law banning human sacrifice was finally passed, since this wasn't fair.

Rodents were destroyed by drowning, although rich senators often complained to the rat catchers: "*In mari meri miri mori muri necesse est!*" (A mouse is dead in my vast vat of best unmixed wine.)

Most plebs belonged to a funeral club, which paid for their friends to have a party when they died. A relative tried to catch the dearly departed's dying breath in their mouth (or at least that's what they said they were doing when caught kissing the body). The deceased was then ritually called aloud by name three times, just to make sure they were really gone. Rich men paraded the wax heads of their ancestors, and hired actors to mimic them, so that even dead you couldn't get away from the cranky old sods. Prostitutes strolled in the graveyards where they doubled as professional mourners if business was slow. During the funeral procession clowns and dancers could be hired to liven things up, jokes were cracked about the deceased, and onlookers jeered or hurled abuse. A big crowd also gathered around the last moments of a dying beggar, reports Martial, but it was a pack of impatient, hungry stray dogs.

Numerous fancy tombs lined the road outside the city, boasting of the deceased's achievements: "Stop and read stranger, how good I was, etc. And now that you've read, have a happy day." Often the reader scrawled a reply: "Thanks, you too!" Some inscriptions warn: "Don't dare paint advertisements for public games on this tomb!" Others got posthumous revenge on the living by having their epitaphs denounce ungrateful freedmen, disinherit children, announce some crime that an enemy was purported to have committed, or simply state: "I pray that the gods get you!" Others were more subtle, since having told eager heirs to expect a big legacy, left them stunned to receive no mention in the will. Even better was leaving a large debt, which the heirs became liable for.

"You paid Fabius 6,000 a year and he left you nothing in his will," Martial advised a disappointed heir, "but he's really bequeathed you 6,000 a year!"

"The only time a Roman tells the truth is in his will," wrote Lucian, "because he can't be punished for it. Some Romans continue their stupidity even after death, by ordering their best robe to be burnt, or a favorite slave to stand by their tomb." One man's will directed his most beautiful slave girl to appear in the arena, while another's instructed that the two boys he had most loved should fight a duel, which was canceled due to public outrage.

The people were annoyed
two boys would be destroyed
killed in a duel
in a will too cruel
so called Null and Void!

I WAS HIS FAVORITE! NOT YOU!!

Pluto (Wealth) was god of the dead, but also of riches, since you hoped to get an inheritance when someone died, and was often called *Dis* (since he could dis or dismiss you) so you hoped Dis missed you.

One Roman's will, concerned that his sons were a spendthrift and a miser, read: "The first son is not to lose my fortune - and the second is not to increase it!"

Fortune sure changed for Ctessipus the fuller, a slave who'd worked jumping in a urine vat. At a closing-down sale he was tossed in as a 'free gift' with a candelabrum purchased by the noble lady Gegonia. Fascinated by this horrible little man, she made him her lover, and died leaving him his freedom and an enormous inheritance. Slaves who struck it lucky were hugely resented by noble impoverished 'real' Romans.

"Pontilianus, I pretend to believe your lies, like your poems, be beaten at your games, and take the blame for your farts. You say you'll treat me well when you die. I don't want anything," griped Martial, "but die anyway!"

"His pyre was laid, his weeping wife bought myrrh, his bier was ready, the anointer stood by, Numa wrote me down as his heir, and," sobbed Martial, "he got well!"

Widows whose husband's will stipulated a perpetual sacrifice to honor the deceased, got out of it by selling themselves to a very old man, who then freed them. The legal duty to sacrifice was now on the old man, which the widow paid for, until he died, which terminated the obligation. Besides arguing over whether two days after yesterday meant tomorrow, the lawyers obviously had tricks without end.

"I won't marry a woman's riches," Martial wrote, "because the husband should wear the britches!" "But I'd marry an old woman," he added, "if she were older!"

The dead were often buried with both a pair of boots and a lamp so they could find their way to the underworld, and a coin placed under the tongue to tip Charon for the River Styx ferry ride. The cremated had one of their digits lopped off and buried, so instead of paying, gave Charon the finger. "Only children young enough to get a free public bath believe in ghosts, three-headed guard dogs, and underground rivers," scoffed Juvenal, "Or that thousands of corpses could be ferried across in one small skiff!"

The graves were covered with nets to keep the ghosts in, and tubes used to pour ritual libations of wine or blood underground to keep the deceased fed. These spirits were called *manes* (nice-goodies) because they were really rather mean, but no one wanted to upset them. If the ghost did try to return to the house, it was chased off by banging brass pots and spitting black beans at it.

Libitina was the goddess of corpses, but became confused with *Libentina*, the goddess of sexual pleasure, probably when matrons 'died the little death' rooting for the undergod, or perhaps from the *succubus* (lie-down-under), a sexy female ghost who liked to seduce sleeping men.

The Compitalia festival saw the stringing up of Roman puppets and slave's balls as offerings to fool the ghosts which otherwise might claim the living. Missing soldiers, who returned home from war to find that their funeral had already been held, were debarred from entering the front door, but had to come through the roof like a ghost. Some got around this by going through a religious ritual of pretending to be born again, then wearing nappies to be happily suckled. "Phileros just buried his seventh wife in his field, so no land gives a better yield," observed Martial (since Phileros had kept all their dowries).

Time out

Daylight was always divided into 12 Roman hours, so in summer you got 75 minute long hours (4.30 a.m. - 7.30 p.m.), in winter you got 45 minute long hours (7.30 a.m. - 4.30 p.m.), and every other day you were somewhere in between. Moving north, the daylight hours naturally got shorter, so the workers were accused of being lazy because they had a bad latitude. This system of variable hours continued on official Italian clocks right up until the 1700s, and unofficially today on the state trains. The Roman crier announced sunset by observing when the sun was over the *Carcer* (Prison; *incarceration*) column, to which convicts were tethered for a flogging. His announcement of midday was crucial, since lawyers could not present their cases after *noon* (ninth-hour).

The crier calls midday
but I'll pay him to delay
for high noon
has come to soon
so say the sky's too gray!

The first public sundial set up in Rome had been stolen as booty from Sicily, and the Romans never realized that it didn't work at their higher latitude. "My belly's my sundial," grumbled the slaves, who cursed this newfangled invention that made them wait for lunch, "when it rumbles we eat!" "Six hours is enough for work," read one sundial inscription, "because the others say: Have fun!"

Then some drips made a water-clock so you knew what time your drinking party finished after sundown. "It's easier to find agreement between two philosophers," it was commonly joked, "than two clocks!" One enterprising prostitute used this latest technology to time her favors, so was herself nicknamed *Clepshydra* (Water-clock). Court speeches were also timed. "You must be thirsty by now, so please," Martial begged one long-winded loudmouthed speechmaker, "drink from the water-clock!"

Toga Party

There was more to ancient Roman dress than just knotting a bed sheet over one shoulder. The *toga* (covering) was the best article of clothing in a Roman's wardrobe - the early equivalent of your blue jeans with the trendy rips in the knees, or your Dad's tuxedo. The exact shape, either rectangle, oval, semicircle, or all three, and how it was worn, are matters of hot dispute. "A garment of my shape, put on according to my description, has been found by me to present an appearance exactly like that of the toga as seen on statues," each scholar claims, "and my friends have all made similar experiments with equally satisfactory results." An examination of toga-wearing statues leads to the conclusion that the sculptors carved impossible shapes just to bamboozle modern scholars and dressmakers.

We can blame King Tullus Hostilius for adopting the Etruscan toga as his royal robe, since everyone soon copied due to its versatility. It was used by the soldiers as cloaks, by the plebs as blankets, and by the corpses as shrouds. At first everyone wore the toga, until women invented the *stola* (arrayed-garment). "Every year they've something new," Plautus complained, "the thin tunic, the fat tunic, the padded tunic, the under tunic, the shift, the shiftless, the foreign, topless, crotchless, fluffy, wavy, dyed, see-through, nutty bow-wow!" After that, the only women wearing togas were prostitutes and those convicted of adultery, so it must've been an easier garment to take off than to put on. Hence the saying: "Make love, knot wore!" "You send purple dresses to a notorious adulteress," complained Martial, "Give her the present she deserves - a toga!" "When fat Lesbia rises, her stola disappears in the crack of her rump and she pulls it free with a shriek. The solution?" he added, "Don't get up or sit down!" Men also wore a tunic, and Tacitus advised, "Your tunic should come to your knees. Shorter, and you'll look like a soldier, but longer, and you'll look like a girl!"

Beginning as a simple affair, the toga grew ever longer and more complicated, as fashions do. "It makes you hot in summer, cold in winter, and needs one hand to hold it all together," someone trapped under a pile of folds exclaimed, "this isn't clothing, but a mess!" "No matter how many folds I wrap myself in," lamented Horace, "still people laugh because my underwear shows through!" "Happiness is," agreed Martial, "not wearing a toga!" "Today's trendy young dandies don't wear togas," sneered Cicero, "but tents!" "Dancing in a toga," was a common Roman maxim for anything absurd. "My show-off host pretends he sweats, only so he can change his fancy toga eleven times during dinner," complained Martial, "whereas Cinna thinks he's showing off his new white shoes, but we can't see them under his dirty toga hem!" Decrees were issued: "You have to wear a toga!" when no one wanted to, or: "You can't wear a toga!" when everyone wanted to (in a law against extravagance).

MATCH THE TOGA

VIRILIS   SORDIDA   PULLA   PICTA   TRABEA   MOLESTA   LOOSE

Men wore the white woolen toga *virilis*, and *candidates* (bright-whites) running for public office cheated by rubbing it with dazzling chalk dust to look better than everybody else. "My toga is snowy too," complained Martial, meaning that it was threadbare and therefore cold. "Thank you for the new toga," he told his patron, "O how people will laugh when they see it worn with my old cloak!" The dirty toga *sordida*, along with disarranged hair, wild staring eyes and exposed backside, was worn by accused persons in order to make you feel sorry for them. The black toga *pulla* was worn by mourners, and those too lazy to clean the white one. The embroidered toga *picta* was worn by tribunes trying to look like praetors, praetors trying to look like consuls, consuls trying to look like triumphant generals, and triumphant generals. The purple and white toga *trabea* was worn by the early kings, because it was great for disguising wine stains. The pitch-soaked *tunica molesta* was worn by molesters, who were set alight in the circus. Gigolos wore see-through togas to display their wares, which Cicero complained looked more like veils. Magistrates adopted a fashion of parading their rank by wearing their togas lopsided.

Like the ubiquitous Scotsman, the question that most perplexes modern scholars is: "What did a Roman wear under his toga?" Experiments have shown that he couldn't have worn under-drawers, since only one arm is available to part the fly without the toga falling apart - unless a slave helped him. I sheet thee knot!

"The Greeks are smart," bragged Virgil, "but they can't tie a toga!"

How to knot tie the simple toga

Grab a bed sheet, follow this guide to knot tying a toga, and you'll be the best dressed Roman since Aeneas swapped clothes with Dido in an African cave.

Let the toga, which in this case is not far from an exact semicircle, be held behind the figure, with the curved edge downwards.

First, one corner is thrown over the left shoulder, then the other part of the garment is placed on the right shoulder, thus entirely covering the back and the right side up to the neck.

It is then passed over the front of the body, leaving very little of the chest uncovered, and reaching downwards nearly to the feet. The remaining corner is then thrown back over the left shoulder, in such a manner as to cover the greater part of the arm.

The right arm is released by throwing the toga off the right shoulder, and leaving it to be supported by the left alone. This arrangement is seen in many ancient statues and frat house toga parties.

How to knot tie the difficult toga
(Warning - do not try this at home by yourself!)

The more advanced toga proceeds as before: over, behind, around, under, nip and tuck. The toga hangs much lower though, and on some statues is even seen dragging on the ground.

The toga is placed over the back, as in the older mode of wearing it, but instead of covering the right shoulder, it is brought round under the right arm to the front of the body. This is the most difficult part of the dress to explain. Quintilian says, "*Sinus decentissimus, si aliquanto supra imam togam fuerit, nunquam certe sit inferior.*"

The shoulder and the whole of the throat shouldn't be covered, otherwise they will become narrow and that dignity which consists in width of chest will be lost. The part across the chest (*velut balteus*) shouldn't be drawn too tight.

Tassels or balls are seen attached to the ends of the toga, which may have served to keep it in its place by their weight, or may have merely been ornaments.

In the figure, a mass of folds is seen in the middle of the toga. This is handy for hiding and was used by Julius Caesar during his assassination. Of course, it didn't fool them for long.

The back of the toga, if properly worn, should keep the wearer decently modest. Like the Scottish kilt, there is much debate about what the Romans wore under their toga.

Another mode of wearing the toga was the *cinctus Gabinus*. It consisted in forming a part of the toga itself into a girdle, by drawing its outer edge round the body and tying a knot in front, while at the same time covering the head. It was worn for sacrifices, declaring war, and avoiding tax collectors.

12 THE GODS MUST BE LAZY

The ever-practical Romans signed contracts with their gods that specified the relevant obligations of each party: *"Do ut des."* (Do me or I'll do you!) In return for a *sacrifice* (sacred-make), the god was bound to bestow some favor, and if this wasn't forthcoming, the aggrieved Roman was quite within their right to give the defaulting god's statue a damn good thrashing. Prayers were spoken aloud, with silent prayer reserved only for offensive, indecent, erotic, or magical uses, which Christian practice later adopted.

Each god went by several names and it was important to mouth all of these at ceremonies. "Accept our prayer, what's yer name," they chanted as a standard escape clause, "whether you be god or goddess," since with some it was pretty hard to tell. Any mistake made during the ritual meant it had to be repeated, so the wily Romans also offered a preliminary insurance-sacrifice that covered blunders in advance.

Every Roman worshiped their own household *lares*, which were usually cheap clay figurines of twin drunk boys (larrikins) holding drinking cups, sewn up in a stout dogskin pouch. This saved them having to go to the temple, unless there was a free feast on, and while they were away the *penates* guarded their pantry.

"For telling Juno about my affairs," Jupiter told the nymph *Lara* (Blabbermouth), "I'm removing your tongue, and ordering Mercury to escort you to the Underworld!" Mercury raped Lara en route, who gave birth to the Lares, and became worshipped as the Silent Goddess on the *Feralia* (Wild-thing festival).

Adopt-a-god

The original Roman gods called *numens* (nodders) were rather boring, like *Janus* (Door), *Forculus* (Door handle), *Cardea* (Door hinge), *Limentinus* (Door mat), *Spiniensis* (Weedkiller), *Robigus* (Mildew), *Cloacina* (Sewer), *Sterculinus* (Crap), *Muta* (Silence), *Fortuna* (Luck), *Fraus* (Bad luck), and *Fessona* (Rather boring), so they imported the gods of their defeated foes. "Hey," the Romans shrugged, "the more fighting on our side, the better!" The Greek Zeus became *Jupiter* (Jove), who appears to be the original sex-god, since he seduced mortal women disguised as their husband (Alcmena), a snake (Proserpine), a swan (Leda), a bull (Europa), an eagle (Ganymede), gave golden showers (Danae), slept with a cow (Io), and even gave birth himself (Minerva and Bacchus). Unaccountably pregnant women would point at their bellies, boasting, "By Jove!" As a baby, Jove had been suckled by a goat, which explains his identity crisis, and he married his own sister, *Juno* (meaning

160

Youth, since she lied about her age), who was also his mother oddly enough (unless you'd rather believe the version where Jove seduced his mother when they were knotted together as two snakes). Although ultimately responsible for whatever happened on earth, if the other gods got too mad at his decisions, Jove could shrug, "Don't blame me, it was Fate!" He also had an evil twin, *Vejovis* (anti-Jove), who you worshiped just so he wouldn't hurt you, like a sort of divine protection-racket.

Jove's day began with one priest giving him his wake-up call, while others mimed the bathing and anointing of his statue using ridiculous gestures, as yet another announced the names of the worshipers who'd bothered to turn up. Women acted as hairdressers for Juno by moving their fingers as if through her hair, but respectfully stood well away from her statue, giving her a nice air-do, and then holding up a mirror for her approval. Other priests summoned the gods to give good behavior bonds, offered legal briefs and explained cases to them. "The gods enjoy my plays," boasted a decrepit retired old actor who performed for them, "even if men no longer do!" Women hung about Jupiter's statue, hoping to make love to him without being caught by scowling Juno.

"The poets' tales of the gods' origins are ridiculous," scoffed Lucian, "They say that Saturn cut off the Sky's testicles with a sickle and the spilt sperm formed Venus, the goddess of love. Saturn then swallowed all of his own children, except for Jupiter who was swapped with a stone. Jupiter carved open Saturn's belly to free the gods, then proceeded to rule by engaging in illicit love affairs with all and sundry. The Roman homeland of *Latium* (Hiding) was named because Saturn hid there from Jupiter. Without intercourse with her husband, Juno mothered the wind-child Vulcan, who was tossed out of heaven by Jove and fell down to earth which left him crippled. Somehow the sculptors saw the gods, so were able to make statues of them, so we know Jove's got a beard, Mercury's got a moustache, Apollo's got neither, Neptune's hair is blue, and Minerva has green eyes. We can but laugh at their ignorance, and weep at their folly!" "It's easier just to play along," advised his fellow skeptic Seneca. "The Roman god Saturn who swallowed his children is really the Greek god Cronos," explained Cicero, in support of religion, "who is actually *Chronos* (Time) because time devours all things!"

All the gods were schizophrenic with split personalities, and Mt Olympus was their asylum. For example, Jupiter was the stormer, sower, stopper, seducer, smiter and smoter. Venus was the lucky, horny, killer, mother and virgin.

Jupiter, Mars and Quirinus were originally the Capitoline *triad* (three amigos), but the fun-loving Etruscans decided Jupiter would prefer sharing his temple with Juno and crafty Minerva who became the Capitoline *ménage a trois* (threesome). Minerva was also known as *Pallas* (Pal-lass, sort of like Girl-friend although she was more of a Tom-boy). Jove had swallowed the pregnant mother of Minerva, the goddess of wisdom, so nobody would be smarter than him. However, Vulcan's axe blow to cure Jove's splitting headache subsequently birthed Minerva from his brow by frontal-lobotomy caesarian-section. "That's just Minerva's mother," Jove ex-plained, whenever his belly rumbled, "giving me some advice!" Minerva took up flute playing, but when she noticed how ugly it made her big cheeks puff out, she instead took up sword fighting.

Right: The rather cheeky so-called Venus 'Beautiful-bum.'

Found in the emperor Nero's Golden House (50 BC).

As the avenger of cuckolded husbands, Juno inflicted terrible punishments on Jove's many lovers, so he often had to hang her up with anvils tied to her feet, to make her behave. The handsome Trojan prince *Ganymede* (Glossy-cunning-genitals), called *Catamite* in Latin, was picked up by Jove posing as an eagle to be his new Troy-boy cupbearer. "Juno won't like that!" the Greeks exclaimed, while Martial pointed out, "Ha! She'll be happy to no longer stoop to play the part of a boy!" Juno's ceremony involved slave-girls dressed as matrons being chased from her temple. The bosom buddies whipped each other with fig tree branches, and not to beat around the bush, employed these to make out in an in-delicate lesbian fertility rite. The milky sap mi-micked insemination.

Right: Mirror (Viterbo)

Juno got her own back on Jove when she was stalked by the flower goddess Flora, who deflowered her, so Juno gave birth to Mars, the god of war and gardening.

Vulcan (the ugly, sooty, limp god of fire and forgers) had been forced to marry Venus (the goddess of harlots) for a joke, which shows that Greek priests had a dirty sense of humor. His temple stood outside Rome to stop the city catching fire, but it still often did. The ever-practical Romans didn't shout, "Fire!" when there was a fire but, "Water!"

Vulcan used a net to catch his wife Venus in bed with Mars, and embarrassed them in front of the other gods. "Look," he pointed, "they have normal sex!" "Vulcan, you can make a fool of me too," joked Mercury, "in the same way!"

Mercury (*Hermes*) eventually forced Venus (*Aphrodite*) to have sex with him in order to get her stolen sandal back, and their union produced the double-sexed *Hermaphrodite*.

Above left: A satyr's attempt to rape a sleeping nymph ends with the surprise discovery that he's picked on a hermaphrodite - who's about to give him a severe beating, or even worse! **Above right:** Pan tries Mercury's trick with less success as Venus gets ready to wallop him with her sandal - while Cupid holds his head straight so she can get a good shot! (Marble statues, from Rome and Delos.)

Venus was often depicted with mischievous *Cupid* (Desire) suggestively stroking Mars' sword and *vagina* (scabbard). She was assisted by the *Graces* (Thanks) called Beauty, Love and Pleasure so that artists could paint pictures of three naked women, although the Christians later changed Pleasure's name to Chastity and gave her a see-through miniskirt. Flora's Games saw the city courtesans display themselves naked in lascivious dancing and the magistrates didn't dare to stop the indecent spectacle for fear of making the year barren.

Mars was honored with an annual horse race around the Campus Martius. "Go slower," yelled the jockeys, "slower!" since the winning horse was sacrificed. The tail was chopped off as a lucky charm, while two gangs of plebs fought over the head, which the winners nailed to a wall as a trophy on their side of town.

Diana was the loopy virgin goddess of fertility, and a keen huntress, but also patroness of the SPCA. Juno tipped out her arrows, boxed her ears, and sent her howling back to Jove. "You're another one of his illegitimate brats," she hissed, "go crying to Papa!" Diana's priest was a runaway slave, confined to stay in her sacred grove. He was succeeded whenever another runaway slave challenged him, by breaking the branch off a sacred tree, to hit him over the head with. The position carried quite a high turnover rate.

Mercury was the god of thieves and liars, so represented the Roman merchants. Neptune was the god of puddles, until the Romans finally learnt how to sail. Then he took over the sea, and his brother Jove's bad habits, by seducing mortal women disguised as a dolphin, a bull, a horse, mounting a ewe (to beget a lamb which became the famous Golden Fleece), bedding the hideous snake-haired Medusa, and even his own grandmother, which shows just how desperate he was for a date. Neptune created the first horse, but it took a few bumbled attempts (which resulted in the camel and elephant).

Sol (Sun) was the only god with a decent day-job, while his sister *Luna* (Moon) worked nights. The Christians found it impossible to stamp out celebration of the Sun's birthday on the 25th of December's midwinter solstice, so took it over as the Son's birthday of Jesus Christmas.

Ovid's *Metamorphoses* (0 BC)

Ovid was the notorious self-styled Doctor of Love, whose poem *Metamorphoses* (Changes) crammed 250 Greek myths into one nonstop Roman fable.

"In the beginning was Chaos," Ovid's poem began, as an *etiology* (cause) for the world, "so land, air and water were mixed into a big bouncy mess, and you would've had to swim through air, walk on water, and breathe dirt. Then some god (I'm not sure who) split them up and made man from clay."

It was a Golden Age without Iron (or laws, criminals, or even judges) followed by an Iron Age with Gold (which everyone fought over). Jove visited earth and was outraged when *Lycaon* (Wolf) served a cooked human for dinner, so turned him into the world's first werewolf (*lycanthropy*). "I'd destroy the wicked human race with a hail of thunderbolts," Jove growled, "if I wasn't worried that the fire might rage out of control and set Heaven ablaze as well!" He instead flooded the place, so dolphins were swimming in the trees, while anchors plowed the fields. Only Deucalion and Pyrrha survived. They prayed to the oracle

Themis (Justice), who intoned, "Cover your heads, take off your clothes, and toss your mother's bones behind you!" "I'm not messing up my mother's bones," complained Pyrrha, and Deucalion chided, "I think she means Mother Earth, who has stones for bones!" The couple threw the stones, which turned into Romans, and this is the reason that Romans are so tough!

Jove placed a cloud over the maiden Io's head so he could rape her under cover of darkness. Juno noticed that Jove was missing so looked under the cloud to see what he was doing. Thinking quickly, Jove turned Io into a cow, and pretended to be patting her. Juno demanded the cow as a present, and Jove didn't refuse for fear of looking guilty. Juno knew something was up, so set 100-eyed Argus to guard the cow. The cow wrote in the dust with her hoof, and told her father how she'd been changed. "Alas," cried her father, "now you will have a bull for a husband and calves for children!" Jupiter killed Argus, and uncowed Io. Juno stuck Argus' 100 eyes onto the tail feathers of her sacred bird, the peacock, to keep an eye out.

"Your mom's a liar when she says your dad is the sungod," boasted Io's son to Phaeton, "but I was nearly born as a cow!" *Phaeton* (Bright) complained to his mother, who made his father promise to play with the boy. Phaeton demanded to drive his dad's sun-chariot across the sky. The reluctant sungod agreed, and rubbed suntan lotion on his son to stop him getting sunburnt. Phaeton lost control of the chariot and the fiery steeds charged across the sky. They went so low as to set the earth on fire, and burnt the Ethiopians, which is why they are all black. In order to save the earth, Jove blasted Phaeton out of the chariot with a thunderbolt, who fell to earth like a falling star. His tomb was inscribed: "Here poor Phaeton lies - who raced across the skies - but his journeying - left him burning - like a side of fries!" It took the sungod a day to build a new chariot, but fortunately the fire kept earth warm until a new sun arrived.

Jove decided to fix the burnt forest and noticed the maiden *Callisto* (Sexy) sunbathing. "Hmm, my wife will never know about this," Jove grinned, "or if she does - it will be worth it!" Jupiter dressed himself as the goddess Diana, kissed the unsuspecting girl, and then raped her. The real Diana soon came along, and Callisto fled, thinking it was Jove returning for seconds. Diana proved she was herself by stripping off to bath, and invited Callisto to become bare, which revealed her guilt. The virgin Diana didn't know what lost maidenhood meant until her worldly nymphs informed her, and she ordered Callisto out of the pool. Jealous Juno then turned Callisto into a bear, and Jove complained, "You can't bear her!" Jove turned Callisto into the Bear Constellation, and Juno spat, "Must you bare her heavenly body!"

Jove turned himself into a bull, carried the beguiled maiden *Europa* (Moon-face) away on his back, and named the country where he raped her as Europe to make up. ("Juno turned Io into a cow," joked the poet Martial, "so that's when Jove should've turned into a bull!")

"You detain me with your nonstop chatter while Jove is seducing nymphs," Juno told Echo, "so I curse you to repeat only the last words spoken!" Echo fell in love with a boy, who called out to her:

"Is anybody here?" "Here!"

"Where? Are you hiding?" "Hiding!"

"Well, will you come out and kiss me?" "Kiss me!"

"Where are you? Are you teasing?" "Teasing!"

"What? Do you think I'm a fool?" "Fool!"

"Grr! Then you won't sleep with me?" "Sleep with me!"

"Bah! I'm going, and won't come back!" "Come back!"

"Why? So you can call me an idiot?" "Idiot!"

"That's it, I'm off for good!" "Good!"

"My bow's bigger than yours," boasted the god Apollo to Cupid, who replied by shooting him with a wee love-arrow. Apollo immediately fell in love with Daphne, who Cupid shot with an anti-love-arrow. "Gods, please make him leave me," prayed Daphne, who suddenly twigged. "Why did you make like a tree and leave?" complained Apollo, who kissed her trunk and knotholes as the world's first tree-hugger. "You'll always be my tree," he declared, "and all Rome's great generals will wear your laurel leaves as a victory crown!"

"Minerva and Diana are virgins" complained Venus to Cupid, "and now Proserpine wants to be one too!" Cupid shot a love-arrow at Pluto, the god of the Underworld, who fell madly in love and dragged Proserpine down to his dark abode. "I'm not letting any cereals grow," Ceres told Jove, "until you do something about the rape of our daughter!" "Why don't you call things by their proper name?" complained Jove, "It isn't rape - but an act of love!" "Although our new son-in-law has no other qualities to recommend him," Jove added, "it is still a great thing to be the brother of me!" Jupiter ordered his sister and brother to share his daughter, so Ceres had her for half the year (summer) and Pluto the other half (winter) in the world's first joint child-custody arrangement.

"If you don't tell anybody I stole these cows - I'll pay you one cow," Mercury told an old man, who swore, "That stone will talk before I do!" Mercury returned in disguise, crying, "Help me find my stolen cows - and I'll pay you two cows." The old man told him, so Mercury turned him into a stone, crying, "So! You betray me to myself!"

"My poem is complete," Ovid finally concludes, "and not even Jove, time, sword, nor fire shall destroy it!"

Upon being banished by the emperor Augustus for doing something (too naughty to mention), Ovid dramatically tossed his poem into the fire because, he announced, it was unfinished. (This was in dramatic imitation of Virgil - except Ovid really had plenty of spare copies!)

166

Herc the jerk

Hercules' temple was built by the *Forum Boarium* (Cow Market) because he was a notorious cattle-rustler, and the notice on the front door read: "By Order - No entry to any dogs, flies, or women!"

For those that found religion too boring, the Oracle of Hercules let you pray to a dice board, and then try your luck. For every throw of the dice there was an interpretation written, so you could play until you rolled something you liked. The keeper of Hercules' temple once challenged the god to a dice game, rolled for both of them, and beat himself. Much to the priest's chagrin, Hercules had won a night with the prostitute *Fabula* (Miss Myth), who was locked in the temple on a gilded bed. In the morning she explained, "The god said I have to marry the first man I see in the market!" This happened to be a childless old millionaire, who married Fabula as ordered, then dropped dead and left her his entire fortune. The gullible plebs promptly began worshiping fabulous Fabula as a god's girlfriend.

According to the Greeks, Hercules was killed by his wife *Deianeira* (Man-killer), whose name should've been a tip-off, and ascended to heaven where he married Hebe. In Greek, *Hebe* can mean *pubes*, so their poets had much fun euphemistically joking about "Hercules' hairy wife."

Right: Hercules wrestles an opponent who grabs his Hairy Wife! (Herculaneum.)

Hercules' Sanctuary was served by a virgin priestess until she died, since he'd once tried to sleep with 50 sisters in one night (jokingly known as his 13th labor), but could only make 49, so she represents the frustrated last sister still waiting her turn.

The shrine of Hercules the Woman-Hater was served by a priest who mustn't bed women for a whole year. Consequently, no one wanted the job but old men. Once when a young man got the job, he spent all his time hiding from his girlfriend, until she eventually caught him drunk and had her wicked way. "Will Hercules be mad at me?" he asked the oracle of Delphi. "A man's god a do," she answered, "who a man's god a do!"

Once, the sexmad hoof-footed forest god *Faunus* (Lover-boy) spied Hercules and his girlfriend *Omphale* (Belly-button) celebrating the rites of Bacchus. After everyone had passed out drunk, Faunus crept into the cave where they were sleeping, intent on seducing Omphale. Feeling about, he found her dress, and gingerly raising it, mounted her from behind. To his astonishment he found that the drunken lovers had mixed-up their clothes and it was Hercules he caused to awake with an almighty outraged roar. For this reason, Faunus hates clothes.

"All worshipers must come to my rites naked," he insists, "so you can't fool me again!" Having learnt his lesson, the sexmad Faunus soon thought of a safer way to molest women, and took to chasing them in their dreams!

Right: Faunus kids around (A sculpture from the Pope's Secret Collection).

Right: Rear of an Etruscan engraved bronze mirror depicting queen Juno adopting the adult Hercules by letting him suck on her breast, while old bald-headed Silenus sprawls out above, sucking on a wine cup (350 BC). In another version the infant Hercules bit Hera's teat, and as she shrieked, the milk squirt from her breast sprayed across the sky to form the *Galaxy* (Milky Way).

Saturn alias

Roman *religion* (tied-up-in-knots) kept *Saturn* (Sullen) permanently trussed in his temple, but let loose once a year for the *Saturnalia*, to cause chaos when joke gifts like mud pies were exchanged, gambling was allowed, and slaves lorded it over their masters. Of course if they were too cheeky, they got a damn good thrashing when it was over.

"Saturnalia once lasted a week," Seneca complained, noting the constant chaos in Rome, "but now lasts a year!" The soldiers elected a mock-king and this lucky man got to do whatever he liked, drinking the best wine, eating the shiniest gold and bedding the prettiest wives. The only hitch was, at the end of the month he was killed.

Patrons gave their clients presents as a payoff. "Postumus, every time I tell someone about the presents you gave me, they answer: I know, he already told me," griped Martial, "If you want me to praise you - shut up!" "Sextilianus, the dish you usually send me at Saturnalia, you've sent to your mistress," he added, "and instead of buying me a new toga, you bought her a new dress! You enjoy free love affairs, since they're paid for by me!"

Martial's *Epigram* 8.71 on the *Ten years of Saturnalia* reads:

"On the 1st year of Saturnalia my patron sent to me: four pounds of silver plate. On the 2nd year of Saturnalia my patron sent to me: three pounds of silver plate (I'd hoped for more than four). On the 3rd year of Saturnalia my patron sent to me: two-and-a-half pounds of silver plate. On the 4th year of Saturnalia my patron sent to me: two pounds of silver plate. On the 5th year of Saturnalia my patron sent to me: one pound of silver plate. On the 6th year of Saturnalia my patron sent to me: an eight-ounce oblong dish. On the 7th year of Saturnalia my patron sent to me: a half-pound cup. On the 8th year of Saturnalia my patron sent to me: a two-ounce dessert-spoon. On the 9th year of Saturnalia my patron sent to me: a snail-pick lighter than a needle. On the 10th year of Saturnalia my patron sent to me: nothing! ...Let's start at four pounds again!"

"The Saturnalia gifts that Umber didn't want, he sent to me," grumbled Martial, "A sponge, a napkin, a cup of beans, a bag of olives, a black flagon of must, a jar of figs, tablets, toothpicks and dried prunes. These were carried by eight porters, when he might have sent a single boy with some silver plate!"

"I received a long and impressive procession," declared Lucian, "First was the slave who'd overheard his master talking, so ran to tell me in advance, and demanded a fee in advance. Next came a dozen slaves insisting that they'd each reminded their master of me, recommended expensive gifts, and picked the very best one. They all departed with a tip, and even grumbled that I should've paid more. Finally the present arrived - a beggarly scarf or flimsy undergarment!"

"Poor Umber used to send me a cape, but now he's rich he sends me," Martial carped, "capers!" "I did once receive a shaggy barbarian cloak, which was useful," he grudgingly admitted, in case you thought he always complained about gifts, "but *so* unfashionable!"

"Why did you present me with me snow in winter?" demanded an outraged patron, to which Martial answered, "So you'll retaliate by sending me a thin summer toga!"

Disgusted with the quality of his Saturnalia presents, Martial finally penned two books containing over 350 gift ideas, each with a poem to go with it, stretching from the old standby, a pair of socks, to the ubiquitous back-scratcher.

Book 13 covers food and drink, of which Martial advised, "Try presenting bad wine as good vinegar!" Leeks: "If you've eaten, give shut-mouth kisses!" Mushrooms: "Gold doesn't squash, but these do!" Toothpaste: "Let me taste a young girl's mouth, and not polish purchased teeth!" Hay: "Rob your mule to pad your mattress!"

Book 14 suggests: cymbals, seashell, ear-pick, wig, hair dye, candle, condom, dumbbells, leather cap, a bag for straining snow, skin-scrapper, whip, Priapus-shaped breadrolls, sausage, whips, broom, sponge, truss, feathers, a monkey, a dwarf mule (doesn't hurt if you fall off), a German barbarian mask (to scare the children), a marble hermaphrodite, a boy "made smooth by youth, not pumice stone," or a girl from Gades "whose shimmy will make a eunuch masturbate!"

Right: A typical Roman *cista* (box) lid-handle shaped as an acrobatic Gades girl.

For the ladies he recommended the Bosom-band (14.66): "I shrink from big-breasted women," or Bust-hugger (14.134): "More than a handful's a waste." Chamberpot: "I'm called with snapping fingers, but the dozing slave lingers, with a pillow as my rival!" Bedspread: "What good's a warm bed, with your cold wife!" Bedroom lamp: "I watch, but don't tell!" "When they complain that there are no coins in the money-box," Martial advised, "say that the box itself is the gift!"

"Buy my book," he shamelessly suggested, "then just send one of my poems as a present, instead of a gift!" And for those too mean to even do that, he added, "Just send a blank page!"

Chattin' with Saturn

"Saturn grant me wealth," asks the poet Lucian in his *Chattin' with Saturn* satire, who replies, "Ask Jupiter for that, I only rule for seven days, and take charge of drinking, feasting the slaves, singing stark naked, and being pushed headfirst into cold water with soot on your face. I can let you win at dice and drinking games, so you'll get a sausage as first prize, and be able to give silly orders like making the loser carry the flute-girl around the table three times or shout out self-abuse.

My *Gift Laws* are: No one shall work, except the cook and baker. The rich shall give gifts to the poor, especially to poets, who deserve a double share. The gift-bearers shall demand no greater tip than a cup of wine. A jar of wine, a hare, or a bird, is not a good enough gift. In return, the poet shall send the rich man a poem. The rich man shall read the poem with a glad countenance. Any poor man who sends expensive gifts to a rich man shall receive 250 strokes with a cane.

My *Banquet Laws* are: The rich can't drink better wine than everyone else by saying they have tummy trouble or a headache. The wine-waiter will remember to fill everyone's cup. No one shall present lyre-players who are still learning. All gambling shall be with nuts ("Gambling with nuts may sound safe," Martial observed, "but it has often cost boys their buttocks!" like a flogging - or worse!).

Rich men who don't comply will be punished: Their favorite wine-server will grow whiskers and go bald, while the poor will close their eyes, so that the rich have nobody to admire their expensive things!"

"Lets drink then," Lucian tells Saturn, "and I'll publish this conversation so everyone knows what to do!"

Revival festivals

The New Year feast of the Wet Nurse *Anna Perenna* (Annual Perennial) was celebrated by couples sleeping outside and drinking as much wine as possible. Each cup represented the number of years you had yet to live, and most lost count.

Mars once asked Anna, "Fix me up a hot date with Minerva?" She agreed, and on the big night, after bedding Minerva, Mars raised her veil for a kiss. To his horror, Anna's ugly old face was grinning back at him. *Fraus* (Fraud) was similarly represented as a beautiful woman with hidden deformities to surprise the unsuspecting suitor. Drunken girls, who lost their virginity before their wedding night, sang ribald songs in Anna's honor:

Minerva's willing manner
as eager Mars did span her
made him lift her veil
only to wail
you got my ban Anna!

Right: Satyr trying to steal a girl's wine cup (South Italian vase).

Ceres (Cereal) invented corn to replace acorns for supper. Her corny festival was celebrated by setting foxes' tails on fire, since once a fox caught raiding chickens was wrapped in straw to be burnt alive, but unfortunately escaped and torched all the crops. Nine days sexual abstinence was required, so girls pleased their boyfriends in other ways, which saw their fathers reluctant to give them the traditional good morning kiss. They uttered nonstop obscenities, swearing that foul language had cheered sad Ceres after her daughter was raped.

The most gruesome feast was the *Fordicidia*, a sacrifice of the pregnant cows whose gutted embryos were burnt in the temple of Vesta when the Vestals wanted veal. Naked drunkards celebrated the *Lupercalia* (Wolf) festival by running about striking women with bloody thongs in order to make them pregnant. This ritual proved so popular that the Pope couldn't stamp it out, so in AD 494 renamed it the Festival of the Purification of the Virgin Mary. "We were once banned from riding in carriages, so retaliated by refusing to bear children," boasted the Ausonian women, "and aborted ourselves with secret thrusts!" The exasperated senate let them ride in carriages again, and the women instituted the festival of *Carmenta* (Crazy) to celebrate. The secret name of Rome was guarded by the goddess *Angerona* (Angina) who wore a gag over her big gob, and can't be mentioned. It was *Roma* spelt backwards, which means *Love*, so they must've been kidding, since anyone saying it was executed. No one could remember what the goddess *Furrina* did, or why her festival was celebrated. Any ideas?

Drunk and disorderly

The Greek *Dionysus* was adopted as both *Bacchus*, god of wine, and *Liber*, god of wine and orgies, which made for twice as many drinking parties, and just so there was no Greek funny business between them, the Romans gave Liber a girlfriend, *Libera*. You couldn't miss them, since Liber was paraded about as a gigantic phallus on a cart, lewd rites were performed at crossroads, and the most moral matron of each city crowned the immoral member.

You got drunk at the *Vinalia Priora* (New Wine) festival, and recovered at the *Meditrinalia* (Healing) festival by drinking more wine to cure old hangovers with new.

Right: A drunkard carrying his party-wreath, wine-jug, and two slaves home.

Silly girl," Juno told Semele, "I bet your new lover is just a mortal man pretending to be the god Jupiter so he can bed you!" Outraged, Semele demanded that Jupiter appear as his real self, so he did, and she was burnt to a crisp. However, Jupiter saved the child from her womb, sewed it up in his own groin, and gave birth to the 'twice-born' god Bacchus. To keep the secret from Juno, Jupiter dressed Bacchus in girl's clothes and had him raised by a herd of goats. Bacchants (followers of Bacchus) enjoyed excessive wine, music, dancing, sex, and *sparagmos* (ripping apart animals with their bare hands to eat raw).

172

Below: Bacchus gets the three Graces drunk (From the Pope's Secret Collection).

CHEERS!

Left: Bacchus got Vulcan drunk so he would free Juno from his trap-chair. Silenus lugs the wineskin in rivalry with donkey dong. (Francois Vase)

The Latin word for *phallus* (penis) is *fascinum* (favorable), because they were fascinated by it, and large phallic symbols were erected on walls inscribed: "*Habitat felicitas*" (Happiness is here!) although one perplexing inscription reads: "*Hang ego cacavi*" (I shat on this one!). Protective penis amulet charms were worn by everyone, from children to triumphal generals, who also dangled one below his chariot to ward off envy.

Phalluses were erected at places of danger, like crossroads, so you could see what was coming. The power could be increased by combining two symbols, such as a phallus with a head or hand. The other defense against the Evil Eye was laughter, and big phalluses were considered funny. Men grabbed their testicles if bad luck was sighted, while women gripped a piece of iron.

Left: Mosaic Evil Eye attacked by a centipede, trident, sword, cat, bird, snake, dog, scorpion, and dwarf's penis, inscribed: "Same to you," intended to deflect any malevolent intentions.

Phalluses were also depicted with wings, or legs, or even sporting their own phallus. Other depictions include a phallus-nosed centaur, phallus-tongued masks, Mercury wearing a five-phallus hat, phallus-shaped drinking flasks, a phallus vase-stand (with two balls), and a chariot race pulled by four phalluses. Many of the phalluses had bells hanging under to generate luck (with little dings and big dongs).

Proud Priapus

The bakers' *Fornacalia* celebrated putting a bun in the oven by baking lewdly shaped Priapus rolls, and was known as the Feast of Fools, since the priests posted the festival date, but the bakers couldn't read so always caroused on the wrong day.

The god *Priapus* (Penis) guarded gardens. Intended as a scarecrow, his wooden statue sported an erection bigger than himself and if that didn't deter trespassers, the groundsman could use it as a club to beat some respect into them. He was inscribed with a warning: "In garden, no pardon - I'm hard in!"

Horace tells of two witches dancing around an illegal fire, the heat of which caused the wooden Priapus to split with a resounding crack.

The wooden statue of Priapus
guarding garden grass
sees two witches dancing
whose fire burns his ass!
They lost teeth and hair and fled in fear
from Priapus' attack
when he let off a mighty fart
which is why he has a crack!
- Horace, *Satire* 1.8

Right: This humorous vase painting has a humiliated Priapus used as a bird perch.

A thief entered by stealth
but the garden lacked in wealth
so the cheeky sod
stole the god
Priapus couldn't save himself!
- Martial, *Epigram* 6.72

I've only got two nuts
since my harvest filled the guts
of a cheeky maid
in Priapus' glade
not scared by the putz!
- Martial, *Epigram* 7.91

Below: A satyr teases Priapus, while Faunus chases a sleeping woman through her dreams. Somnolent women were supposedly less disdainful to his advances. (Sarcophagus relief, Pope's Secret Collection, AD 180.)

Encountering Vesta asleep in his garden, Priapus couldn't believe his luck. He crept up, and was about to mount her, when a nearby donkey gave a loud bray. Awakened in fright, she fled in disgust, which is why his sacrifice is an ass rump. Priapus insisted, "Roast the tell-tail!" "No, the real reason he hates asses is because we had an argument about who has the largest genitals," reported the talking donkey (whom Bacchus gave the power of speech), "and Priapus lost!"

Right: Faunus plays the goat.

Awkward St Augustine (420 AD)

When Christianity took over, Augustine penned his book *City of God against the Pagans*, which exposed the Roman gods as demons in disguise. "There are more pagan gods than positions, but by making them job-share, the Roman priests leave none unemployed," Augustine complained, "so instead of one god for Land, it's split into *Rusina* (Fields), *Jugatinus* (Mountain tops), *Collatina* (Hills), and *Vallonia* (Valleys). *Agenoria* (Anger), *Stimula* (Stimulation), *Strenia* (Strenuous) and *Murcia* (Lazy) are all worshiped at state expense, but *Quiet* (Shutup!) is left outside the city. *Pecunia* (Money) is worshiped as *Aesculanus* (Bronze) and his son *Argentinus* (Silver), but I'm only amazed he hasn't got a son called *Aurinus* (Gold) to rule over them all!"

"Only one pagan god is really needed," he snorted, "and that's *Felicitas* (Happiness). Perhaps they couldn't see her due to the crowd?" "The pagan gods are supposedly placated by the shameful acts performed on stage," scoffed Augustine, in reference to popular plays, "even though some priests claim these aren't divine rituals, but poets' drivel. But if Jupiter wasn't really an adulterer, surely he'd strike them down with a lightning bolt for their cheek? The Romans let the poets slander gods, but not men. The Greeks let poets slander everyone!"

"Did the Romans have to adopt the Greek healing god Aesculapius because Jupiter was too busy fornicating to learn medicine?" laughed Augustine, "Even so, women still had stillborn babies, but I suppose that Aesculapius will argue that he's a doctor, not a midwife?"

"The pagans say that virgins tend Vesta's fire, because nothing's born out of fire, or a virgin," he added, getting heated, "except smoke when her own temple burns down!" "*Fortuna Barbata* (Lucky Beardess) presides over a young man's first chin fuzz, but that's a feminine name, and whoever heard of a bearded lady?" Augustine scoffed, "Yet I've seen full bearded men mocking wispy-faced youths praying to her for a decent set of whiskers! But even if it's true that making fun of Barbata will give you a scraggy beard, her power extends no further. The pagan gods can't grant eternal life! Bacchus gives wine - but can't give water!" "Not only is it easier to sacrifice to my one God," Augustine insisted, "it's also a lot cheaper!"

When Augustine wasn't complaining about Roman religion, he complained about Roman history. "Rome's troubles began when *Discord* (Nuisance) started the Trojan War," he explained, "but she was probably angry because the Romans celebrated their Gracchi murder spree (120 BC) by building a temple to Concord, when Discord had done all the work!" "The Greeks say that Troy was destroyed because King Priam's father didn't pay Apollo for building the city walls," Augustine griped, "But surely since Apollo can predict the future, he already knew he'd be ripped-off? And why would the gods be mad at Paris' adultery with Helen, when they do worse themselves? After all, the Romans were born from the adultery of Venus!"

"Scripture (*Genesis* 6.4) says that the apostate angels lay with the daughters of men and begat a race of giants," he added, "so maybe the Roman story that the god Mars fathered Romulus isn't so ridiculous after all. If Mars isn't his Dad, then Rhea Silvia should be punished as a Vestal virgin who broke her vow!" "And you can't make a man like Romulus into a god!" scoffed Augustine, who would've been amazed to find himself made into a saint.

Augustine's made a saint
so pagans make a complaint
He says God's city
tops Venus' titty
but we say it's ain't!
(They're pagans, not poets!)

"The gods must've been asleep when the Gauls took over Rome, so it's lucky the geese were awake," Augustine snorted, "Did their honking wake the gods up, so that they at least saved the citadel? Rome sunk to the level of Egyptian animal worshipers when they started honoring their geese in annual ceremonies!" "The pagan priests hid in hollow statues to fool the believers," scoffed another Christian, "and one even passed himself off as the god Saturn, to engage in intercourse with his unsuspecting pious ladies, till he betrayed himself, in a moment of transport, when he couldn't disguise the tone of his voice!"

"Which god gave Rome her empire - Jupiter or Victory? Or the goddess External Aggression, since she did all the toil?" Augustine taunted, "They worship Fear, Pallor and Fever, so why not Aggression? Aggression started the war and Victory finished it, while Jupiter took a holiday! Victory should have a son called Triumph, since the Romans like parades so much!" "I think my God probably let the Romans rule because they weren't so bad," Augustine finally decided, "although maybe he had some other reason."

"Janus appears to be the only god that doesn't get in trouble, so he's made two-faced," explained Augustine, "since the other depraved deities have all lost face!" "The two-headed god Janus is ridiculous," fumed the monk Arnobius (AD 300), "since the pagans say he's the world, the year, the sun, the Janiculum hill, the first king, Hecate's son, Fons' father or Juturna's husband. Just what does Janus do?"

"A sexy nymph always told her gullible suitors that she'd follow them into the bushes, because she was too embarrassed to make love in an open field, and when they turned around she'd be gone," explained Ovid, "but she couldn't play that trick on Janus, because his other head saw where she hid, so he raped her in a bush! That's what Janus does! So watch your back!"

"The Romans worship the Five Planets, so the rest of the sky must be angry," snorted Augustine, "especially when they gaze down to see Priapus' ridiculous erection of propitiated!"

The Romans named their six known planets because: 1. Mercury was the fastest (as the gods' messenger), 2. Lovely Venus was seen only at early evening or morning (on her way out for a night of lovemaking, or sneaking home again), 3. Mars looked bloody red (from fighting), 4. *Terra Mater* (Mother Earth) was dirty, 5. Jupiter was the biggest, and 6. Old Saturn was the slowest (still fleeing from Jupiter).

The French still use Roman gods for the days of their week: Saturn-day, Sun-day, and Moon-day, but Mars-day, Mercury-day, Jove-day, and Venus-day were hijacked in English by similar German gods: Tius-day (war), Wodens-day (cunning), Thors-day (thunder), and Frey-day (love).

Vestigial virgins

The Vestal virgins had two jobs: keeping the sacred fire of *Vesta* (Veiled), goddess of the hearth, burning, and being a virgin. Their symbol "VV" looks like a pair of *rumas*, but they actually worshiped a phallus that they lent to victorious generals to hang under their triumphal chariot. Any Vestal who let the fire go out was whipped, but it was illegal to draw her blood, so a piece of wet spaghetti was used. The pontifex maximus disciplined her naked, under a veil, in the dark, just so there was no funny business. A Vestal caught not being a virgin was executed, but since it was illegal to kill her, she was buried alive. It was also illegal to starve a virgin, so she was sealed in a cave with a piece of bread, a bowl of milk, and a lighted candle. "Don't eat or drink, and leave the candle burning," she was advised, "so you won't hang about!" The plebs waited outside, taking bets on how long she'd last, and how many screams she'd make. The more humane and sophisticated Greeks appreciated the tricky problem of making sure virgins stayed that way, so gave this job to menopausal widows. Then, if they did fool around, nothing showed for it.

No need to call the surgeon
when a Vestal starts to burgeon
the eunuch stud
is a dud
'cos she's a pregnant virgin!

A Vestal had a 30 year career, starting with the pontifex maximus announcing, "I seize you, beloved!" so she couldn't struggle as she got a bad haircut to make her look ugly. The first ten were spent learning how to be a virgin, the second ten being a virgin, and the last ten teaching the new Vestals how to be virgins.

Many wealthy families wanted a daughter to be one, because she had the privilege of saving the condemned criminals she met in the street, a useful perk in any crooked clan. The job paid well and she got front row seats at the games, but had to give up perfume, flowers and frilly dresses. Corpses, strangers, iron swords, spots struck by lightning, the number 36, and babies (especially her own) were all bad luck for a Vestal. The *Palladium* was a small statue of Minerva hidden in a barrel, with a handy identical wine barrel next to it, supposedly to fool would-be burglars.

At the Vestal's rainmaking festival, they tossed old men off the bridge into the Tiber River, but this looked like too much fun, so they were made to substitute straw dolls instead. "This tradition comes from homesick Greeks," explains Ovid, "who were too mean to pay for a funeral, so just tossed their corpses into the river, and then boasted that they were floating back to Greece for a proper burial!"

In 420 BC, the Vestal virgin Postumia was charged with unchastity, due to her gay attire and happy manner. "I know you're innocent," chortled the pontifex maximus, "but dress more dowdy, and stop cracking jokes!"

The Vestal virgin Postumia
was ordered to look gloomier
and not wear weavage
to cleave her cleavage
but something a little roomier!

Postumia's jokes: "What do bad Vestals sing? C'mon baby, light my fire!" "How did the Vestal find the missing sacred flame? In Vesta gate!" "Where does a Vestal get her money? In Vesta mints!" "What did the banker tell the Vestal? In Vesta wisely!" "How many Vestals does it take to light a sacred fire? Two, one to light it, and one to get whipped for letting it go out!" "What's the most expensive part of the temple of Vesta? The Vesta bill!" "How does a Vestal pay to relight the sacred flame? Has a whip-around!" "How does a Vestal show her authority? By the power in Vesta'd in me!" "What do you call a Vestal's appendix? A Vestagial organ!" "How do Vestals look bigger? A padded Vesta!"

In 114 BC, when Rome lost a battle in Thrace, a lightning bolt killed a girl's horse and blasted her clothes off. "This means," the soothsayers declared, "the Vestals must be acting lewdly at knights!" A special commission set up to investigate uncovered Aemilia and Licinia sleeping with numerous knights. "You're the only one," they'd told each lover, who was dumped for another, "who'll be in trouble if we're caught!" Finally, so many men were involved, that they couldn't help but be exposed. The prosecutor, Longinus, asked the famous legal question, *"Cui bono?"* (Whose good?), but should've asked, *"Cui bonobo?"* (Who's a sex-mad chimp?) since they were all monkeying around. "I only had a single man and wouldn't have been caught," cursed Marcia, who was also found guilty, "except for those other sluts!" Aemilia was accused of letting the fire go out, but cleared herself by restarting it with her dress.

The Vestal Tuccia proved her virginity by carrying some water in a sieve. Although this sounds impossible, a Roman sieve newly woven from horsehair has a film of animal grease, so if you have steady hands you might hold it long enough to show that Vesta's on your side. You can try this at home using a sieve soaked in olive oil to see if the theory holds water.

> The Vestal virgin's taught:
> first - don't let the fire aught
> second -
> don't be fecund
> third - don't get caught!

Sibyl quibble

The old hag Sibyl offered her *Sibylline Books* to King Tarquin for a bag of gold. He baulked at the price, so she held a fire sale, burning them one by one. "Okay," he agreed, his curiosity piqued, "I'll buy three for the price of nine!" They contained sacrificial instructions, disease remedies, and an oracle collection, so were a Cookbook, First-aid manual, and Complete Fortuneteller, all rolled into one. The priests tried to decipher the bizarre gobble-de-Greek composed in acrostics, where the initial letters of each verse spelt out a secret message. For example:

> **D**ivine Sibyl's prediction:
> **U**se cat pee on this affliction
> **P**isces seeks love
> **E**at boiled dove
> **D**oubt not my contradiction!

180

Extra pages were suspected of being added, to support private political agendas, since these actually made sense. "I tricked Apollo by offering him sex if he made me immortal," complained Sibyl, as she faded away to a nagging voice, "but forgot to ask for eternal youth!"

The will of the gods could also be determined by observing the pecking of the sacred chickens, or the *auspices* (birds-flying). "Knock the roof off your house," the augurs ordered one surprised man, "it's blocking our bird view!" Augurs interpreted bird cries, such as the owl (*twit-who*), chick (*peep, cheep*), woodpecker (*tat-tat*), or hen (*book-book*), to sound out divine messages (in this case about the augur himself): "*Twit who peep tat cheep book!*"

"All foreigners, slaves, and women," the *hauspex* (gut-gazer) priest chanted at the beginning of all animal sacrifices, in order to get rid of moochers, "Scram!" The animal's liver was inspected, and if it was good enough for the god, everyone ate the rest. If it wasn't good enough, then another animal bought it, and everyone had a second course. "I don't know how one liver-diviner can meet another," Old Cato snorted, skeptical of their pretense, "without laughing in his face!"

Right: Bronze model of a sheep's liver (100 BC).

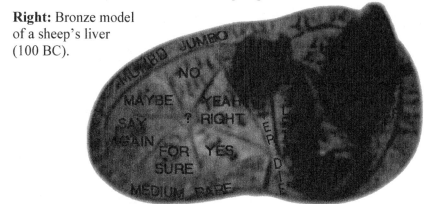

Once, during a ceremony, the priests threw the animal entrails straight into the fire in order to speed things up as there was an enemy approaching the city walls, and because the Romans won that fight, it became Mars' new rite. "Pigs and goats deserve to be sacrificed because they gnaw the grape vines," wrote tenderhearted Ovid, "but what did the nice fluffy sheeps do wrong?"

"If the gods feast on *ambrosia* (immortality) and nectar," the sacrilegious Martial wondered, "why would they want our raw entrails and green wine?" "*Prometheus* (Forethought) once split a sacrifice into two parts and offered Jove first choice," explained the priests, "who was tricked into picking a bag full of bones!" The Romans felt justified in continuing this deceit, so burnt the bones for the gods, and ate the meat themselves. "You might have the best meat," laughed Jove, "but you'll have to eat it raw!" Prometheus stole fire from Jove, who was so outraged that he swore an eternal curse on mankind and created: Woman!

"You're guaranteed a laugh, watching the sacrifices," explained Lucian's *Sacrifices* satire, "The gods sell anything: Health for a calf, wealth for four cows, or a royal throne for 100 bulls - while the poor man can propitiate the gods simply by kissing his own hand. The poets say that in each god's heavenly house, they dine on divine wine - but if a pious mortal below makes a sacrifice, the gods gather around to inhale the smoke and lick up the spilt altar blood like flies! The priest says those who sacrifice must be clean, but he stands there all bloody, just like the Cyclops, cutting up the victim, removing the entrails, plucking out the heart, pouring the blood about the altar, and doing everything possible in the way of piety. Meanwhile the animals bellow plaintively, which I must suppose is a religious noise!"

Offerings to *Hecate* were made at crossroads, where beggars and itinerant philosophers often stole the food scraps off the altar for dinner. This early form of drive-through takeout was jokingly known as a "Hecate Supper."

Oracular utterances

Greece got rich from the famous oracle at Delphi. "Jupiter released two eagles from opposite ends of the earth," the Greeks insisted, "and they smacked into each other at *Delphi* (Womb), so it's the private part of the world!" Apollo replaced a mountain snake (*monty python*) with a *pythia*

(snaky woman) who got high inhaling the smoke of laurel leaves, or volcanic vents, and spoke with a forked tongue. The god Apollo rode the possessed woman like a pony, digging his spurs into her flanks, which caused her hoarse shrieks and convulsions. A scribe recorded her mad ravings, which were then interpreted as divine utterances. A young girl originally had the job, but then a woman over 50 was employed because they rave madder, longer. Finally three worked in shifts so that one was always available if the others had passed out.

First on leaves she nibbles
then hot wine she dribbles
and a priest awaiting
Pythia's prating
scribbles Sibyl's quibbles!

"Myrtale chews laurel leaves, not to be possessed," Martial wryly observed, "but to cover her drunken breath!"

The Delphic oracle often spoke in riddles. "Go to war," the oracle told King Croesus, "and a mighty empire will fall!" (His own!) "What sex will my wife's baby be?" asked a man, and the oracle replied, "Boy-no-girl!" "Who fathered the baby?" he added, and the oracle answered, "You-not-neighbor!" When Sparta asked who would be best to guard a statue that they had stolen from Argos, the oracle said, "Thieves!" Sometimes the oracle went on strike and answered all questions with, "I'm not answering until the priests get paid!"

The Italian oracle at Cumae let the suppliant draw lots for a response. If they weren't happy with the answer, the priests let them draw again, but this time the rigged-disc read: "The god says you can't ask the oracle again!" which avoided the embarrassing questions of cult-followers.

In 280 BC, *Brennus* (King) led the Gauls to sack Delphi. The short Greeks thought to hold them at the river, but were surprised when the taller Gauls simply waded across.

"The barbarians commenced to slaughter children, eat babies and drink blood," according to Pausanias, in his greasy *Guide to Greece*, "The Greek women proceeded to commit suicide, then found that the Gauls still ravished them, whether they be dead, dying, or even still alive but shamming. Many women died from lack of sleep, due to the long queue of Gauls lined up to sleep with them. In revenge, gangs of wild women laid ambushes and speared the half-naked Gauls as they marched on Delphi. The gods displayed their displeasure by making loud thunder, so the Gauls couldn't hear each other think. A loopy Gaul mistook his comrades for Greeks and furiously attacked them. More and more barbarians joined in the big free-for-all until the whole army was at each other's throats. The dumbfounded Athenians watched the Gauls beating themselves up, and then hurried out to help chase the losers off. Brennus killed himself by drinking too much unmixed wine!"

"I assure you," Pausanias adds, "that's what really happened."

The Gallic army decided to split in two, so one half could keep fighting, while the other half took Delphi's gold back to Gaul, where they placed their comrades' share in a temple. Unfortunately, their comrades never returned, but it was finally claimed by another gang of barbarians - the Romans.

The Christian historian Eusebius claimed that the emperor Augustus visited Delphi and found the oracle was silent. "Why don't you answer?" Augustus angrily demanded, and the priestess replied, "Jesus has just been born and sent me down to Hell, so don't come back here again asking your stupid questions!"

Portentous prodigies

The Romans recorded the yearly prodigies and portents, some as follows, and with possible interpretations:

1. A shower of stones = The stoning got out of hand again.

2. The oracular scrolls shrunk in size = The priest forgot to take the scrolls out of his toga when he washed it.

3. A wolf snatched a sentry's sword and ran off with it = The slob sentry was not only asleep on duty, but hadn't even washed the blood off his sword, which attracted the hungry wolf.

4. The shores were lit up by numerous fires = Someone held a beach party.

5. Two moons were visible in daytime = Too much unwatered wine had been drunk.

6. Shields appeared in the sky and the sun fought with the moon = Way too much unwatered wine had been drunk!

7. A hen turned into a cock, and a cock into a hen = A fowl mix-up.

8. Hot water flowed from cold springs = Who peed in the pool?

9. A four-footed snake was seen = Someone saw their first lizard.

10. A wolf ran through Rome, chased by excited pursuers = The poor wolf had been hoping to mooch a handout.

11. A statue of a cow was mounted by a bull = The bull really needs to get out more.

12. An ox said, "*Roma cave tibi!*" (Rome beware!) = Or maybe, "*moo!*"

13. A pig was born with the face of a man = Time for a new swineherd.

14. In the temple of Juno a crash followed by a dreadful roar was heard = The priest was drinking out the back again, and tripped over his robes onto the incense urns.

15. Hair appeared on the statue of Hercules = Time for the gardener to chop the weeds off its head.

16. A foal was born with five feet = A sure winner in the chariot races.

17. Three chickens were born with three feet each = Oh no, not drumsticks for dinner again?

18. A woman changed her sex = Another cross-dresser was caught.

19. It rained blood = The bird being sacrificed escaped with a neck wound, and sprayed the crowd as it flew away.

20. A statue frowned = Someone saw a statue of Tarquin the Arrogant.

21. The hut of Romulus burnt down = Crows dropped flaming fragments of meat on it that they'd snatched from an altar.

22. The chariot of Minerva crashed while being returned from the circus races to the Capitol = Minerva was drinking driving.

23. An ox walked up three flights of stairs, then frightened by the tenants' screams, leapt out the window = This one I can't explain.

24. A senator went into convulsions and was possessed by a god = He faked it to stop a law he didn't like being passed.

25. Dogs gathered outside the pontifex maximus' house at night and howled = The pontifex will soon howl too, and throw his boot at them.

26. A statue wept or sweated = Some drunkard had urinated on it.

27. Ears of wheat grew out a woman's nose = She was caught shoplifting in the vegetable market.

28. A slave-girl bore a boy with four hands, feet, eyes, and ears, and double private parts = She was a double-dealing two-timer.

29. A boy was born without aperture in his fundament = This is a genuine miracle, since Rome's never been short of a *podex* (asshole).

30. A woman was discovered with double private parts = And no fundamental aperture (*podex*).

31. The ceremonial banquet spread for a goddess was devoured by a dog before it had been tasted = An impious doggess.

32. Light shone so brightly at night that people got up and began working as though it was dawn = The water clock needs adjusting.

33. When taking the auspices, the sacred chickens flew out of their coop and hid in the forest = Auspices are off today.

34. Every year lots of things were struck by lightning, the most common portent of all = Used to explain almost anything.

Everything in Rome was corrupt, even the gods, so it was common to bribe them with the promise of a new temple in return for victory, and often cheaper to lose a battle. Whenever an earthquake was reported, all business was suspended on dint of religious grounds. This became so common and annoying that an edict was issued forbidding anyone to report earthquakes.

Cursory Curses

Your enemies could be cursed by inscribing what you wanted done to them on a thin sheet of lead (usually made from stolen lead waterpipes) as a *defixio* (fixed) curse tablet, rolling it up, and giving it to the gods of the underworld. Since these gods lived underground, you had to either bury your tablet, drop it down a well to them, or give it to a deceased friend for hand delivery. You could hire a professional scribe to write your curse for you, since they were experts in bad language.

Many curse tablets have been recovered, inscribed with such wishes as: Fix whoever stole my property, fix my lover who jilted me, or even fix the chariot races (which was the most common curse by far).

If you preferred taking matters into your own hands, a wax image of your opponent was used. Melting it induced them with a desire to mess around with you, but stomping on it made them regret walking all over you. We know that they must've worked, because the senate kept passing laws against using them.

Many curse tablets were written in advance, with a gap left to insert the recipient's name (some of which were so long that they had to be squashed or written sideways). In case you ever need it, here is a multipurpose curse (you just need to fill in the names):

"This is the spell. I appeal to Mercury, Jupiter, Pluto, Nemesis, various water nymphs, and any restless spirit who has died an untimely death. I curse _ _ _ _ _ whose mother is _ _ _ _ _ Make them headless, footless and powerless. Make them cold and hard as this curse tablet. Also, I conjure the spirit to make _ _ _ _ _ whose mother is _ _ _ _ _ not to have any sexual pleasure except with me. Let them not eat or drink, nor go out or find sleep without me. Drag them by their hair and heart until they no longer stand aloof from me. Also, under the power of necessity, I ask that my _ _ _ _ _ chariot team may win, and the enemy _ _ _ _ _ chariot team lose a wheel, tangle their reins, and be sent to destruction. Also, may this power undo the spell of anyone who has put a curse on *me*! If a restless ghost does this for me, I shall set you free."

Good luck with your cursing!

The *Gorgon* (Terrible) head was popular in Etruscan art for scaring off evil and was perhaps modeled on the mother-in-law. "Medusa the Gorgon once had such sexy blonde hair that Neptune couldn't resist raping her in Minerva's temple," wrote Ovid, "So Minerva turned her hair into snakes to avenge the insult!" The Romans adopted gorgons as gargoyles to protect Christian churches.

Our Gorgon will protect you from the above curse in case your enemy read this book before you!

13 CONCLUSION

We've followed Rome's rise from a gang of outcasts, runaway slaves and criminals hiding in a mud-hut fort by the Tiber River who gradually expanded their farmland to rule all of Italy. Once they plowed into the sea and there was nobody more to fight, they began farming fish, which were an expensive delicacy.

Next begins the world conquest of Sicily, Spain, Greece, Africa, and Asia, until eventually there's no one left to loot, so the Roman warlords turn on each other. But that's another story... (see p.199)

Perhaps Rome can be most objectively summed up by the only tribe they couldn't be bothered conquering, funnily enough, the Irish. "But oblige me by taking away that knife. I can't look at the point of it," wrote James Joyce, "It reminds me of Roman history!"

He also wrote: "Read the road roman with false steps ad Pernicious from rhearsilvar ormolus to torquinions superbers while I'm far away from wherever thou art serving my tallyhos and tullying my hostilious!"[9]

Right: Cranach's *Lucretia* (AD 1535).

Jimmy must've liked the Romans, since he called his famous banned pornographic novel *Ulysses*, instead of Odysseus.

Macaulay's popular ballad *Lays of Ancient Rome* recalls how Mars lay Rhea Silvia, Appius Claudius tried to lay Virginia, and sexmad Sextus lied to lay Lucretia.[10] Victorians liked quoting his rhyming couplets. The *Prophecy of Capys* celebrates Rome's victory over King Pyrrhus: "The Roman soldiers cheer - shield sword and spear - every ear - far or near - hears Rome's name with fear!" However, a prophetic warning is added: "O men beware this omen - more than any other foeman - tribunes bite - and senators fight - Roman now hates Roman!"

I hope you've enjoyed this book, and if someone has read it aloud to you for an authentic historical experience, they've sure earned their freedom!

---

[9] *Finnegan's Wake* 467.34, possibly written in Etruscan while chewing laurel leaves. The allusions are to Rhea Silvia, Tarquin Superbus, Tullus Hostilius, and the Tullianum (prison). It makes about as much sense as Roman history ever does.

[10] Sextus fought Horatius at the Tiber Bridge: "Every man's a traitor - unless he makes Rome greater - I'll meet my fate - before the gate - we all die sooner or later!"

Authorized version

Brett Clark, the author, is rather overqualified to write Roman history because he's read half of Gibbon (the footnotes), watched *Gladiator* twice, and saved Caesar on many campaigns in the Age of Empires (Rise of Rome) computer game. Majoring in Classics and Ancient History, Brett's work was praised by his professors for being "too anecdotal," and "a bit of a riff."

Right: The author saves Caesar yet again from a computer-generated ass-assin during an Age of Empires campaign, and notes, "It's not until you campaign with Caesar that you realize he's not so good at fighting as he is at claiming credit!"

To research this book, Brett followed Aeneas' trail from Turkey to Italy. His report is as follows: "Salve, Dear Reader,

Turkey and Greece are nice places, except for the Turks who insist, "Turks are nicer than Greeks!" then add, "Nobody has stabbed you yet, have they?" and the Greeks who reply, "Greeks don't have to be nicer than Turks!" Fighting at Troy continues, especially with cabdrivers that charge double fare to Istanbul Airport - but our altercation was cut short by the Tourist Police, who took the driver off at gunpoint!

Greece's Olympic Airways is famous for passenger complaints, who often have to tell the stewardesses off for smoking on the plane. Greece retains the lascivious customs of its ancestors, including free x-rated movies in the hotel rooms - so don't let your mother channel surf. Sailing south, I found that the archaeological isle of Delos has been deserted for the adjacent party-island of Mykonos, where the wine flows freely and hungover archaeologists keep missing the only early-morning daily excursion boat. Most of the sacred shrines were built over by luxury condominiums when the Romans converted it from a holy site to a slave market long ago.

Crete hasn't changed much in 3,000 years, where drivers still stick to the middle of the road. "That way you've got *two* choices for turning," they explain, "when we come straight at you head on!"

The Trojans Aeneas left behind in Sicily have become *Mafia* (Braggarts) and left for Hollywood to make movies. The Aetna volcano is still scaring tourists, but not the pigheaded locals who keep rebuilding their shacks on the cooled lava flows.

The Carthage fruit market is still full of "Romans," because that's what the Arabs call pomegranates (named after the people they first got them from). Many Roman remains have been uncovered on Byrsa Hill and are displayed in the Carthage Archaeological Museum where they've been broken up for use as crazy paving or plastered into the perimeter walls. The arms and heads of statues poking out of the wall seem to make good coat hooks. The excavated ruins are protected from weathering by a thick layer of weeds, and cameras can get into the archaeological sites at a cheaper price (1 dinar) even than students (3 dinar), which seems rather unfair. The locals are trying to rebuild the Roman aqueducts, but really need a good centurion with a fast whip to increase productivity.

Italian drivers are crazy, so I blended right in by speeding, swerving, and running red lights, only to be stopped by the polizia for having a dirty number plate. The Italian entry to the Underworld, Naples, has saved you a journey by moving Hell above ground. Cerberus occupies nearly every alleyway, in the form of three stray vicious dogs looking for a bite. Baia has sunk into the sea, but diving expeditions allow murky viewing of underwater ruins, rubbish, and floating oddities from the leaking sewerage pipes. Also, note that the toppings on Italian pizza are so heavy it's sold by weight, painted-up African prostitutes act as convenient milestones by standing at intervals along the roadside, and wine is cheaper to drink than soda pop.

Right: The author plays the Greek drinking game *cottabos* and loses his shirt. Roman drinking parties always elected a Master of the Cup, who told the party how much wine they could drink, in order to stop the more violent Romans getting so drunk that they killed everybody!

Heading north to the Etruscan hill towns of Tuscany, I found the acropolis of *Volterra* (Hill-land) occupied by the state prison, but Norchia occupied only by sheep. Ruined *Vulci* (Swamp) is described as the "Etruscan Pompeii" but without the volcano. The museum attendants enjoy shouting, "No photo!" unless they're gabbing on their cellphones or congregating for a ciggy break (which is most of the time).

The trip from Turkey to Italy really isn't too bad, so Aeneas must've exaggerated just to impress Queen Dido. In fact, I've found Rome to be pretty safe and the only – ack!" [Report cut short!]

Ancient Authors mentioned in the text

Aelian (AD 200) wrote *Alien* (Weird Animals). The Mysterious Case of the Disappearing *Garum* (Fish-sauce) saw slaves accused of stealing from the locked pantry keep a nocturnal vigil and apprehend the real thief – an octopus who entered the house through the toilet!

Appian (AD 160) wrote *Roman History* in the Appian way.

Aristotle (320 BC) was a prolific Greek philosopher who claimed, while fleeing from a mob at Athens: "The Athenians murdered Socrates - so I don't want them to sin against philosophy twice!"

Augustine, Saint (AD 430) wrote *Confessions*, which is the autobiography of a Manichaean who became a Christian while still having a good time.

Augustus, Emperor (AD 14) wrote *Deeds of the Divine Augustus*.

Bentley (AD 1700) wrote *Exposé of Fake Ancient Manuscripts*, which caused huge controversy by exposing fake ancient manuscripts that ushered in modern classical criticism (scholars insulting each other).

Byron, Lord (AD 1800) was a clubfooted bisexual poet ("Mad, bad, and dangerous to know") who sailed his boat the *Hercules* to help the Greeks fight the Turks, but died of flu on the way.

Caesar, Julius (44 BC) wrote *Civil War* and *Uncivil War*.

Camoes (AD 1550) was exiled from the Portuguese Royal Court for womanizing, lost an eye fighting, and wrote his epic poem the *Lusiad* in the solitude of prison (to became Portugal's National Poet). His epitaph read: "Camoes' cameo was to live poor and neglected, and so die."

Cassius Dio (AD 220) wrote *Roman History* which compressed 1000 years into 1 book (and was perhaps written by Dio Cassius).

Cato, Old (140 BC) was a cranky old Censor who hated Greeks, so wrote the first *Roman History* in Latin.

Catullus (50 BC) wrote *Poems* lamenting a failed love affair with Lesbia who left him for her husband.

Chaucer, Geoffrey (AD 1400) was influenced by Ovid ("Venus clerk, Ovyde, who's sown wondrous weed – the great god of Love's seed!") to write *The House of Fame* (about Aeneas' adventures), *The Physician's Tale* (recounting the Decemvir Appius Claudius' attempted rape of Virginia), *Troilus and Criseyde* (about two lovers during the Trojan War), and *The Legend of Good Women* (including Clytemnestra, Dido, and Lucretia).

Choerilus (450 BC) "I'm sorry, but I'll have to write about what happened to me today," complained the epic poet Choerilus, "because all the old heroes have already all been written about!"

Cicero (40 BC) was a Republican orator who published great *Speeches*, *Philosophy*, *Letters*, and some awful *Poems*.

Claudius, Emperor (AD 54) was encouraged by Livy to write several *Histories*, but the solemnity of his first public reading was ruined by a fat senator whose seat broke. Whenever he punished an enemy, Claudius liked to quote Homer: "Let him first attack, but be sure to get him back!" Claudius added three new letters to the Latin alphabet, insisting "they were most necessary," and probably were too, due to his incessant sniffing, coughing, burping, slobbering, drooling, and other bodily noises.

Dante (AD 1300) wrote the Christian *Divine Comedy*, which consists of *Inferno* (Hell), *Purgatory* and *Paradise* (Heaven).
Virgil's ghost guides Dante through the Nine Circles of Hell. Limbo contains the Greek philosophers (Socrates, Plato, and Aristotle), and the great poets Homer, Horace, Ovid, and Lucan. Virgil introduces Dante, who boasts, "The Poets treat me almost like I'm number six in their group!" "I'm better than Ovid, because he writes about changing shape," adds Dante, "but I'll write about EX-changing shape (between a man and a reptile)!"
The Circle of Lustful Lovers contains Helen, Paris, Dido, Cleopatra, and Achilles (Dante hadn't read Homer, since he couldn't read Greek, and so didn't know that Achilles was supposed to be a fighter, not a lover). The Circle of Fraudsters contains Jason (who left his wife Medea), and Odysseus and Diomedes (who tricked the Trojans with the Wooden Horse). Satan chews on the traitors Cassius, Brutus and Judas (so betraying Caesar seems twice as bad as betraying Jesus).
Dante upset so many of his contemporaries by placing them in Hell that he was forced to flee for his life, and today many small Italian towns bear his statue and the proud claim: "Dante hid here!"

Eratosthenes (200 BC) was a Librarian of Alexandria who was the first to call himself a "Literary Critic," but was nicknamed by his rivals a "B-grade Smart-ass." His *Round the Earth* calculated the angle of a stick's shadow against sunlight in a well's bottom to give a circumference of 250,000 *stadiums* (a disputed length). Dismissing mythological dates, his *Chronology* instead used the (supposedly) historically accurate dates of the Trojan War.

Eusebius (AD 330) wrote his *Church History* to apologize for Christianity, and revised it whenever he changed his mind.

Fracastoro (AD 1500) wrote his patriotic Latin poem *Syphilis, or the French Pox* to blame the disease on France, instead of Italy (which had a bad dose) or Spain (blamed for bringing it back from America). "Haw! I've got more kids than the goddess Leto," bragged Niobe (in Ovid's *Metamorphoses*), which provoked Leto to kill all Niobe's children, including her eldest son, Syphilis. Fracastoro boasted that Juno cured the shepherd Syphilis with Holy Wood sap (which he sold to sufferers at great profit, but which later proved to be ineffectual).

Gellius, Aulus (AD 180) began his *Attic Nights* as a book of anecdotes to while away nights in his attic, and finished it to keep his kids quiet.

Geoffrey of Monmouth (AD 1150) wrote *British Kings History*, which runs from Aeneas down to King Arthur and the wizard Myrddin - whose name sounded too much like the French word *merde* (poop), so was renamed Merlin. "I ain't wrote in fancy language," boasts Geoffrey, "so you won't have to look any big words up!" Geoffrey's claim that the heads of a decapitated Roman legion were tossed into a river near London was considered nonsense until a large pile of skulls was discovered in the riverbed in AD 1860.

Gibbon, Edward (AD 1794) wrote *The History of the Decline and Fall of the Roman Empire*, which is "a revolution which will ever be remembered, and is still felt by the nations of the earth," and was "the triumph of barbarism and religion." Gibbon was a born-again Pagan historian with a hydrocele (testicle the size of a watermelon) who blamed Christianity for Rome's fall. "It is melancholy to say it, but the chief, perhaps the only English writer who has any claim to be considered an Ecclesiastical Historian," wrote Cardinal Newman, "is the unbeliever Gibbon!"

Greek Anthology (700 BC-AD 600) contains 4,000 poems written in Greek (many by Romans).

Herodas (350 BC), often called **Herondas** to fool his enemies, wrote humorous *Mimes*.
The Go-between: An old woman who advises a girl to take a lover is rewarded with a jug of wine.
The Flogging: "Teach my truant son not to go to school," a mother orders the schoolmaster, "and flog him with your oxtail!"
The Dildo: A desperate woman missing her sex-toy is outraged to find her friends sharing it.

Herodotus (420 BC) wrote *History*, which invented the genre.

Horace (8 BC) wrote abusive *Satires*, and *Writing Poems Made Easy*.

Homer (700 BC) is credited with composing the *Iliad* and *Odyssey* from an oral tradition of old bards' tales, so that anomalies abound, for example: Iron and bronze weapons co-exist, chariots are used as taxis to transport warriors to the battle, and many heroes get killed several times.

Homer was a sensitive poet, concerned to show us charming small details of his warriors' lives, before graphically killing them (ex. "So-and-so had tended sheep as a boy. The spear smashed through his teeth and pierced the back of his skull spraying black blood as the dark mist covered his eyes!").

Jerome, Saint (AD 420) translated the *Bible* into *Vulgar* (Mob) Latin, and was chased out of Rome for dallying with the widow Paula.

Joyce, James (AD 1922) wrote *Ulysses* as an experimental Irish retelling of Homer's *Odyssey*.

Ulysses travels through Dublin visiting Nestor's School, an Underworld funeral, the Brothel of Circe, the one-eyed patrons of Cyclops' Pub and the tempting Siren barmaids, while Penelope sleeps with a suitor ("and yes I said yes I will Yes!").

"Tell me about Pyrrhus," demands longwinded schoolmaster Nestor of a pupil, who answers, "Pyrrhus, sir? Pyrrhus, a pier."

Parallels abound (ex. Homer's "Wine-dark sea" copied by Joyce as "Snot-green sea").

Finnegan's Wake is an experimental Irish "lambdad's tale" with "a bed as hard as the thinkamuddles of the Greeks and a board as bare as a Roman altar. Are you roman cawthrick 432? -- Quadrigue my yoke. Triple my tryst (*sic*)."

Juvenal (AD 130) wrote *Satires* and claimed that his bombastic style was better than epic and tragedy combined.

Livy (AD 17) wrote *Ab Urbe Condita* (From the Foundation of the City) as a monumental Roman history in 142 books. Livy's annalistic style liked listing annual prodigies and portents (see p. 184).

Lucian (AD 160) was a witty and prolific comic satirist whose 80 titles include: *Jove Rants*, *The Talking Cock*, *Philosophies for Sale*, *Alexander the Charlatan* (exposing a fellow fraudster), and *The Mistaken Critic* (a nefandous attack on a critic who laughed at Lucian's use of the word "nefandous").

Macaulay (AD 1840) wrote *Lays of Ancient Rome* praising heroic deeds in doggerel lines easy enough for Victorians to quote. "Does the smoke belching from those factory chimneys," young Macaulay asked his mother, "come from the fires of Hell?"

Macrobius (AD 430) wrote *Saturnalia* about Christian senators at a drinking party who reminisce on Rome's great Pagan past.

Martial (AD 100) wrote *Epigrams* mocking Roman social mores. "My rooftop garret is so drafty," Martial complained, "that even the Wind God wouldn't want to live there!"

Milton (AD 1650) wrote *Paradise Lost* and *Found*. Teased as 'Mother Mary' for his long hair, Milton won fame penning *Epitaph on the admirable Dramatick Poet:*

Now that Shakespeare's left the room
Heavenward his sepulchers zoom
But his immortal art
Lives in our heart
So each of us becomes his tomb!

As the 'Secretary of Foreign Tongues,' Milton wrote propaganda to justify Oliver Cromwell's execution of King Charles. Unfortunately, the Restoration saw the restored king issue his death warrant. "Book as a killer," Milton urged, "whoever kills a book!"

Nero, Emperor (AD 68) wrote *Poems*. "Everyone thinks Nero copied his poems," wrote Suetonius, "but I saw his notebook and it was filled with crossings-out!" Nero's last words: "A great artist dies with me!"

Nestor (AD 200) rewrote the *Iliad* as a lipogram (by missing a different letter from each book). Therefore Book 1 couldn't mention **A**chilles or **A**gamemnon or M**a**rs, Book 2 **B**ees or **B**attles or **B**ig Ajax, Book 3 **C**ows or A**c**hilles or He**c**tor, and so on.

Ovid (AD 17) wrote *Lovers' Letters, Lovers' Adventures, Making Love Made Easy, Makeup for Maids, Breaking-up Made Easy, Feasts,* and *Metamorphoses* (Changes). After Ovid was exiled by Augustus (for an unmentionable sexual intrigue) he wrote: *Sorrows, Sad Letters from the Black Sea,* and finally *Dirty Bird* (an angry curse poem).

Pausanias (AD 150) wrote *Guide to Greece*. Ancient Romans were keen tourists, as attested by the many graffiti left carved onto famous monuments.

Petronius Arbiter (AD 60) wrote the *Satyricon* (Satyr-satire) about the humorous sexual misadventures of an amoral bisexual cad made impotent by the phallic god Priapus. The urbane Petronius was titled 'Arbiter of Elegance' in Nero's court, until forced to commit suicide. Before dying he broke all his best cups so Nero couldn't have them.

Philostratus (AD 230) was four different poets from the same family who wrote *Sophists Lives, Gym Exercises,* and *Love Letters* (half to boys). In *Big Heroes,* cunning Odysseus' ghost recounts the Trojan War to Homer, on condition that he's praised in the *Iliad*.

Pindar (450 BC) wrote *Victory Songs*. In recognition of the poem Pindar had written about his ancestor, Alexander the Great left only Pindar's house standing when he destroyed Thebes.

Plautus (180 BC) wrote Roman *Comedies*. The 30 plays of Plautus (copied from Greek originals) were so successful that another 100 plays pretended to his authorship.

Pliny, Old (AD 79) wrote *Natural History*. Pliny says he has recorded 20,000 facts from 2,000 books (but this is a severe underestimate). Ever curious, Pliny died by investigating the eruption of Vesuvius too closely.

Pliny, Young (AD 110) wrote *Letters*. "Salve Emperor Trajan, I'm not sure what to do with the Christians. I caught some and asked them several times to change their minds. They refused, so I executed them, not for being Christians - but for being so stubborn! Vale, Young Pliny."

Plutarch (AD 120) wrote *Parallel Lives*. "Not only have the Romans copied Greek myths and events," wrote the Greek biographer Plutarch, "but also their very lives!" "Romulus copied Theseus, Numa copied Lycurgus, Poplicola copied Solon, Coriolanus copied Alcibiades, and Camillus copied Themistocles," he proved, in a series of comparisons, "except the Greeks did it better!"

Polybius (200 BC) wrote *Roman History* that explains to the Greeks how the Romans conquered the world. "Only pathetic people won't want to read my book," wrote Polybius.

Quintilian (AD 90) wrote *Oratory Made Easy*.

Seneca, Young (AD 65) wrote *Essays* and *Tragedies*. He was banished by the emperor Claudius for seducing the emperor Caligula's sister, so wrote *Clemency*. On Claudius' death, he wrote *The Pumpkinification of the stupid Emperor Claudius the Clod*. Seneca was recalled to tutor the emperor Nero, who finally ordered his suicide.

Shakespeare, William (AD 1600) wrote the poem *The Rape of Lucrece*. In his play *Coriolanus* Shakespeare blames Coriolanus' problems on his mother, who had taught him to win at all costs (even if it's for the wrong side). Shakespeare's play *Troilus and Cressida* is a humorous send-up of the Trojan War depicting the Greek 'heroes' as violent, lustful fools. "Helen is a whore fought over by a lecher (Paris) and a cuckold (Menelaus)," while Achilles' slave-girl (Briseis= Briseida=Cressida) leaves her Trojan lover Troilus for the sexier Greek Diomedes. "He not only took my girl," weeps Troilus, "but my horse too!" The pimp Pandarus gives us our word *pander* (procurer, or go-between in illicit love affairs), while "False as Cressida" became a byword for sexual betrayal.

Silius Italicus (AD 100) filled his retirement by writing the longest Latin poem, *Punica*, detailing Hannibal's Punic invasion of Italy.

Sotades (250 BC) penned an obscene version of the *Iliad* and the *Katabasis* (Going Down is Hell).

Timolaus (300 BC) inserted a new line after each line of the *Iliad*. Here's how the revised poem starts [with Timolaus' additions]:
"Sing, goddess, the anger of Achilles [who was mad over a girl] and its devastation on the Greeks [because they fought the Trojans without him] who were hurled down to Hades [by Hector's pointy spear]."

Theopompus (320 BC) was a "trouble-maker" historian (exiled for incessantly denouncing the moral depravity of leading politicians). Theopompus was such a keen student that his teacher said: "Most require the spur, but Theopompus needs the bit!" (Probably because he beat his teacher in an Oratory Contest.) He made the world's first historical epitome by condensing Herodotus' *Histories* down to just two books. However, his *History of Philip 2nd* was 58 books long, but when Philip 5th chopped out all the digressions (about barbarians and other things, such as: "The Macedonians by day were men-killers, but by night were men-kissers!") there were only 16 books left. An enemy poet wrote *Three-Heads* (a defamatory attack on three Greek cities) in the same style as Theopompus (which got Theo in a lot of trouble), although he really did write the *Attack upon Plato*.

Valerius Maximus (AD 30) wrote *Unforgettable Gettables*, which illustrated various Roman moral principles (Gratitude, Chastity, Cruelty, etc), he'd copied from various sources.

Varro (27 BC) was a prolific Roman scholar who penned over 600 books (2 survived).

Vegius (AD 1428) wrote *Book 13* of the *Aeneid:* "Having killed Turnus, Aeneas posts Pallas' belt back to Evander at Pallanteum. Aeneas rules for three years, and is then raised to heaven by Venus as a star."
As a young boy Vegius was so obsessed by Virgil that most of his everyday speech was copied from the poems. The Middle Ages interpreted the *Aeneid* as an 'allegory of the soul', which therefore needed to end in heaven, not earth. Many other *Book 13*s were also penned, but Vegius' was accepted because he so closely mimicked every aspect of his idol's style. Adding the happy ending changed Virgil's tragedy into a comedy.

Virgil (19 BC) wrote various *Poems*. Virgil lost his farm during the Emperor Augustus' proscriptions, but for writing such great poems about Augustus he was soon rewarded with another.

Epitaph

Last words from a collection of tombstones:

"Here lies the jolly old clown Protogenes, slave of Clulius.
The last joke was on him!"

"Aulus Salvius Crispinus
- flattened by a wall while eating lunch!"

"Here am I, Lemiso, laid to rest. I didn't stop slaving
until death gave me a break!"

"To the memory of M. Antoninus Terens of Micenum
Elected to the highest offices in his city
Most celebrated importer of pigs and sheep."

"I'm Callicratia: lived 105 years, birthed 29 kids,
saw 0 die & never used 1 walking stick!"

"Here I lie,
the famous woman who laid only one man!"

"To Allia from your lovers two
it's just not the same without you!"

"Here lies Pontia Prima.
Do not touch!"

"Timon the misanthrope, lie I below
Go, and revile me, traveler - only go!"

"HMHNS"
[*Hoc Monumentum Haedes Non Sequeter*]
(The heirs will not have this monument!)

"Though you're in a hurry, stop and read this little stone
Here lie the bones of Bretus Andruicus Clarcius the poetaster
I thought you'd like to know. Bye!"

THE BLOODY FUNNY HISTORY OF ROME 2
WORLD CONQUEST
233 PHOTOS, MAPS, ILLUSTRATIONS, AND CARTOONS

This lasciviously illustrated and hilarious book carries the reader on a first-class sedan tour of Roman history, from the conquests of Alexander the Great which created the Hellenistic world that Rome inherited, to the invading herds of Hannibal and the battles for world domination culminating in extravagant debauchery, decadent luxury and undreamt wealth - and the funny thing is they say it's all true! There are asides on Roman culture, and synopses of Herodotus, Cato, Plautus, Athenaeus, in fact snippets of almost every ancient writer from Diogenes the Dog and Ovid the Doctor of Love to mad Nietzsche and Mommsen. Everything is covered, from the philosophers' drinking party to Cybele rites, or uncovered, from the prostitutes' positions to Bacchanalia frenzy. The casual reader will laugh as they learn, while the expert will smile as familiar episodes show their funny side. If your ancient Greek slave reads you only two books on Rome - this should be the other one!

"Witty and irreverent, but well-informed, I can well imagine its taking on a cult status with educated readers (especially with university students) fond of a good joke."
W. Jeffrey Tatum
Professor of Classics
Florida State University

"Readers can expect much that is clever in combination with the odd gross moment. You'll quite literally find sex, drugs, and rock-n-roll within these pages, but students of Roman history will recognize the depth of Clark's knowledge. Hannibal's Drinking Song is a stand-out!"
Tom Stevenson
Professor of Classics and Ancient History
University of Queensland

"A heady mix of schoolboy history and Pythonesque humor. Seemingly, Clark is able to present every amusing anecdote from the entire Loeb Classical Library."
James Grout, Encyclopaedia Romana

"Clark has a knack for bringing the obscure, bizarre, and deliciously titillating corners of Rome into full light. Bloody Funny? Bloody brilliant, I say!"
Jeffery B. Knapp
Associate Professor of Humanities and Latin
Tallahassee Community College

AVOID THE STAMPEDE - ORDER ONLINE!